IRISHNESS AND WOMANHOOD IN NINETEENTH-CENTURY BRITISH WRITING

Dedicated to my mother, Berenice,
who sang me Toorah Loorah.
"And I'd give the world if she could sing
That song to me today"

Irishness and Womanhood in Nineteenth-Century British Writing

THOMAS TRACY
Grambling State University, USA

ASHGATE

Published by
Ashgate Publishing Limited
Wey Court East
Union Road
Farnham
Surrey, GU9 7PT
England

Ashgate Publishing Company
Suite 420
101 Cherry Street
Burlington
VT 05401-4405
USA

www.ashgate.com

British Library Cataloguing in Publication Data
Tracy, Thomas J.
Irishness and womanhood in nineteenth-century British writing
 1. National characteristics, Irish, in literature 2. National characteristics, British, in literature 3. English fiction – 19th century – History and criticism 4. Irish in literature 5. Women in literature 6. Ireland – In literature
 I. Title
 823.8'0935299162

Library of Congress Cataloging-in-Publication Data
Tracy, Thomas (Thomas J.)
 Irishness and womanhood in nineteenth-century British writing / by Thomas Tracy.
  p. cm.
 Includes bibliographical references and index.
 ISBN 978-0-7546-6448-2 (alk. paper)
 1. English fiction—Irish authors—History and criticism. 2. English fiction—19th century—History and criticism. 3. National characteristics, Irish, in literature. 4. National characteristics, British, in literature. 5. Nationalism in literature. 6. Women in literature. 7. Ireland—In literature. 8. Irish question. I. Title.

PR8807.N37T73 2008
823'.80935817—dc22   2008042449

ISBN: 978-0-7546-6448-2

Mixed Sources
Product group from well-managed forests and other controlled sources
www.fsc.org Cert no. SGS-COC-2482
© 1996 Forest Stewardship Council

Printed and bound in Great Britain by
TJ International Ltd, Padstow, Cornwall

Contents

Acknowledgements

In writing this book I have incurred many debts of gratitude, the most important of which I would like to acknowledge here. First, there were the friends and colleagues from the University of Oregon who were there at the beginning of this project and whose advice and suggestions were instrumental in its ever coming to light. Foremost among these was my mentor Ian Duncan, who provided invaluable direction and insight. I would also like to express deep thanks to Keiko Kagawa, Randy McGowan, Mary Ann Peters, David Sandner, Dick Stein, and Richard Stevenson. The colleagues at Grambling who have helped and encouraged me in this project through sometimes difficult conditions include Chimegsaikhan Banzar, Danielle Boudreau, Bernie Evans, Uju Ifeanyi, Robert Kendrick, Jim Kim, Beatrice Mackinzie, Charles Snodgrass, Linda Ward, and Hugh Wilson—thank you all. I also appreciate the people at Ashgate whose help and professionalism made this a better book, including especially Ann Donahue, as well as Seth Hibbert, and all the hard workers at the Burlington desk editorial department. I will furthermore always be grateful to my family, who believed this project would come to fruition at times when I didn't believe it myself: Kathy, Sue, Mike, Michelle, Emma Rose, Maggie, and Mikey; Joe, Vicki, and Alex; Willie and Kate; Taylor and Travis; Tim and Maureen—gone but not forgotten—and above all Miss Nancy, a Southern belle who is something of a wild Irish girl herself.

Chapter 1
A Long Conversation

Introduction

> [Sydney Owenson's (Lady Morgan's) sentiments are] mischievous in tendency, and profligate in principle; licentious and irreverent in the highest degree … If … she could be persuaded to exchange her idle raptures for common sense, practice a little self-denial, and gather a few precepts of humility, from an old-fashioned book, which, although it does not seem to have lately fallen in her way, may yet, we think, be found in some corner of her study; she might then hope to prove, not indeed a good writer of novels, but a useful friend, a faithful wife, a tender mother, and a respectable and happy mistress of a family.[1]

In his dismissal of Lady Morgan's novel *Woman: Or Ida of Athens* (1809), a novel advocating the cause of liberty in Greece, John Wilson Croker invokes some central terms of the debate in Britain over a cause much closer to home: the "Irish question." The Anglo-Irish Croker's attack invests the political values of Lady Morgan's position with a distinctly sexual charge. Furthermore, his frequent comments on Lady Morgan's books over the next twenty years retain a primary focus on the themes of sexual anarchy and gender deviance which he initiated in this, the first number of his influential journal. In later reviews he increases his causticity and drops his ironic suggestions that she might become an acceptably domestic wife and mother (though not, alas, a good writer), at one point famously asserting that her social ideals and class pretensions are the ravings of an "audacious worm." In all of his commentary on Lady Morgan and her work, including *Ida of Athens*, her travel books *France* and *Italy*, and her national tales, Croker equates the progressive political and social vision she expresses with socio-sexual impropriety, and attributes her egalitarian "promiscuity" to a root cause: Gaelic Irish anti-domesticity.

The reason Croker troubled himself to respond so vehemently and over such a long period of time to an "audacious worm" was, however, only nominally precipitated by the appearance of *Ida of Athens*, a novel then regarded as minor and now largely forgotten. Croker was responding rather to the enormous popularity and influence of the ideals expressed in Lady Morgan's earlier novel, *The Wild Irish Girl* (1806). In it, Lady Morgan created a powerful heroine who embodied Irish nationhood and who, through her union with the English hero, represented a re-imagined distribution of power between Britain and Ireland, as well as between men and women. *The Wild Irish Girl* had a tremendous, if often unintentionally

---

[1]   Croker, John Wilson. Review of *Woman: Or Ida of Athens*, in *The Quarterly Review* 1 (1809), 52.

negative impact on subsequent developments in British literature and politics.[2] Its influence can be traced in the historical romances of Walter Scott and beyond, as well as in the political debates over issues such as Catholic Emancipation in Ireland, Repeal of the Union between Ireland and Great Britain, and social and urban reform in England. Beyond this, Irishness became a crucial term in the elaboration of an idealized *British* national culture. Croker's reviews of works by Lady Morgan, and her responses to them, were contributions to a dialogue on Union engaged by many influential commentators throughout much of the nineteenth century, including those featured most prominently in this study: Maria Edgeworth, James Kay Shuttleworth, George Cornewall Lewis, Friedrich Engels, Edmund Burke, John Croker, William Makepeace Thackeray, and Anthony Trollope. The main focus throughout this book will be to examine the implications of this long-standing debate on the cultural ideals which played an important role in shaping British national identity.

The study begins by closely investigating two Irish novels which construct imagined Unionist identities and which offer crucially different representations of Irish womanhood, but whose differences do not receive sufficient acknowledgement: *The Wild Irish Girl* and Edgeworth's *The Absentee* (1812). As Edgeworth's critique of Lady Morgan's social vision, the latter novel provides some of the first evidence that Croker's characterization of Lady Morgan's philosophy as sexually and politically deviant adheres to a consistent pattern. *The Wild Irish Girl* offers a useful starting point for examining this dialogue, but any discussion of the British writing of Ireland must recognize the impact and influence of Edgeworth's foundational *Castle Rackrent* (1800), which inaugurated the Irish national tale tradition. *Rackrent*'s significance lies in its encapsulation of the public history of Ireland (or at least an Ascendancy version of it) in the private history of the Rackrent family. Written at the time of the Union of Great Britain and Ireland, in which the interests of both the Anglo-Irish Patriot Party and the Catholic majority of Ireland were subordinated to the primary *British* interests of simultaneously containing Napoleonic aggression and Irish republicanism, *Castle Rackrent* is the story of a Big House in decline. Thady Quirk's "personal" memoir, which Thomas Flanagan in his masterful reading describes as an elegy for the Protestant nation,[3] pessimistically encodes the disintegration of Anglo-Irish society (a society which in many ways constitutes the British colonial presence)

---

[2]   Lady Morgan's novel went through seven editions in the first two years after its appearance (Newcomer 33), and made such a cultural icon of the harp-playing Lady Morgan that *Punch* magazine was still relatively obsessed with her well into the 1840s, long after her most productive period. R.F. Foster notes that "in early *Punch* ... Lady Morgan's *conversaziones* were also fair game [for the magazines frequent satire]" (Foster 1993, 173), and in W.M. Thackeray's *Punch* Prize Novels satire of Charles Lever (1847), jokes about Lady Morgan abound (see "*Phil Fogarty, a Tale of the Fighting Onety-Oneth,*" in *Punch* 13 [July–December 1847], 56 *ff*).

[3]   Flanagan, Thomas, *The Irish Novelists 1800–1850.* New York: Columbia University Press, 1959, 69–79.

as an *effect* of Union. The family's extortionary landlording policies, known as rack-renting, bring ruin to their tenants, while their wastefulness brings ruin upon themselves; both groups are then exploited by a rapacious (and Catholic) middle class. Submerged within the text, moreover, is a thoroughgoing anti-domesticity. The only marriages represented in the text are failures, and childless at that. The wives are greedy and the men, in the absence of any well-regulated women, are recklessly improvident. The gentry's disorderliness engenders a similar disorder in the lower classes.[4] Edgeworth will revisit these Burkean themes in more refined detail in later novels, and in repeatedly doing so reveals her ongoing project of engaging Lady Morgan's novels and their depictions of powerful women who exert a positive influence on society through their actions in the public sphere.

Lady Morgan, at this time still known by her maiden name Sydney Owenson, adopted many of the devices used in *Castle Rackrent* in elaborating her liberal social vision in *The Wild Irish Girl*, and in the process transformed the national tale both generically and ideologically. She reimagines Union as the comic resolution to her narrative, encoded in the egalitarian marriage of the English hero and the Gaelic Irish heroine. She also argues for a reappraisal of the colonial past, and a transformation of the political dispensation in the future. The hitherto subjected Gaelic Irish, as embodied in her heroine, Glorvina, are given a "beautiful voice" in her inclusive new society, and for the first time empowered politically. The partners in the reimagined Union share power and responsibility equally.

The social implications of these themes have been largely ignored by modern feminist literary historians, or in some cases misinterpreted. Julie Anne Miller, for example, argues that both Edgeworth and Lady Morgan offer "an inadvertent critique" of Union by expressing "anxiety about the repressive power dynamics within the institution of marriage," and that "Edgeworth's and Owenson's novels of Union expose the way colonial control is secured and obscured through the privatization of power relations in marriage."[5] Such an appraisal ignores fundamental differences in the social and political worldviews these two authors express, differences of which contemporary critics such as Croker were acutely aware. While Lady Morgan does indeed expose the ways in which power relations are secured in marriage, it is anything but inadvertent and decidedly not obscurantist: her work consciously seeks to transform the power relations. In one of the many innovations for which she was one of the most influential (though often reviled) authors of her time, Lady Morgan invokes Shakespeare's second

---

[4]   For a valuable discussion of *Rackrent*, see Daniel Hack's "Inter-Nationalism: *Castle Rackrent* and Anglo-Irish Union," in *Novel: a Forum on Fiction* 29:2 (1996), 145–64. Hack notes the novel's Anglo-Irish hegemonic implications as well as its anti-domesticity.

[5]   Miller, Julie Anne. "Acts of Union: Family Violence and National Courtship," in Maria Edgeworth's *The Absentee,* and Sydney Owenson's *The Wild Irish Girl*," in *Border Crossings: Irish Women Writers and National Identities*, ed. Kathryn Kirkpatrick. Tuscaloosa: University of Alabama Press, 2000, 14–15.

history tetralogy,[6] a group of works which Scott later invoked as the model of national historical fiction. Her purpose is to expose the initial overturning and subsequent reinforcement of traditional gender roles in the Henriad, which it utilizes as a means of validating the hierarchical social, political, and colonial order. Against the model of the Welsh temptress undermining the rebels' cause in *Henry IV Part 1* and Hal reasserting a righteous male dominance in *Henry V*, Lady Morgan juxtaposes the radically altered relationship of Horatio and Glorvina. (The Henriad is often invoked in the dialogue surrounding the "Irish question" throughout the century, in novels such as Edgeworth's *Ormond* and Trollope's *An Eye for an Eye*.) Edgeworth, on the other hand, seeks to "secure and obscure" normative gender ideals in the process of endorsing an equally repressive social and political system. She directly engages Lady Morgan in each of her Irish novels following *The Wild Irish Girl*, taking issue with that and Lady Morgan's subsequent novels' educational, gender, and political philosophies. In *The Absentee* and *Ormond* she seeks to contain Lady Morgan's radical themes through her own elaboration of ideals famously promulgated by Edmund Burke, in which the political and social structures of the nation are modeled on and derive their authority from the sanctified, domestic, patriarchal family.

Thus, *The Wild Irish Girl* establishes new and crucial terms in a debate with profound and wide-ranging implications. Lady Morgan's reimagination of social, political, and gender hierarchies en*gender*ed a dialogue whose ramifications can best be understood by placing a central focus upon the conceptions of idealized femininity within it, since her heroines were read not as powerful or progressive by critics like Croker and Edgeworth, but deviant. Edgeworth's Irish novels appearing after *The Wild Irish Girl* also offer a prescription for the (gradual) assimilation of two distinct cultures through the device of the allegorical marriage. However, the two cultures assimilated in Edgeworth's novels are not the English and Gaelic Irish who are united in *The Wild Irish Girl*, but the (metropolitan, imperial) British and the Anglo-Irish, whose ethnic and cultural roots are unmistakably *English*. To counteract Glorvina's influence, Edgeworth presents alternative examples of properly domesticated and largely voiceless Anglo-Irish heroines, and in her final Irish novel, *Ormond*, paints a picture of a Gaelic Irish anti-domesticity characterized by mothers breeding their children to a life of idleness, vice and crime (a stereotype which persisted throughout the nineteenth century). There is thus a strong line of demarcation separating the projects of Owenson and Edgeworth, who "mark their political differences from one another," in Katie Trumpener's phrase, "precisely in the way they order and recombine the same generic repertoire."[7] One of the more important themes addressed in the later novels of Lady Morgan and Edgeworth

---

[6]   The group of plays known as the (second) Henriad that includes *Richard II*, *Henry IV Parts 1* and *2*, and *Henry V*.

[7]   Trumpener, Katie. "National Character, Nationalist Plots: National Tale and Historical Novel in the Age of *Waverley*, 1806–1830," *English Literary History* 60 (1993), 685–731, 688.

was the conceptualization of anti-domesticity as a type of moral contagion, and the characterization of Gaelic Irishness (by Edgeworth) as a medium in which this contagion is engendered and spread. While again promoting a social hierarchy that relegates the Gaelic and Catholic Irish to child-like dependency in *Ormond* (1816), Edgeworth, following Burke, portrays deviant morality as the product of the authority and example of a diseased gentry class (significantly embodied in this novel, as elsewhere throughout her fiction, by a Gaelic Irishman who renounces Catholicism for the sake of material and social gain). Lady Morgan addresses this motif in *Florence McCarthy* (1817) and refutes it by directly attributing Ireland's social woes, as well as the spread of contagious physical disease, to the material conditions produced by British colonial policy[8].

The terms of the dialogue initiated by *The Wild Irish Girl* echoed throughout the nineteenth century in the work of later and influential commentators, including two of Britain's most popular and highly-regarded novelists, and, perhaps surprisingly, a co-founder of the international workers' movement. But in an intermediate stage of the conversation, Edgeworth's strategy of depicting Irish moral contagion as arising from unregulated desire in *Ormond*, which Lady Morgan refutes in her novel *Florence McCarthy*, was implemented in the 1830s by authorities such as James Kay (later Sir James Kay Shuttleworth) and George Cornewall Lewis. In arguments made before several Parliamentary and Royal Commissions, including one which led to the formation of Britain's national police force, these commentators directly and persistently equate Irish anti-domesticity with physical and moral contagion, and utilize the motif of anti-domestic Irish mothers breeding their children to a life of crime to argue for either the quarantining or expulsion of Irish immigrants from Britain's rapidly industrializing cities. Ironically, the authors of these reports and witnesses before the committees made the same linkage between physical and moral disease as did Lady Morgan in *Florence McCarthy* (but which Edgeworth did not). However, the *causes* of physical disease Lady Morgan identifies – squalor, filth and deprivation resulting largely from colonial policy – are instead characterized as *effects* of moral contagion by Kay and Cornewall Lewis. The reports of these committees further suggest that Irish anti-domesticity threatens to infect the English working classes, with whom Irish immigrants are in close contact in their poor urban neighborhoods, and thence the rest of British society. But these arguments and rhetorical strategies were by no means confined to rarefied political milieus. Various aspects of the relationship between James Kay's 1832 pamphlet *The Moral and Physical Condition of the Working Classes Employed in the Cotton Manufacture in Manchester*, and Friedrich Engels' *The Condition of the Working Classes in England* (1845), reveal how Engels utilizes Kay's metaphor of Irishness as a disease to argue for an international (workers') culture

---

8   She also in this novel creates a thinly-disguised character based on Croker himself, who represents the class of corrupt official middlemen who often manipulate the owners for their own ends, which are to wield the real political and economic power in Ireland to their own material benefit and the further suffering of the Irish peasantry.

to replace the British national cultural identity elaborated by Kay. Kay's work was extremely influential, as is evidenced by his prominence in the compilation of the Parliamentary reports, and well beyond the Houses of Parliament, as Engels' open acknowledgment of its effect on his own work makes clear. Kay, in advocating the factory-owners' interests, demands an end to government interference in business and markets, and an end to government welfare programs. He also proposes turning charity back over to benevolent associations and faith-based organizations, and most importantly, the removal of the Irish from Manchester. Such a program would allow profits to "heal" England's social woes, for in Kay's view, the Irish immigrants who were reducing wages by competing for industrial jobs brought with them not only physical diseases such as cholera, but, more dangerous to England, a moral contagion that destroyed the English workers' family life and values. Engels, on the other hand, argues that the economic system itself forced Irish immigration into British cities, and that the conditions imposed upon these immigrants naturally produces "drunkenness and sensual pleasure" as well as prostitution and crime, a situation which will lead to the war of "each against all" and the proletarian class versus the property-owning class. Engels, while decrying the degradation visited on the working classes, welcomes the hastening of the final crisis, which he likens to that of a physical disease and considers ultimately salutary. For Engels, the severity of the "condition of Irishness" will eventually lead to the healing of the working classes.

Edgeworth and Lady Morgan's dialogue may thus be observed not only to have had an influence on policies affecting the rule of Ireland and the treatment of Irish immigrants in Victorian Britain, but in the larger debates about the changes taking place in industry and its effects on modern life, down to the nature and benefits of capitalism itself, and the shape British society should take. Questioning the rigidities of the hierarchical boundaries of gender, class, and ethnicity in the manner of Lady Morgan, who herself was careful to retain those hierarchies even while arguing for expanded conceptions of them, also evoked reactions in the journals and commentary that helped shape public opinion of the day. Some of these observers painted progressive social ideas as a threat to the social structure, and in some cases as downright anarchical. In Croker's criticism, dating from the first decade of the nineteenth century to the 1830s, he develops his characterization of Lady Morgan as licentious and Jacobin, the latter being a term with a strong emotional charge in the political context of that time (akin to calling someone a Communist in the America of the early Cold War period, or a supporter of terrorists in the early twenty-first century), to dismiss her nuanced political positions wholesale. Edmund Burke had memorably portrayed the revolution in France in the personal terms of an invasion of Marie Antoinette's boudoir, and the term Jacobin connoted an anarchic and violent overturning of the social order, a rude assault upon the domestic patriarchal family at its core. Despite its inaccuracy in reference to Lady Morgan's politics, which were far from being anti-aristocratic, the term "Jacobin" is still applied to her even by sympathetic modern critics, a fact which belies a failure to carefully consider the exact nature of her arguments and fully appreciate why they were regarded as so dangerous by Croker and others, and why they continued to be invoked throughout much of the century in the ongoing project of constructing British national identity.

Lady Morgan's and Edgeworth's arguments also reverberate in works by William Makepeace Thackeray, for example, where the figure of the Irish woman again plays a crucial role. Thackeray's journalism often concerned itself with Irish politics and literature, and one of his chief complaints against romance recalls Croker's objection to Lady Morgan's "dangerous" sentiments. In reviewing historical romances by the Anglo-Irish writers Charles Lever and Arthur Lover, he charged that the radical themes often expressed in romance cannot be contained by the gesture toward social harmony in the comic ending. For Thackeray, a contagious anti-domesticity is a product of social class, but it eventually becomes apparent that Irishness is a marker of the class which produces it. Thackeray, it should be remembered, was (after the appearance of *Vanity Fair*) the only British novelist to rival Charles Dickens in popularity and stature. Early in his career he attributed the inassimilability of the Irish to their premodernity, and asserted in reviews and in his fiction that this cultural primitivism was a product of British colonial policy. His views were transformed over time, however, in large part owing to developments in Irish republicanism, which he characterized as ingratitude and intransigence.

In Thackeray's fiction, the novels *Barry Lyndon* (1843) and *Pendennis* (1848) notably engage the national tale tradition and its representations of gender ideals in constructing a normative British cultural nationalism, with increasingly anti-Unionist undertones that parallel the evolution of those sentiments expressed in his journalism. The hero of *Barry Lyndon* is depicted as inassimilable into British metropolitan society essentially because his Irishness renders him culturally primitive, a fact which Thackeray attributes in his *Irish Sketch Book* (1842) to the social structure resulting from British policies that have kept Ireland in a state resembling that of premodern European nations. But also present in this novel is a thoroughgoing Irish anti-domesticity. Barry acquires his aversion to working for a living from his mother, who also inculcates his snobbish, social-climbing manners. In *Pendennis*, his first novel following *Vanity Fair*, Thackeray represents Irish inadmissibility to the now-dominant British middle class as a product of ethnicity: the Irish "weren't made" to inhabit the same sphere as that to which his hero, Pen, belongs. Thackeray constructs in *Pendennis* an ideal in the English hero's mother against which the model of Mrs. Barry may be measured, and in the marriage plot prominently features an anti-domestic Irish woman against whom Laura, the English heroine Pen finally marries, irresistibly draws comparison. Pen's mother's objections to the sexually deviant and social-climbing Emily Costigan also echo Croker's disapproval of Lady Morgan's own marriage, since older women from the lower social classes seeking unsuitable marriages are potentially disruptive of the social order. Thus, in a year marked by social upheaval and unrest throughout Europe, and one which found Thackeray at the height of his popularity and influence, Irishness figures crucially (and negatively) in a novel strongly advocating a British cultural nationalism characterized by ethnic exclusivity and rigid, idealized gender norms that conform to the status quo.

In the Irish novels of Anthony Trollope, an increased pessimism regarding assimilation similar to Thackeray's is traceable. Trollope attributes much of the responsibility for the deteriorating prospects of a successful Union to the British. He too reprises the formal and ideological strategies of Lady Morgan's national tale, but rewrites the comic resolution in order to condemn British colonial policy. The marriage plot becomes in these novels a seduction plot. In his first novel, *The Macdermots of Ballycloran* (1847), Trollope characterizes the problems of assimilation he represents as remediable. *An Eye for an Eye* (1879), on the other hand, represents a full-circle return to the pessimism and irony of *Castle Rackrent*. The death of the hero represents the end of the corrupt colonial enterprise, but the confinement of Mrs. O'Hara, an embodiment of Irish nationalism, in "a private asylum in the West of England" (1) represents the insuperable alienation and forceful suppression of a large segment of the Irish population, a circumstance Trollope denied in *The Macdermots*. Thus the marriage plot structure utilized by Lady Morgan to express great hope for a future in which Britain and Ireland are united, provides Trollope a fitting means by which to chronicle the death of those hopes.

Discourse and the Novel

One of the salient features of these British novels which take the Irish in whole or in part as their subject (aside from Lady Morgan's, which, not coincidentally, all the others engage), is that they do so solely in the context of a British identity. The marginalization of Irish voices, even in novels that overtly and relatively sympathetically consider the "Irish Question," is indicative of how many nineteenth-century Britons could only conceive of the Irish in what Terry Eagleton and others have called "evolutionary triumphalism." In Trollope's *Phineas Finn; the Irish Member* (1869), for example, although Phineas is charming, the reader is never really encouraged to sympathize with him. His ambition in both politics and love are always obviously self-serving and somewhat less than heartfelt. Laurence Fitzgibbon, another Irish MP in the novel, is totally unscrupulous as well as totally devoid of any ambition beyond a determination to enjoy life to the fullest. Phineas's political career follows his romantic career – he is fickle and primarily looking for advancement in every move he makes (with the character Violet his wooing is ultimately revealed to be blatant adventuring for personal gain). The actual substance of Irish issues such as tenant rights is dismissively portrayed in this novel as "something of which no English reader will desire to know much".[9] But unfortunately, *Phineas Finn* goes beyond trivializing Irish political

---

    [9]   *Phineas Finn, the Irish Member* (1869). Oxford: Oxford University Press, 1992 (2:341). Neil McCaw points out that Trollope himself suggested in his *Autobiography* and elsewhere that "success [as an author] in England was not to be achieved by fiction that dealt with the politics of Ireland so conspicuously [as Trollope's first two novels, which were relative commercial failures, had]." See "Some Mid-Victorian Irishness(es): Trollope, Thackeray, Eliot" in *Writing Irishness in Nineteenth-Century British Culture*, ed. Neil McCaw. Aldershot (UK): Ashgate, 2004, 129–30.

and social issues. The nadir is perhaps reached when the Church of Ireland tithe problem is described as "one of those matters which seem to require the interposition of some higher power … to clear away the evil – as famine comes, and men are driven from want and ignorance and dirt to seek new homes and new thoughts across the broad waters … and war comes & slavery is banished from the earth."[10] Trollope here treats the famine as the consequence of God's mercy, as opposed to other possibilities (such as His indifference, or wrath, or perhaps British colonial policies, or some combination of these or other factors). Furthermore, as Eagleton noted in a discussion of Trollope's *Castle Richmond*, this type of Malthusian remark "undoes the results of human folly."[11] Not only is any British culpability expunged, but the famine, rather than being deplored for causing death, suffering, and hardship the likes of which modern Europe had never seen, is lauded for having providentially provided the impetus for near-savages on an overcrowded island to escape and breathe free in more auspicious (and more distant) climes. This response a mere twenty years after the fact, despite its posture of high-minded Christian acceptance, expressed in language and cadences that seem consciously to echo the American President Lincoln's second inaugural address, unlike that speech betrays a coldness and lack of sympathy towards Trollope's fellow-members of the human race, his countrymen, which the Irish were under the Union. And Trollope had lived and worked among these "countrymen" for many years in his career with the Post Office. One wonders whether he would have exhibited the same degree of stoicism had a disaster of similar relative magnitude befallen England. In any event, clearly this Union has failed to become the imagined community that is a modern nation. *Phineas Finn*, like most nineteenth-century British novels, makes no mention of the repeal movement, republicanism, or home rule (let alone attempt to examine Irish positions or sentiments and their reasons for them on these issues), because it is only able to conceive of Irish cultural identity as "West British." The customs, manners, and mores of the Irish people are not matter for absorption into the body politic, but rather markers of inferiority that attach to characters like Corny O'Shane, Barry Lyndon, and Laurence Fitzgibbon. However, it is not my intention here to claim a self-righteous moral superiority and sneer at authors from an earlier epoch for their backward, unenlightened attitudes a century and more after the fact. Far from it – I get immense enjoyment from much of their work, and I appreciate the fact that these writers also had many admirable qualities as human beings. Trollope, for instance, was deeply troubled by the immorality of British actions toward the Irish (as evidenced in *An Eye for an Eye*), Kay worked tirelessly to promote public health and later as an educational reformer, and Thackeray was actually much more sympathetic to the Irish than many, indeed most, of his countrymen (and *Pendennis* is an underappreciated novel with some brilliantly realized comic characters – notably Major Pendennis). But the cultural nationalism to which they subscribed had consequences both immediate and long lasting, and should be understood for what it was.

---

[10] *Phineas Finn, the Irish Member.* op. cit. (2:181).

[11] Eagleton. *Heathcliff and the Great Hunger.* New York: Verso, 1995, 388.

In the chapters that follow I hope to demonstrate that nineteenth-century attempts to impose British culture on Ireland, the coding throughout the century of Irishness as the antithesis of an idealized British national identity, and a general inability to see Ireland and the Irish through anything other than a colonial lens, were integral (though sometimes unconscious) parts of a long-running project of cultural nation-building. Put another way, I will argue, basing my claims on the evidence of a wide range of cultural artifacts including novels, journalism, and political documents, that many British commentators of the nineteenth century practiced what constitutes a form of "Orientalism." In his classic study, Edward Said defines Orientalism as "a kind of Western projection onto and will to govern over the Orient" that manifests itself in innumerable cultural productions, from the social sciences to the fine arts.[12] Even more important to my thesis, however, is Said's premise that the identification of the Other is central to how one defines oneself. In his Introduction, Said claims that "without examining Orientalism as a discourse one cannot possibly understand the enormously systematic discipline by which European culture was able to manage – and even produce – the Orient politically, sociologically, militarily, and imaginatively during the post-Enlightenment period ... European culture gained in strength and identity by setting itself off against the Orient as a sort of surrogate and even underground self."[13] As Britain's "first colony," the 'Orientalizing" of Ireland, the Irish, and Irish women in particular, parallels, and was every bit as pervasive as was Orientalism in Britain's interactions with Eastern cultures, and furthermore figured perhaps more prominently in the construction of British national identity. It seems an inescapable conclusion that this process was in some ways analogous to the developments in the United States' expansion across the North American continent. The almost total eradication of the Irish language and the imposition of customs and manners more closely follow similar developments in Wales and Scotland in previous centuries. But the policies of willful neglect and marginalization of the "natives" who had previously been driven onto the least profitable lands directly contributed to the Famine, and the resulting diaspora (which had actually begun previously, but was greatly accelerated by this catastrophe) constitutes Ireland's own "Trail of Tears." It is therefore important to take a close look at the ways in which the British "wrote" Irishness in the nineteenth century.

The project of constructing national cultural identity takes place across a range of discourses, and in making my case I examine how various tropes and conceptualizations migrated across discursive boundaries to show not only how one genre or discourse influences others, but how they all reinforce each other as well. While the overall structure is chronological in order to trace the "thread" of the conversation as it developed, the chapters are not strictly chronological. Specifically, after having traced the development and the migration of the trope of contagious anti-domesticity from Edgeworth's novels to the nonfiction work

---

[12]   Edward Said. *Orientalism*. New York: Vintage, 1979, 95.

[13]   Said. 1979, 2, 3. Linda Colley, in the Introduction to her magisterial *Britons: Forging the Nation 1707–1837*. New Haven: Yale University Press, 1992, makes a similar point: "[M]en and women decide who they are by reference to who and what they are not" (7).

of Kay and then to that of Engels, I backtrack a bit (chronologically speaking) to cover the journalism of Croker and Thackeray and on into Thackeray's fiction and beyond with a focus upon the use of Irish anti-domesticity in the construction of an idealized British national culture. The glances at non-fiction and journalism give evidence of the power and pervasiveness of the phenomena we are dealing with. The preponderance of my attention throughout the book, however, will be focused on the novel, because to a great degree a nation's boundaries – what it includes, and what it excludes – are conceptualized and elaborated in its fictions. Timothy Brennan persuasively argues that nations

> are imaginary constructs that depend for their existence on an apparatus of cultural fictions in which imaginative literature plays a decisive role. And the rise of European nationalism coincides especially with one form of literature – the novel…It was the novel that historically accompanied the rise of nations by objectifying the "one, yet many" of national life; and by mimicking the structures of the nation, a clearly bordered jumble of languages and styles.[14]

Benedict Anderson himself suggests that the novel is the exemplar of cultural nationalism *par excellence* when he asserts that it "mimics the structures of the nation," in Brennan's phrase, by imagining a delimited social space full of representative institutions and characters:

> [W]e see the "national imagination" at work in the movement of a solitary hero through a sociological landscape of a fixity that fuses the world inside the novel with the world outside. The picaresque *tour d'horison* – hospitals, prisons, remote villages, monasteries, Indians, Negroes – is nonetheless not a *tour du monde*. The horizon is clearly bounded.[15]

---

[14]   Brennan, Timothy, "The National Longing for Form," in *Nation and Narration*, ed. Homi Bhabha, 49. Brennan's formulation of "a clearly bordered jumble of languages and styles" invokes the concept of heteroglossia taken from Mikhail Bakhtin's "Discourse and the Novel," and this and other insights from Bakhtin's work pervade my study. That authors of novels (and narrators of nations) juxtapose various "languages," and by the ways in which they place them in the context they've created assign relative values to them – that authors, in a word, dialogize the speech acts represented in their works – is an implicit assumption made throughout this book. See *The Dialogic Imagination: Four Essays by MM Bakhtin*, ed. Michael Holquist. Austin: University of Texas Press, 1981. As is perhaps also evident, my discussion throughout this book also draws heavily on Michel Foucault's insights into the emergence and role of various discourses and their domains in the distribution and exercise of social power. See especially *Discipline and Punish*, trans. Alan Sheridan. New York: Vintage (Random House), 1995, and *The History of Sexuality* vol. 1, trans. Robert Hurley. New York: Pantheon Books, 1978.

[15]   Anderson, Benedict. *Imagined Communities: Reflections on the Origins and Spread of Nationalism*. London: Verso, 1991, 30. Anderson's idea of historical time as represented in the modern, realist novel clearly resonates with that of Bakhtin's concept of the historical time chronotope, and as I argue below, Lady Morgan's *Wild Irish Girl* presents the Union of Great Britain and Ireland as an event that takes place in historical time in an otherwise Romantic novel. See "Forms of Time and Chronotope in the Novel," *The Dialogic Imagination*, 84–258.

It is not merely coincidence, in other words, that modern conceptualizations of society and culture were formed simultaneously with the great age of the novel. Our sense of history's diachronic properties is itself "novelistic," as Anderson asserts: "The idea of a sociological organism moving calendrically through homogenous, empty time is a precise analogue of the idea of the nation, which is also conceived as a solid community moving steadily down (or up) history."[16]

The subtle yet compelling quality of narrative makes authors of novels (along with, in more recent times, filmmakers) the most influential participants in discursive conflicts around nationhood: stories have the power to transform social structures and to shape what it means to be the member of a national culture. Ian Duncan claims that "by 1850 in Britain the novel was the ascendant form for the representation of a national cultural identity."[17] However, that the novel has this power seems to have been recognized implicitly by the creators of the great political reviews which arose in the beginning of the nineteenth century as well.[18] Describing their project in phrases more characteristic of their own era but which nevertheless reveal a preoccupation with cultural identity, such as "the instruction of morals and taste," *The Edinburgh Review* and *The Quarterly Review* were veritably obsessed with novels and their impact on readers. Indeed, a large part of the reviews' *raison d'être* was the expropriation of what was assumed to be the immense cultural authority of the novel from female authors and readers, who had with the recent dramatic rise in literacy come to be perceived as dominating the field,[19] for the purpose of restoring that authority to reviewers in the male-dominated "republic of letters."[20] In a rationale typical of many throughout the period, for instance, in a review appearing in *The Quarterly* of Edgeworth's *Tales of Fashionable Life*, the reviewers justify their project by citing the great reach of fiction: "If the importance of a literary work is to be estimated by the number of

---

[16]   Anderson, 26.

[17]   Duncan, Ian. *Modern Romance and Transformations of the Novel: The Gothic, Scott, Dickens*. Cambridge: Cambridge University Press, 1992, 2.

[18]   The political power and influence of these reviews has been well documented. See particularly John Klancher's *The Making of the English Reading Audiences, 1790–1832*. Madison: University of Wisconsin Press, 1987, and Peter F. Morgan's *Literary Critics and Reviewers in Early 19th-Century Britain*. London: Croom Helm, 1983.

[19]   For the perception of the novel as a field dominated by women by the end of the 18th century, see the pioneering surveys of J.M.S. Tompkins, *The Popular Novel in England 1770–1800*. London: Methuen, 1932, and John Tinnon Taylor, *Early Opposition to the English Novel: Popular Reaction from 1760 to 1830*. New York: King's Crown Press, 1943. Ian Watt, in his landmark *The Rise of the Novel* (Berkeley, University of California Press, 1957) estimates that the production of books nearly quadrupled over previous centuries in the period of 1792–1802, and agrees that women were predominant among the exponentially higher number of readers (37, 43–5).

[20]   This argument is convincingly made by Ina Ferris in *The Achievement of Literary Authority*. Ithaca: Cornell University Press, 1991, Chapter 1.

readers it attracts, and the effect which it produces upon character and moral taste, a novel or a tale cannot be deemed a trifling production."[21]

The novel derived much of its burgeoning popularity in the late eighteenth and early nineteenth centuries through its incorporation of the tropes of melodrama and romance, as the tremendous success of the novels of Ann Radcliffe, among others, demonstrates. As noted above, a large part of the newly expanded audience was female, and the tropes these readers were familiar with soon proved popular with male readers, too, as Sir Walter Scott's literary preeminence, beginning with the publication of the Waverley novels, attests – the Waverley series consisting of historical novels which featured a young, ordinary, and sometimes female central character such as Jeannie Deans, whose personal concerns encapsulated larger, public issues.[22] As Scott's novels as well as those of Radcliffe make evident, the tropes of romance often thematize social and sociological concerns (in the novels of Radcliffe and the female Gothic generally, one of the main thematic elements was often specifically women's plight in the patriarchy). Thus, a crucial aspect of what the appropriation of "feminine" conventions into newly "masculinized" genres brought to the novel, in addition to popularity and wide influence, is the emphasis upon individual psychological and emotional states, and the encoding of public, political concerns in private, personal plots. By juxtaposing formal and generic elements, the novel called for a new way of reading, and seeing, and hence a new way of imagining community. Such aesthetic intertextuality had parallels in theatrical melodrama from the eighteenth and early nineteenth centuries, whose artistic practices had developed in part because of prohibitions on content on the "legitimate" stage, and which gave rise to "illegitimate" productions in which folk and current popular traditions were overlaid with "establishment" dramaturgical and fictional structures.[23] While these generic developments were largely a result of commercial considerations in the theater, the novel often exploited this new generic intertextuality for a radical and much more serious moral purpose (though commercial considerations were not irrelevant), as will be seen when we examine novels in subsequent chapters, beginning with Lady Morgan's work. Moreover, the authors examined in this study consciously exploited the "romantic" conventions

---

[21]   *Quarterly Review* 2 (1809), 146.

[22]   See Duncan's *Modern Romance* for the role romance plays in the modern "realist" novel, as well as Scott's incorporation of romantic tropes in his fiction; see also Ferris 1991, et al.

[23]   For histories of the use of melodramatic signifiers in 19th-century drama, as well as the continued use of these tropes in modern film, see Thomas Elsaesser's "Tales of Sound and Fury: Observations on the Family Melodrama," in *Monogram*, No. 4. London: British Film Institute, 1972, reprinted in *Film Theory and Criticism*, eds Gerald Mast et al. New York: Oxford University Press, 1992, 512–35, and Christine Gledhill, "The Melodramatic Field: An Investigation," in *Home is Where the Heart Is*, ed Christine Gledhill. London: British Film Institute, 1987. The "illegitimacy" of female authors and novels in general, of such concern to the great 19th-century political reviews, not so coincidentally parallels developments surrounding stage melodrama.

of the novel in order to engage other works of fiction. As Leo Braudy has noted regarding the study of genre in film, formal structure carries signification, and can thus be deployed to comment upon representation itself.[24]

Interspersed with the chapters discussing particular novels will be others examining literary criticism, political discourse, and works of social reform, all of which both directly and indirectly take up the issues contested by Lady Morgan and Edgeworth. As alluded to previously, the purpose of these chapters is to demonstrate the power and extent of a pattern, which crosses temporal, political and discursive boundaries, and in which the construction of British national identity centers upon the representation of Irish women. It is my hope that, taken in its entirety, this book will have identified a "genealogy" which has not yet been noted in the fields of literary or cultural studies, nor in the developing field of Irish literary and cultural history.

---

[24]   Braudy, Leo. *The World in a Frame*. New York: Doubleday/Anchor, 1977, 111.

Chapter 2
The Mild Irish Girl:
Domesticating the National Tale

The Wild Irish Girl: Owenson

At the outset of the newly-created Union of Great Britain and Ireland, hopes were high in some quarters that the joining of these two nations, despite their troubled past, would lead to an eventual recognition of the Irish people's rights, and allow them to more fully participate in not only their own government, but the larger British culture as well. An early disappointment came immediately following the Act of Union on January 1, 1801, when the intransigence of King George III and large segments of the English population, with the enthusiastic support of the Tory party, forced Pitt the Younger to renege on his promises of Catholic Emancipation. The popular and longest-serving Prime Minister in British history up to that time resigned as a point of honor. Yet Sydney Owenson, daughter of an English mother and Gaelic Irish father, still regarded the Act of Union as an event of great promise. There still existed much prejudice in England against the Irish, as the Pitt debacle had shown. Ireland was associated not only with backwardness and insurrection, but also with sublime ruins and landscapes which captured the Romantic English imagination. Owenson seized on these latter aspects in order to write a polemic that she hoped would soften British predispositions against the Irish.

In *The Wild Irish Girl*, the language, religion, and traditions of the Gaelic Irish, embodied in the heroine Glorvina, wholly seduce the English adventurer Horatio. Revolutionary movements such as the United Irishmen are acknowledged, but ascribed to a misguided patriotism, recuperable through the reversal of long-standing and injurious colonial policies. As a means of beginning to integrate the Gaelic Irish into the British social body, the plot of Owenson's novel directly addresses issues of colonial guilt and reparation. Horatio frequently expresses regret that his ancestor murdered Glorvina's and dispossessed her family of their land during the Cromwellian wars. The resolution of the Oedipal conflict between Horatio and his father, who had been promised Glorvina in marriage, points towards a restoration of the inheritance. Beyond this restoration, the allegorical marriage suggests a transformation of the colonial settlement from one largely characterized by absenteeism and mutual ignorance and hostility, to a relationship of reciprocal responsibility and equal rights shared by settler and native, with the blessing of the "parent" society of the colonist. Just as important, Owenson's two lovers also seek the blessing and assimilate the values and traditions of the parent society of the colonized or dispossessed, represented in the person of the dying Prince (Glorvina's father). Furthermore, and crucial to Owenson's vision, the new cultural and political dispensation is embodied in a transformation of *ancien-régime* sexual arrangements.

Owenson's treatment of Roman Catholicism highlights the way in which *The Wild Irish Girl* seeks to recuperate native culture in the eyes of the colonists. Religious difference was seen as a major obstacle to the assimilation of the Irish and English into a unified British nation, and indeed, has bedeviled the relationship between "settler" and "native" until today. Owenson, unlike many of her contemporaries however, portrays the Catholicism strongly associated with the Gaelic Irish not as a dark force motivating a hostile, primitive, alien people, but as a positive, if picturesque, precursor to the more enlightened Protestantism of the Established Church.[1] Ina Ferris has argued that "all the energies [of *The Wild Irish Girl*] are drawn to the same point: the vindication of Gaelic culture as the origin of the nation, the repository of the true 'ancient Irish' character."[2] Owenson's hero, Horatio, is the second son of an English earl sent to Ireland by his father to study law as atonement for some unspecified sins of his youth. Horatio finds Catholicism, as he does the Irish language, landscape and customs, *seductive*: "What a religion is this! How seducingly it speaks to the senses. What a captivating, what a *picturesque* faith! Who would not become its proselyte, were it not for the stern opposition of reason – the cold suggestion of philosophy!" (original italics).[3] Horatio here asserts the *aesthetic* appeal of Gaelic Irish culture, using terms which move from the erotic (Catholicism "seducingly speaks to the senses") to a more polite, aesthetic containment ("picturesque"). Roman Catholicism, in this figuration, becomes a kind of ruin on the cultural landscape which Horatio at this point reads in a way that Katie Trumpener has characterized as "aesthetiquarian: the more ruins, the more beautiful."[4] Jaded by the excesses of a prodigal youth in English society at home and on the Continent, he is at first merely anxious to relieve his *ennui* by touring the countryside. By examining the ruins more closely under the tutelage of Glorvina, however, Horatio (presumably along with the implied English reader) moves beyond a merely touristic understanding of Gaelic culture.

Prejudiced at the outset, Horatio begins to understand Catholicism as an earlier cultural stage of British Protestantism, analogous to the pagan religions and traditions that have been superseded by Christianity and modern Western culture.

---

[1]   An indication of English suspicions toward Catholicism was its frequent portrayal as a sinister and primitive force in popular Gothic novels of the period. For two of the most popular examples see Ann Radcliffe's *Mysteries of Udolpho* and Matthew Lewis's *The Monk*. Anti-Catholic feeling sometimes manifested itself violently, as in the 1788 Gordon riots.

[2]   Ferris, Ina. "Writing on the Border: The National Tale, Female Writing, and the Public Sphere," in *Romanticism, History, and the Possibilities of Genre*, eds Tilottama Rajan and Julia M. Wright. Cambridge: Cambridge University Press, 1998, 96.

[3]   Owenson, Sydney (Lady Morgan). *The Wild Irish Girl*. London: Oxford University Press, 1999, 50. All subsequent references to the novel will be to this edition.

[4]   In "National Character, Nationalist Plots: National Tale and Historical Novel in the Age of *Waverley*, 1806–1830," *English Literary History* 60 (1993), 701.

When his long conversation with the local priest, whose learning and charity are emphasized, is interrupted by a peasant whose needs the priest immediately breaks off to minister to, Horatio muses: "As I rode along reflecting on the wondrous influence of superstition. I could not help dwelling on the strong analogy which in so many instances appears between the vulgar errors of this country and that of the ancient as well as modern Greeks."[5] The novel suggests that with the assimilation of the English and Irish cultures, Roman Catholicism will be superseded peacefully, in the natural course of events. Horatio is surprised and delighted to hear Glorvina describe some of the peasants' religious beliefs as "ignorant prejudices" and assert that Catholics adhere to their religion for social, not spiritual and doctrinal reasons:

> Of the many who are inheritors of *our* persuasion, *all* are not devoted to its errors, or influenced by its superstitions. If its professors are coalesced, it is in the sympathy of their destinies, not in the dogmas of their belief. If they are allied, it is by the tye of temporal interest, not by the bond of speculative opinion; they are united as *men*, not as sectaries; and once incorporated in the great mass of general society ... their affections, like their privileges, will be in common ...they will forget they had ever been the *individual* adherents of an alienated body.[6] (original emphasis).

Glorvina argues here that the extension to the Gaelic Irish of the *political and social* privileges enjoyed by other British subjects will remove the causes of sectarian division between Irish and British. This is a progressive insight. Owenson's point that church affiliation is mainly a symbol of cultural identity recognizes that the divisions and alienation associated with it stem from the *political and social* "disabilities" attached to Catholicism. At the very least, she attempts to complicate the overheated dialogue concerning religion and transform it into something beyond partisan name-calling (although the references to ignorance and superstition clearly indicate her own allegiance in the matter of religion).[7] Glorvina's theology (she doesn't convert from Roman Catholicism) is left suspended. When Horatio asks her outright whether she does not "receive all the doctrines of [her] church as infallible," she does not reply directly. Horatio informs the reader in a narratorial aside that "in a few words she convinced me that on the subject of religion, as upon every other, her strong mind discovered itself to be an emanation of that divine intelligence, which her pure soul worships 'in spirit

---

5   *The Wild Irish Girl*, 130.

6   Ibid., 187–8.

7   Owenson's observation that a professed allegiance to religion is often the way in which members of social groups assert cultural identity is also ahead of its time. Priests and others working with Irish immigrants in Great Britain make similar observations a generation later in Henry Mayhew's *London Labour and the London Poor*, a groundbreaking sociological work that first appeared as a series of articles in the *Morning Chronicle* in 1849–50.

and in truth.'"[8] The novel evades the fact of actual religious conversion, but while it implies a gradual erosion of adherence to the Catholic faith, this is brought about by reforms in the secular realm (that is, social, economic, and political) with which the novel is primarily concerned.

Owenson's portrayal of Catholicism indicates that *The Wild Irish Girl* represents a dynamic Ireland at a moment of historical transition, which is further reflected in the narrative's movement between generic registers. Katie Trumpener argues that fictional historiography underwent a generic change shortly after the publication of *The Wild Irish Girl*, from the premodern national tale (which in her formulation Owenson's text epitomizes) to the modern historical novel, inaugurated by Walter Scott's *Waverley*. This seems too schematic a distinction in the case of *The Wild Irish Girl*. Trumpener argues that historical stages are represented in the national tales as "geographical," while in the historical novel they are represented as "temporal." She locates the action of *The Wild Irish Girl* purely within what Mikhail Bakhtin has identified as the adventure-time chronotope, which for Trumpener situates Owenson's work securely in the genre of the national tale:

> The national tale before *Waverley* maps developmental stages topographically, as adjacent worlds in which characters move and then choose between ... In contrast, the historical novel ... finds its focus in the way one developmental stage collapses to make room for the next and cultures are transformed under the pressure of historical events.[9]

However, the clear-cut distinction Trumpener draws is problematic in the case of *The Wild Irish Girl*. In the first place, in Bakhtin's analysis, characters residing in the adventure time chronotope (time/space) do not undergo any development or change – they emerge from the adventure exactly the same (psychologically or morally) as they entered it. This is clearly not the case with Horatio. Glorvina's eventual acceptance of the conqueror's heir also represents development. Owenson's portrayal of Catholicism as a precursor to modern religion, analogous to Greek paganism, also suggests historic, and therefore generic, transition. In other words, the events that take place in *The Wild Irish Girl* do not take place exclusively "outside of history." While Ireland is largely represented in the Romantic register in *The Wild Irish Girl*, as the sublime landscapes and heightened sensibilities of the protagonists suggest, its suspension in adventure time is clearly attributed to dynamic material and cultural causes, which are furthermore transformed with the comic resolution – Horatio and Glorvina's union, situated in historical time. Trumpener's formulation, then, must be adapted to account more accurately for Owenson's novel. To encourage a reappraisal of the colonial past, Owenson represents an Ireland suspended in adventure time in order to emphasize the effects of that past, and includes copious footnotes and anecdotal historical evidence in

---

[8]   *The Wild Irish Girl*, 187.

[9]   In *Bardic Nationalism: The Romantic Novel and the British Empire*. Princeton: Princeton University Press, 1997, 141.

the work to document the presumed causes. She thus argues in *The Wild Irish Girl* that the stasis and stagnation pervading Irish economic, political, and social life are produced by an alienating and repressive colonial policy that can and should be replaced by an equal and inclusive Union. Horatio and Glorvina's union represents a moral and psychological breakthrough for each partner, particularly Horatio, whose development continues throughout the novel in historical time. Owenson implies that Ireland will enter a new developmental stage at the commencement of such a Union.

But if indeed *The Wild Irish Girl* points to the eventual predominance of Anglicized beliefs and customs, is Owenson, like Edgeworth, engaging in a project of Anglo-Irish cultural hegemony? Liz Bellamy asserts that "[*The Wild Irish Girl's*] unproblematic union of Ireland with England provided an allegorical celebration of political union while it suppressed the hegemonic implications of the latter act."[10] This is true to a certain extent, but while the allegorical marriage is pointed to in *The Wild Irish Girl*, it never actually takes place – in other words, Union is suggested, but not represented. Clearly, some very specific transformations must precede any "true" Union. What Owenson is proposing here is quite progressive – some would say radical – in that it is a much more inclusive and expansive conception of British national identity, one that has only been embraced, in fact, quite recently.

Most importantly, and not only from the standpoint of the responses it elicited, Owenson's idealized transformation extends to, indeed hinges upon, the realm of gender relations. The significance of this fact has not received adequate recognition from modern feminist literary historians (although it was acutely perceived by some contemporary readers such as Croker and, as will be seen below, Edgeworth). Perhaps because Owenson's heroines have long been recognized as thinly veiled embodiments of the public persona she herself adopted upon achieving fame, they have sometimes been dismissed as arguing not for the empowerment of women, but for the aggrandizement of Sydney Owenson.[11] However, these characters are not merely self-serving projections of an idealized Lady Morgan. The heroines of Owenson's Irish novels all play a crucial role in the expression of her social and political vision (and in *Florence McCarthy*, Morgan's response to Edgeworth's *Ormond*, the heroine exerts more authority than the male hero). Through Glorvina,

---

[10]   Bellamy, Liz. "Regionalism and Nationalism: Maria Edgeworth, Walter Scott, and the Definition of Britishness," in *The Regional Novel in Britain and Ireland, 1800–1990*, ed. K.D.M. Snell. Cambridge: Cambridge University Press, 1998, 63.

[11]   Terry Eagleton sums up the response: "[Owenson's] exuberant self-fashioning as the wild Irish girl, with its excess and extravagant narcissism ... the critics ... view as grotesquely pretentious." But Eagleton does not acknowledge any further importance to this expanded imagining of female roles than it serving as "a highly calculated critique of a certain species of male realism and rationality." See "Form and Ideology in the Anglo-Irish Novel," in *Literary Interrelations: Ireland, Egypt and the Far East*, eds. Wolfgang Zack and Henry Kosok. Tubingen: Gunter Narr Verlag, 1987, 140.

The Wild Irish Girl argues for increased equality both between Britain and Ireland and between women and men.

In effect, the novel offers a displaced *cultural* solution in its transformed gender relations. Perhaps the most significant aspect of the allegorical Glorvina's character is her embodiment of a progressive, activist, and most tellingly, public character. Her profound learning argues for a much more equal partnership than those typical of contemporary marriages, in fiction or in real life (although Owenson's own marriage a few years later to Sir Charles Morgan reflected the ideals she expressed in her fiction). Far from being subservient, Glorvina schools Horatio in Irish language, culture, botany, and history, while he teaches her painting. It is her imparting of this great learning, and her active role in administering her aging father's estates, that seduce Horatio. As Joseph W. Lew points out, "scenes of language learning and seduction assume prominent positions in the plot and are often intertwined."[12] Horatio, the English adventurer, has been traveling in "Connaught, which [Horatio] is told is the classic ground of Ireland."[13] The sublime landscape, and even more the sympathetic, intelligent, and hitherto misrepresented people of Ireland (as he concludes), begin to seduce the reluctant visitor. Since he wishes to prolong his stay, he adopts a fictitious identity, not however for the purpose of indulging passively in an idyll, but for what he sees as tending to the "mutual advantage" of himself and the natives of the castle and surrounding area:

> Already deep in adventure, a thousand seducing reasons were suggested by my newly awakened heart, to go on with the romance, and to secure for my future residence in the castle, that interest, which, if known to be the son of Lord M----, I must have eventually forfeited ... The imposition was at least innocent, and might tend to future and mutual advantage, and after the ideal assumption of a thousand fictitious characters, I at last fixed on that of ... [the] self-nominated *Henry Mortimer*.[14] (original italics)

The interest Horatio is fearful of forfeiting is not Glorvina's, but that of her father, who implacably hates the conquering English who dispossessed his family. When Horatio asserts that the continued strengthening of affection and interest between himself, the legal holder of the property, and the Prince, who considers himself (as do most of the local people) the legitimate heir to it, will be mutually beneficial, he points to the improvements that must come from reconciliation.[15] Some of these anticipated benefits, suggested throughout the text and in footnotes, include

---

[12] "Sydney Owenson and the Fate of Empire," *Keats-Shelley Journal* 39 (1990), 45.

[13] *The Wild Irish Girl*, 17.

[14] Ibid., 55.

[15] Robert Tracy argues (in "Maria Edgeworth and Lady Morgan: Legality versus Legitimacy") that the novels of both Owenson and Edgeworth didactically urged the establishment of long lasting social order in Ireland through the ruling classes' securing of the consent of the Irish people in addition to the protection of British law (Tracy, 1985, 1–22).

a relaxing of the Penal Laws, the restrictive colonial policies that impede Gaelic Irish learning and participation in politics, agriculture and commerce, as well as a reduction of the continued hostility between English and Irish. In other words, Horatio contemplates an active and positive engagement with the local populace. He renounces the role intended for him, that of absentee landlord like his father, and imagines a close relationship with Ireland and the Irish in the manner of the Prince and his Milesian ancestors[16]: "I raised my eyes to the Castle of Inismore and sighed, and almost wished that I had been born the Lord of these beautiful ruins ... the adored Chieftain of these affectionate and natural people."[17] Horatio's "almost wished" vision becomes his ultimately achieved reality over the course of the novel, as Glorvina's intellectual and spiritual charms seduce Horatio and spur him into active self-improvement.

Horatio's seduction and ultimate attainment of a selfhood that makes him worthy to take the place of the Prince in the affections of Glorvina and the Irish people represents a significant break from literary tradition on Owenson's part. In traditional representations, from the Dido episode in *The Aeneid* to the Wales of *Henry IV Part 1*, the seduction of a colonial adventurer characteristically has clearly negative effects. Against these prototypes, Owenson portrays the attraction of her hero (who, echoing two separate characters from Shakespeare's *Henriad*, assumes the name *Henry Mortimer*) as a process that leads to his intellectual and moral growth. Thus *The Wild Irish Girl* foregrounds a topos long familiar in Western literature – the theme of overturning normative gender roles – but reverses the connotations usually attached to it.[18] Patricia Parker describes the disruption of the social order usually associated with the overturning of normative gender roles: "The sense of ... sexual contest (between Verdant and the Enchantress) ... evokes a recall not only of Mars and Venus but of a whole series of subject males and dominating female figures, from Hercules and Omphale to Samson reclining in the lap of that Delilah who deprives him of his strength."[19]

The implications of this theme in *The Wild Irish Girl* become clear when Owenson's novel is considered in relation to the prototypes. In *The Aeneid*, for example, the gods intervene and Aeneas must leave Dido because she is diverting him from his colonial mission, while in *1 Henry IV* Mortimer is seduced by the Celtic Glendower's daughter and thus fails to come to the aid of Hotspur. The *Henriad* is of particular relevance here. Scott acknowledged his debt to Maria Edgeworth in the "Postscript, which should have been a Preface" to *Waverley*, and many critics

---

[16]   *The Wild Irish Girl* frequently mentions that the Prince, like many Gaelic Irish nobles, also traced his ancestry to conquerors – the sons of Mileseus, who according to legend arrived in Ireland from Spain in the 11th century.

[17]   Ibid., 52.

[18]   Stephen Greenblatt in *Renaissance Self-Fashioning: From More to Shakespeare* (Chicago: University of Chicago Press, 1980) has demonstrated the colonial significance of this trope in his discussion of the Bower of Bliss episode in Spenser's *Faerie Queen* (Chapter 4).

[19]   Parker, *Literary Fat Ladies: Rhetoric, Gender, Property*. London: Methuen, 1987, 57.

have commented on Edgeworth's influence on Scott since. Connections between Owenson and Scott, on the other hand, have rarely been made. However, Ina Ferris takes note of some important parallels: "Scott ... may playfully recall Morgan's Glorvina in the introductory chapter of *Waverley*...but his own harp-playing Flora and the journey structure of the novel have strong affinities with Morgan's popular tale."[20] Still another point of contact between *Waverley* and *The Wild Irish Girl* are the ways in which both novels make use of the *Henriad*. The significance of Owenson's invocation of Shakespeare's second history tetralogy is great not only for its probable, though unacknowledged, influence on Scott (as well as writers such as Edgeworth and Trollope). Recognition of just how she reworks its gender themes provides a key insight into her cultural project.

A short scene in *1 Henry IV* and the comic ending of *Henry V* together provide a model of the complete reversal of normative hierarchies and their subsequent re-establishment. These diametrically opposed scenes serve as a thematic frame upon which the ideology of the *Henriad* rests. In the first of these episodes the rebel leader Mortimer provides a contrast to Prince Hal, "the mirror for all Christian kings," by allowing himself to be seduced in his Welsh "bower" by the daughter of Owen Glendower, a seduction which appears to rely on his failure to speak her language.[21] In the bower with his Welsh wife, Mortimer fumes impotently: "This is the deadly spite that angers me – / My wife can speak no English, and I no Welsh."[22] He still is seduced, however, and in the midst of preparations for war, Mortimer allows his wife (through her father's translation!) to persuade him to cast aside all duty:

> Glendower:
> She bids you on the wanton rushes lay you down .
> and she will sing the song that pleaseth you
> And on your eyelids crown the god of sleep,
> Charming your blood with pleasing heaviness,
> Making such difference 'twixt wake and sleep
> As is the difference betwixt day and night
> Mortimer:
> With all my heart I'll sit and hear her sing.[23]

The imagery in Glendower's speech thematizes the leveling of differences in this scene. It records the blurring of the boundaries between wake and sleep produced by the Welsh woman's song, and the erasure of the difference between night and day in the hour of the dawn. This imagery also reinforces the obliteration of the gender hierarchy upon which the social order is based – that which Hal forcefully reinscribes in the scene of his wooing. In the comic ending of *Henry V*, it will be

---

[20]   Ferris, Ina. *The Achievement of Literary Authority*. Ithaca: Cornell University Press, 1991, 123.

[21]   *Henry IV* 1.3.1.190*ff.*

[22]   Ibid., lines 191–2.

[23]   Ibid., lines 213, 215–19, 222.

remembered, Hal masters his wife by means of "Englishing" her; that is, imposing his language on his victim of conquest. Henry completes his cultural conquest by forcing Kate to violate the customs of France and kiss him, thus repeating a familiar English pattern of extirpating the language and customs of conquered peoples.[24] It is clear, however, that while Shakespeare suggests linguistic community or commonalty in this scene and a leveling of differences, the power relationship remains vertical and hierarchical, with England and English on top.

Parallels between Owenson's hero and Shakespeare's Mortimer are evident in the manner by which Horatio meets Glorvina. As he gazes on the ruins of the Castle of Inismore, the last remaining portion of Glorvina's patrimony that has not been appropriated by Horatio's ancestor, Horatio is seduced by the singing of the harp-playing daughter of the Celtic chief with the "beautiful voice."[25] In Owenson's re-imagining of the scene, however, he climbs the wall of the Castle in order to seek out a relationship which throughout the novel will challenge him on many levels: "Directed by the witching strain ... I climbed, with some difficulty, the ruins of a parapet wall ... [which gave] me, when I stood on it, a perfect view of the interior of the apartment."[26] Although Glorvina is here the object of his gaze, Horatio falls from his vantage point on the parapet and requires Glorvina's medical care to restore him to health in a symbolic leveling of hierarchies. Owenson thus argues a middle way between Shakespeare's Mortimer and Hal; that is, between capitulating, or "going native" (and with it completely renouncing dutiful nation-building), and conquest and subjection. Glorvina becomes Horatio's partner and equal, not his colonial subject.

Like the great learning which makes her so effective in the public sphere and so thoroughly seduces Horatio, Glorvina's sympathy and nurturing, two qualities which the novel foregrounds, have been cultivated not through the development of her piety and domesticity, but by the development of her intellect. Father John, who has been largely responsible for her upbringing, explains the philosophical rationale behind such an education:

> I only threw within [Glorvina's] power of acquisition, that which could tend to render her a rational, and consequently a benevolent being; for I have always conceived an informed, intelligent, and enlightened mind, to be the best security for a good heart; although the many who mistake talent for intellect, and unfortunately too often find the former united to vice, are led to suppose that the heart loses in goodness what the mind acquires in strength.[27]

---

[24] See Michael Neill for a useful discussion of the intersection of language, gender and cultural conquest in this scene. Henry's limited ability to speak French is even foregrounded in the last act of *Henry V*, a detail which suggests its unimportance to a king who boasts that he is "so good a proficient in one quarter of an hour that I can drink with any tinker in his own language" (*1 Henry IV* 2.4.17–19).

[25] The literal translation of "Glorvina" from the Irish.

[26] *The Wild Irish Girl*, 52.

[27] Ibid., 79.

This expression of educational philosophy, obviously endorsed by the novel, aligns Owenson with the radical views of Mary Wollstonecraft, who likewise argued that the neglect of girls' intellectual development had negative consequences for their moral development. Many conduct books and novels, including ones written by Maria Edgeworth,[28] suggested that the development of piety and domesticity was the best means of ensuring female virtue. Other books on girls' education stressed the attainment of "accomplishments" which were chiefly designed to attract a husband.

Wollstonecraft, on the other hand, argues in *A Vindication of the Rights of Woman* (1792) that the failure to develop intellectual strength in girls weakens women's morality: "[T]he minds of women are enfeebled ... [and] books of instruction, written by men of genius, have had the same [negative] tendency as more frivolous productions ... Weak, artificial beings ... undermine the very foundation of virtue, and spread corruption through the whole mass of society."[29]

Glorvina has been thoroughly educated in what at the time were considered masculine studies: the natural sciences (including botany, a subject in which she impressively lectures Horatio, and the practice of medicine), history, philosophy and classical languages. The result is a spiritual and moral strength clearly superior to anything Horatio has yet encountered. Her elevated intellect and spirit are repeatedly asserted to be what seduces him. At the same time the novel recognizes that the resulting new equality for women will be unsettling, but nevertheless may still be embraced by people with traditional attitudes. A peasant informs Horatio that even the local people who are devoted to Glorvina fear her: "[E]very mother's soul of us love her better nor the Prince [her father]; aye, by my conscience, and fear her too; for well may they fear her, on the score of her great learning."[30] Glorvina, unlike many traditional "heroines," is not merely passed as a possession from one male to the next. She clearly shares power in the rule of her people, first with her father, and upon her marriage with Horatio. The social and cultural implications of this formulation seem worthy of more recognition than Owenson enjoys from modern critics.

The Mild Irish Girl: Edgeworth

As many commentators have noted, the relationship between Horatio and Glorvina, which develops into love and a true union of equal partners, allegorizes the relationship between Great Britain and Ireland. The metaphorical implications of the union of these two characters, in which the female character is so expansively conceptualized, suggests a far more complex and interdependent relationship than the kind envisioned in the works of a more influential writer of Irish national

---

[28]   Marilyn Butler's biography of Edgeworth features a thorough discussion of these conduct books.

[29]   *A Vindication of the Rights of Woman* (1792). London: Penguin, 1992, 80–81.

[30]   *The Wild Irish Girl*, 41.

tales – Maria Edgeworth.[31] The influence of *The Wild Irish Girl* on Edgeworth's subsequent Irish novels is palpable. But for Edgeworth, Owenson's re-imagining of traditional gender relationships represents a radical overturning of the social order. Furthermore, the Gaelic culture and tradition embodied by Glorvina and celebrated in *The Wild Irish Girl* are too suffused with dangerous and radical content, much of which directly invokes the violent (and ongoing) conflicts between the two cultures. Edgeworth therefore seeks to reclaim in subsequent novels the public and the political issues Owenson had so "deftly taken from her and placed in their colonial context,"[32] and to translate them once again into private and domestic equivalents, there to deradicalize them.

Edgeworth's Irish heroines who occupy Glorvina's position in the allegorical union are divested of almost all agency outside that of reproducing the patriarchal social order. This accords with other influential, conservative constructions of Anglo-Irish cultural identity. Edmund Burke's *Reflections on the Revolution in France* articulates a social order modeled on and rooted in the domesticity of the patriarchal family, which he invests with an inviolable sanctity:

> We have given to our frame of polity the image of a relation in blood, binding up the constitution of our country with our dearest domestic ties, adopting our fundamental laws into the bosom of our family affections, keeping inseparable and cherishing with the warmth of all their combined and mutually reflected charities our state, our hearths, our sepulchers, and our altars."[33]

Diedre Lynch has argued that Burke's "matrocentic[ally] inflect[ed] statecraft… aimed to homogenize the public and private meanings carried in the words 'home' and 'domestic' … and to make home life underwrite the authority of administrative institutions."[34] Lynch asserts that women writers of the early nineteenth century also "[e]ngaged in just such rewritings (re-inscriptions of relations), produc[ing] plots that disarticulated 'mother' and 'country.'"[35] Lynch here echoes Gary Kelly's argument that "throughout anti-Jacobin fiction there is a tendency not only to reduce large political and public issues to their everyday, domestic, commonplace consequences in individual domestic experience (a tendency found in Burke's *Reflections* and fully developed in the Romantic historical novels), but also to actually translate the political and public issues into private and domestic equivalents."[36]

---

[31] Edgeworth was certainly more influential with contemporary critics, including Scott, Jeffrey, Croker et al. Modern commentators have almost unanimously agreed with only minor qualifications (such as that of Ina Ferris noted above).

[32] Joseph Lew, op. cit. "Sydney Owenson and the Fate of Empire," 41.

[33] Burke, Edmund. *Reflections on the Revolution in France* (1790), ed. Conor Cruise O'Brien. London: Penguin, 1986, 30.

[34] Diedre Lynch. "Nationalizing Women and Domesticating Fiction: Edmund Burke and the Genres of Englishness," *Wordsworth Circle* 25 (Winter 1994), 45.

[35] Ibid., 46.

[36] Kelly, Gary. *Women, Writing, and Revolution, 1790–1827*. Oxford: Clarendon Press, 1993, 289.

The gender plot of *The Absentee* is an example of such rewriting and translation. *The Absentee* furthermore betrays a significant preoccupation with what Lynch describes as the Burkean themes of "migrant maternity, disinheritance, and sexual improprieties,"[37] and also offers an instance of Edgeworth appropriating and rewriting familiar genres, including that of the comically-structured Owensonian national tale and the traditional Irish *aisling*, in order to validate Anglo-Irish cultural and political hegemony. The aisling is an eighteenth-century poetic genre, derived from earlier forms, which depicts Ireland as a mythologized female, and in which cultural and Jacobin political objectives often interact.[38] Grace Nugent, heroine of *The Absentee*, takes her name from the subject of an aisling written by the bard Carolan.[39] Owenson's heroine Glorvina sings a translation of "Gracey Nugent" in *The Wild Irish Girl*; significantly, Edgeworth merely alludes to Carolan's song and thus attempts to defuse its radicalism. Meanwhile, she seeks to appropriate the metaphorical value of the heroine of "Gracey Nugent," an aisling which "shares with others of its genre remnants of older Gaelic beliefs and social structures to which the image of a woman who embodied the land and whose espousal conferred sovereignty was essential."[40]

Edgeworth empties out not only any radicalism from the figure of Grace Nugent, but Irishness itself.[41] As W.J. McCormack and Kim Walker point out, Grace's name strongly associates her with Irishness to the initiated reader: "She is one of an attainted family, celebrated in the folk tradition of a displaced and depressed nobility. Her name is inscribed in popular song, the theme of which she reenacts in the novel."[42] McCormack and Walker go on to argue that "this is a Union which seeks to suggest a transcending of differences political, aesthetic,

---

[37]   Lynch, 46.

[38]   The representation of Ireland as a woman was derived from popular folk traditions, and continued in other genres in addition to the aisling. The most famous instance is perhaps Swift's *The Story of an Injured Lady*, which depicts Ireland as a woman who is cruelly thrown over by her lover (England) for another woman (Scotland), and was written around the time of the 1707 Union of Scotland and England (but not published until 1746). Vestiges of the tradition can be traced throughout the nineteenth century, as in *Punch* cartoon representations of a suffering Hibernia being rescued by Britannia from the horrors of the famine, for instance. (See L.P. Curtis's *Apes and Angels* for a definitive study of iconographic representations of Ireland. *Cf.* this tradition with that of the "Bower of Bliss.")

[39]   See C.L. Innes, *Woman and Nation in Irish Literature and Society, 1880–1930*, Athens: University of Georgia Press, 1993, 16–25, for a brief but useful discussion of the aisling tradition. An appendix to the Oxford's World Classics edition of *The Absentee* includes a discussion of the appearance of the aisling "Grace Nugent" in both *The Wild Irish Girl* and *The Absentee*, and also alludes to the Jacobin undertones of the piece.

[40]   Innes, 20.

[41]   As Robert Tracy notes in "Maria Édgeworth and Lady Morgan," Grace's parents are actually English (Tracy, 1985, 13).

[42]   Introduction to the Oxford World's Classics edition of Edgeworth, Maria. *The Absentee* (1812), ed. with an Introduction by W.J. McCormack and Kim Walker. Oxford: Oxford University Press, 1988, xxiv. All subsequent references either to the novel or its introduction are to this edition.

and ontological."[43] However, it might be more accurate to say that the novel *appropriates* the aisling's theme, and that the Union it depicts elides, rather than transcends, the differences McCormack and Walker name.

In a long coda to the novel, the hero establishes the legitimacy of Grace's uncertain origins, because, as the narrator informs us, the hero "Lord Colambre had the greatest dread of marrying any woman whose mother had conducted herself ill."[44] In tracing Grace's ancestry, Colambre discovers that Grace's father, who was killed in the service of the Austrian army (which fought against the Revolutionary French forces of Napoleon), was an Englishman named Reynolds. Grace's mother also was English. The mother's maiden name, St Omar, suggests the name St Omer, site of the English Jesuit college in France where, because of the Penal Laws, Irish priests were trained before the establishment of Maynooth College in 1795. Grace's family then, though English, has submerged associations with France, Jacobite counterrevolution, and Roman Catholicism. But these connections are only hinted at, and rather than establish Grace as a representative of Gaelic Ireland, as some have argued, suggest instead an Ascendancy attempt to co-opt Gaelic legitimacy. In any event, Edgeworth displaces these public and social concerns onto the private (reputed) sexual improprieties of Grace's mother, which the establishment of Grace's legitimate birth puts to rest. Grace's grandfather has disinherited Grace because he is unaware that his son had legally married Grace's mother. The novel repeatedly insists that only a girl raised by a mother who inculcates a proper sense of gender and social duties can be considered marriageable, as when Count O'Halloran warns Colambre that "[i]n marrying, a man does not, to be sure, marry his wife's mother; and yet a prudent man, when he begins to think of the daughter, would look sharp at the mother; ay, and back to the grandmother too, and along the whole line of female ancestry."[45] Colambre enthusiastically concurs. Grace's attraction for the hero is firmly located in her purity and domesticity, qualities purportedly ensured by her maternal lineage, and not in her accomplishments, learning or beauty, in sharp contrast to Glorvina.

The long digression establishing Grace's parentage – fully a fifth of the novel is devoted to it – culminates with an avowal of the mother's virtue:

> When she was told of the … suspicions, the disgrace, to which her mother had been subjected for so many years … that mother … who had, with such care, instilled into the mind of her daughter the principles of virtue and religion; that mother whom Grace had always seen the example of every virtue she taught ... Grace could only express ... astonishment, pathos, indignation.[46]

But her indignation quickly turns to an acceptance of Colambre's suspicion as just: "Grace sighed, and acknowledged that, in prudence, [her presumed illegitimacy]

---

43 Ibid., xxiv.
44 Ibid., 112.
45 Ibid., 222.
46 Ibid., 256.

ought to have been an *invincible* obstacle [to his marrying her] – she admired the firmness of his decision, the honor with which he had acted towards her" (original emphasis).[47]

Marilyn Butler has argued that the Grace plot links *The Absentee* with a more explicitly didactic work Edgeworth wrote with her father, *Professional Education* (1809). One of the main themes in *Professional Education* is that early education is an extremely powerful factor in determining character. According to Butler, the connection between the main plot of *The Absentee* (which chronicles the corrupting influence the desertion of the gentry has on the peasantry) and the Grace plot is only comprehensible in this context:

> [Colambre] knows that as a small child Grace was brought up by her mother. If it is true that this mother was unchaste, the dominant influence on Grace's early education was a corrupt one. Colambre's refusal to overlook this fact is another attempt by Maria to prove that environment and early education determine character.[48]

Butler is correct in connecting the drawn-out narrative concerning Grace's marriageability to Edgeworth's preoccupation with environment and education. Even more significant, however, is the fact that the inculcation of virtue is the *only* aspect of Grace's education touched upon in *The Absentee*. The philosophical rationale behind Grace's education stands in sharp contrast to that evidenced in *The Wild Irish Girl*. Glorvina offers long disquisitions on philology, botany, medicine, and history etc., but Grace is an intellectual cipher, a trait she shares with the heroines of Edgeworth's other Irish novels. In her influential *Desire and Domestic Fiction*, Nancy Armstrong "links the history of British fiction to the empowering of the middle classes in England through the dissemination of a new female ideal," that is, an idealized female virtue and domesticity.[49]

The Grace plot in *The Absentee* offers a classic illustration of Armstrong's argument, with one important difference: the class empowered is an exclusionary Anglo-Irish gentry. Edgeworth's fears of sociosexual impropriety are furthermore resolved by what Mary Jean Corbett calls "the replotting of Irish and Anglo-Irish families on an English ideal." Corbett traces this ideal to "Burke's primary metaphors for political society [which are] heavily dependent on the aristocratic idiom of the landed estate and patrilineal succession."[50] In such a scheme adulterous women threaten to disrupt the social, political, and imperial order, since among other things men could never be absolutely certain of the paternity

---

[47]   Ibid., 257.

[48]   Butler, Marilyn. *Maria Edgeworth: A Literary Biography*. Oxford: Oxford University Press, 1972, 332–3.

[49]   Armstrong, Nancy. *Desire and Domestic Fiction: A Political History of the Novel*. New York: Oxford University Press, 1987, 9.

[50]   Corbett, Mary Jean. "Public Affections and Familial Politics: Burke, Edgeworth, and the "Common Naturalization" of Great Britain," *English Literary History* 61 (1994), 878.

of a woman's child. Stated in positive terms, women "act as the unacknowledged ground for familial, economic, and political legitimacy."[51] But as Ronald Paulson points out in referring to the famous scene in Marie Antoinette's boudoir in the *Reflections on the Revolution in France*, Burke also opposes "a vigorous ('active'), unprincipled, rootless masculine sexuality, unleashed and irrepressible, against a gentle aristocratic family, patriarchal and based upon bonds of love.[52] In Burke's view, both male and female sexuality must be policed by a responsible masculine authority which regulates domesticity. If, conversely, instead of this virtue and authority an example of vice and immorality emanates from the top ranks of society, corruption and licentiousness of the sort traditionally associated with a diseased aristocracy will infect all levels of society below. Burke ascribes political and social chaos *and* the laxity of French morals to the overthrow of the ultimate worldly paternal authority, the king: "France, when she let loose the reins of regal authority, doubled the license of a ferocious dissoluteness in manners ... and has extended through all ranks of life ... all the unhappy corruptions that were usually the disease of wealth and power."[53] Burke's virtuous aristocracy, under the patriarchal authority of the monarch, would regulate both female sexual excess and unprincipled masculine ambition, aggressiveness, and sexuality.

In Edgeworth's Burkean vision, Colambre's renunciation of his own father's absenteeism and prodigality, and Grace's carefully vetted marriageability are what suit them to rule over a docile and grateful Gaelic peasantry, who along with the rest of Gaelic Ireland in *The Absentee* represent the *children* of Union, not equal partners in it. The new society is still rigidly compartmentalized, and all types of economic, social and political opportunity are inaccessible to the overwhelming majority of Ireland's population. Most Irish being Catholics, they are barred by custom, law, and circumstance from obtaining the type of domesticating education Grace received or gaining entrée into the social milieu of Colambre and the property-owning class. Edgeworth, in contrast to Owenson, does not see fit to address these inequities. Nor do any other groups outside the Ascendancy merit consideration as participating as useful, productive, or even legitimate segments of society in Edgeworth's post-Union social body. The Gaelic Irish members of the newly emergent commercial class depicted in *The Absentee*, such as Mrs Rafferty, are depicted as vulgar and grasping and beneath Colambre's (and Edgeworth's) contempt.[54]

---

[51]   Ibid., 880.

[52]   Paulson, Ronald. *Representations of Revolution, 1789–1820*. New Haven: Yale University Press, 1983, 64.

[53]   Burke, Edmund. *Reflections on the Revolution in France* (1790), ed. Conor Cruise O'Brien. London: Penguin, 1986, 33.

[54]   This pattern is consistent throughout Edgeworth's Irish novels, and moreover the hated class of middlemen, a stratum of Anglo-Irish society distinct from that occupied by Colambre and Grace, invariably in Edgeworth's fiction turn out to be recanting Gaelic Catholics, from Jason Quirk in *Castle Rackrent* to Ulick O'Shane in *Ormond*.

Edgeworth's restricted social norms are also evidenced by the gender ideals elaborated through other characters in *The Absentee*, and these patterns provide a striking contrast to the inclusive and expansive roles imagined in *The Wild Irish Girl*. Female power of any kind, particularly sexual, is portrayed in *The Absentee* as unnatural and perverted. Lady Dashfort, with her oft referred-to "masculine boldness,"[55] characterizes the type of sexually and socially transgressing mother Colambre mistakenly fears Grace had. And Lady Dashfort's daughter Isabella restores the figure of the enchantress to the disrepute it enjoyed before Glorvina. Colambre, seemingly just on the point of being seduced (emotionally, at least) by Isabella, is horrified to overhear her avow that "to purchase the pleasure of making [a rival] feel the pangs of jealousy for one hour, look, I would this moment lay down this finger and let it be cut off."[56] The lesson for Colambre is that seductive women like Isabella are monsters. The possible seductiveness of a Gaelic Irishwoman (or Gaelic Ireland in any form) is never entertained in the novel.

But of course Colambre never allows himself to be seduced by either Isabella or Grace. Rather, he makes calculated decisions. First he renounces the apparently unsuitable Grace, then he deigns to possess her, "happy in the hope of winning the whole heart of the woman he loved, and whose esteem, he knew, he possessed and deserved; happy in developing every day, every hour, fresh charms in his destined bride."[57] Her charms, or "accomplishments" of the type satirized by Austen and denounced by Wollestonecraft, will be "developed" in her by Colambre – through his agency, not hers. Grace is not responsible, beyond reproducing suitably domesticated and socially regulated Anglo-Irish male heirs, for accomplishing any of the serious masculine work of nation-building. Her contribution will be her charms, and presumably keeping herself pure so as not to taint his progeny. The nation building pursued by Colambre and his like in Edgeworth's Irish novels is not the creation of a new and more diverse society of Britain, but rather the westward expansion of England at the expense of the marginalized "natives." While the policies of Britain were not as forthrightly brutal as some of those implemented by the United States in its pursuit of its Manifest Destiny, the course followed contributed to the natives of Ireland suffering famine, death, and displacement in the years to come.

---

[55]   *The Absentee*, 97.

[56]   Ibid., 126.

[57]   Ibid., 260.

Chapter 3
Ormond:
From "The Disease of Power and Wealth" to "The Condition of Irishness"

Nineteenth-Century Culture Wars

The national tales of Lady Lady Morgan and Maria Edgeworth go to the heart of the early nineteenth century British "culture wars," and in addition offer important examples of the many ways in which "Irishness" played an important role in the construction of British national cultural identity. Beyond this, the patterns of representation utilized in their Irish novels constitute no less than a new historiography, with which they sought to expand the possibilities of the novel as well as compensate for inadequacies in "factual" history. There has been some excellent critical attention given recently to the historical projects of these women and how their novels contested existing tropes of literary and cultural authority.[1] However, as noted above, at issue for both women in these works is not only the potential of genre but that of gender, and much less attention has been given to the ways in which the national tales of Edgeworth and Owenson (hereafter referred to as Lady Morgan)[2] also contest *each other's* notions of gender ideals, as well as history. It is therefore important to examine each woman's project individually, rather than assume, as many commentators have, that their aims largely coincided. Ina Ferris has noted that "[Morgan's] national tale [is] a generic innovation [that has] been strangely neglected by feminist literary history."[3] Lady Morgan's vision of women's place in society, so vehemently contested by Edgeworth in her fiction (as well as by some of the most powerful and influential of Lady Morgan's contemporary literary critics), has also been neglected by modern feminist literary historians. A detailed examination of Edgeworth's novel *Ormond* (1817) can shed further light on the many points at which her philosophy is at odds with Lady Morgan's social and cultural vision.

---

[1]   See Ferris (1991), esp. Chapters 1–4, and Gamer, Michael. *Romanticism and the Gothic: Genre, Reception, and Canon Formation.* Cambridge: Cambridge University Press, 2000.

[2]   Owenson assumed the title upon her marriage to Sir Charles Morgan in 1812 and published subsequently under that name.

[3]   "Writing on the Border: The National Tale, Female Writing, and the Public Sphere" in *Romanticism, History, and the Possibilities of Genre*, eds Tilottama Rajan and Julia M. Wright. Cambridge: Cambridge University Press, 1998, 87.

Some critics have noted that Edgeworth and Lady Morgan represented the nation in their Irish novels in response to perceived inadequacies of the masculinized discourse of historiography.[4] Yet in what is otherwise one of the most valuable accounts of their critiques, Ferris claims that Edgeworth ultimately assigned greater cultural authority to the discourse of masculinist history than she claimed for her own practice of historiography: "Where Scott absorbs the authority of official discourses like that of history, even as he modifies and on occasion subverts them, Edgeworth challenges such discourses but betrays an uneasiness in so doing that in effect leaves their authority in place."[5] However, even as early as her first Irish novel Edgeworth overtly rejects that authority. In the preface to *Castle Rackrent* (1800), Edgeworth characterizes historical discourse as engaging in excess:

> Of the numbers who study, or at least read history, how few derive any advantage from their labours! The heroes of history are so decked out by the fine fancy of the professed historian; they talk in such measured prose, and act from such sublime or such diabolical motives, that few have sufficient taste, wickedness, or heroism, to sympathize in their fate.[6]

Edgeworth's critique is notable for its utilization of several aesthetically loaded terms, including "fine fancy," "sublime," and "sympathize." The explicit objection to the productions of "professed historians," which her invoking of these terms makes clear, arises from their use of the tropes of romance, a discourse Edgeworth herself regarded as dangerous.[7] Her subsequent Irish novels continue her critique of both genres. It is true, however, that Edgeworth and Lady Morgan both recognized the standard lines of demarcation in the public sphere and sought when publishing works like these to allay some of the gender anxieties so often expressed by male critics.[8] In the preface to *The O'Briens and the O'Flahertys* (1828), Lady Morgan denies anticipated charges of transgressing the boundaries of the separate spheres through any "unfeminine presumption in 'meddling with politics,'" and in a defiant tone claims alignment with the ultimate patriarchal authority, the Bible, in pursuing her project: "[L]ove of country is of no sex. It was by female patriotism [of Queen Esther] that the Jews attacked their tyrants."[9]

Her invocation of Queen Esther is undoubtedly meant to conciliate phallocratic reviewers. But the strong terms Lady Morgan employs along with it ("attacked their tyrants") signal the great ideological divide separating the projects of Lady Morgan

---

[4]   Ferris (1991) and Gamer devote sustained and specific attention to this point, which is also implicit in the arguments of Gallagher, Leerssen, Robert Tracy, Trumpener, and Dunne.

[5]   Ferris. *The Achievement of Literary Authority*, 112.

[6]   *Castle Rackrent* (1800). London: Penguin, 1992, 61.

[7]   See, for example, the preface to her novel *Belinda*.

[8]   The most thorough and influential account of the genre and gender anxieties expressed in the discourse of literary criticism is also Ferris 1991, Chapter 1.

[9]   *The O'Briens and the O'Flahertys* (1827), London: Pandora, 1988, xv.

and Edgeworth. It is precisely the exclusionary Ascendancy class Edgeworth champions whose ruling practices Lady Morgan condemns in her fiction. Therefore it is worthwhile to investigate the particularities of each of their positions more closely than has been done, both for their political implications as well as to better understand how gender ideals were woven into their politics. Katie Trumpener has characterized these positions as "Maria Edgeworth's critically pro-Union Irish novels on the one hand, and the Jacobin-feminist national tales of ... Sydney Owenson (Lady Morgan) on the other."[10] This description, while it acknowledges differences in the two approaches, flattens out important considerations in understanding Lady Morgan's project in particular, as well as what is at stake in this debate, by utilizing undefined and imprecise terms. Lady Morgan herself was also "critically pro-Union," as the allegorical celebration of Union in *The Wild Irish Girl* makes clear. More significantly, her work cannot accurately be described as Jacobin, a term which some of her contemporary political opponents notoriously utilized in order to marginalize Lady Morgan. The most vehement and vituperative of these critics was John Wilson Croker.[11] The very looseness of the term "Jacobin" as employed by Trumpener also allowed Croker and others to dismiss Lady Morgan's positions wholesale and ignore or misrepresent important and specific considerations within her critique. As will be seen in the discussion of *Florence McCarthy*, Lady Morgan's works were far from anti-aristocratic.

Ferris has recognized that the national tale genre as practiced by Lady Morgan engages domestic fiction in the process of contesting historiography and the boundaries of the public sphere, but she asserts that Lady Morgan's project does not challenge normative domesticity:

> Informed by a liberal belief in the public sphere, it operates on the very border of the literary and political, rewriting the trope of the public sphere in the process; and it defines as central to the fable of the subjected nation a form of female authority neither identical with or opposed to the domestic authority rooted in the home and family. [12]

Yet if Lady Morgan does not explicitly contest existing gender norms while rewriting the trope of the public sphere, heroines such as Glorvina and Florence McCarthy certainly alarmed observers such as Edgeworth and Croker. Edgeworth's Irish novels written after *The Wild Irish Girl* offer evidence that her cultural ideals were clearly threatened by the feminism as well as the politics expressed in Lady Morgan's work. I wish to turn now to Edgeworth's novel *Ormond* in order to examine the political, social and gender ideals evidenced within it. Edgeworth's

---

[10] "National Character, Nationalist Plots: National Tale and Historical Novel in the Age of *Waverley*, 1806–1830," *English Literary History* 60 (1993), 693.

[11] Croker's attacks on Lady Morgan are examined at more length in Chapter 7.

[12] "Writing on the Border: The National Tale, Female Writing, and the Public Sphere," 87. Among the more influential accounts of the ways in which the domestic trope figured the nation in women's writing of the period are Kelly 1993, Chapter 5, and Mellor, Chapter 4.

views have been regarded as both moderate and enlightened by her contemporary reviewers in the British cultural mainstream, as well as many modern readers. But as we will see, she represents an infantilized Gaelic Irish population in need of the paternalistic oversight and assistance of the ethnically English Ascendancy, and seeks to uphold the status quo in matters of gender and politics.

Exclusive Inclusion: *Ormond*

Ormond is a Bildungsroman that traces the social and political education of an Anglo-Irish orphan. Like Edgeworth's other Irish novels following *Castle Rackrent* (1800), *Ormond* is a comically structured work in which the hero (and by extension the Ascendancy he represents) establishes his legitimacy as a member of Ireland's ruling class by the means of that education. The marriage plot functions as an allegorical representation of the achievement of a "balanced" social order. The hero's name, Harry Ormond, resonates with historical significance for Anglo-Irish nation-building. The Earldom of Ormond was created by Edward III to protect his interests against "Irish enemies and English rebels." The earldom, comprising the counties of Kilkenny and Tipperary, was held by members of the Anglo-Norman Butler family, who were noted for their retention of much closer ties with England than the Geraldines, who held the other great earldoms of the Pale, Desmond and Kildare. The name of Ormond evokes several historical situations and incidents in which that family played an important role, and of which many of Edgeworth's initiated contemporary readers were likely to be aware. Unlike many absentee Norman landlords, who resided mostly in England when not pursuing wars in France, the powerful fourth Earl of Ormond made his seat at Kilkenny an important center of Anglo-Irish culture and was an advocate of "home rule."[13] The appropriateness of the Ormond name for Edgeworth's hero is increased by the actions of later representatives of the noble family. In the 1640s the Earl of Ormond represented the king in negotiations with the "rebellious" Catholic forces led by Owen Roe O'Neill, not to be confused with his uncle Red Hugh O'Neill, leader of the "rebellion broached on the sword" referred to in the epigraph of Shakespeare's *Henry V* who temporarily defeated Elizabeth's forces under Exeter. The younger O'Neill defeated the English royalists but later was conquered by Oliver Cromwell. In July 1647 Ormond handed over the English army in Dublin to the forces of the English Parliament and left the country. He returned the next year in an attempt to unite the royalist forces in Ireland, but after the execution of Charles I, Ormond was defeated outside Dublin by Cromwell in 1649.[14]

---

[13]   See Kee, Robert. *The Green Flag*, 3 vols. Harmondsworth: Penguin Books, 1989; and Martin Wallace, *A Short History of Ireland.* New York: Barnes and Noble, 1996, 26–38. See especially Simms, 72–81 and Wallace, 36–7.

[14]   See esp. Canny, Nicholas P. *Kingdom and Colony: Ireland in the Atlantic World 1560–1800.* Baltimore: Johns Hopkins University Press 1988.

The strong associations of the name of Ormond with Anglo-Irish culture, autonomy, opposition to Catholic "rebels," loyalty to the crown deriving from ancient ties, and in particular the family's providing a prototypical alternative to absentee landlordism, make it a fitting title for Edgeworth's project and her hero. The title character is furthermore given a first name which vastly increases the allegorical overtones of cultural nationalism in the work. "King" Corny, a Gaelic Irish chief who rules over the obscurely-located Black Islands,[15] insists that all his "subjects" refer to Ormond by the same name of the central figure of Shakespeare's English nation-building second tetralogy, the Henriad: "A horse, decked with ribands, waited on the shore, with King Corny's compliments for *Prince Harry*, as the boy, who held the stirrup for him to mount, said he was instructed to call him, and to proclaim him '*Prince Harry*' throughout the island, which he did by the sound of a horn" (original italics).[16] While there is irony here, it is to be found in the mock-heroic trappings of Corny's title and state, not in the hero's assumption of the princely moniker.

In fact, this scene foreshadows the plot resolution, in which the Anglo-Irish Ormond purchases the estates of the Gaelic Corny and installs himself as a benevolent, progressive landlord. The fact that Ormond purchases, and does not inherit, the estate signals Edgeworth's ongoing anxieties about Anglo-Irish legitimacy.[17] Catherine Gallagher, in discussing *Ennui* (1809), argues persuasively that in Edgeworth's "productivist ideology" she "shift[s] the ground of [Anglo-Irish] entitlement from birth to merit."[18] Among other things, the plot of *Ormond* is concerned with modeling the Anglo-Irish Ascendancy's acquisition of this merit, symbolized in the purchase of Corny's domain. Ormond merits his entitlement by recovering his own fortune, fraudulently appropriated from him in his youth by Ulick O'Shane and used to pay off Ulick's enormous debts. Of great importance for its political symbolism is the fact that the bulk of Ulick's debts are owed to the Annaly family.[19] At novel's end Ormond becomes the owner of the property

---

[15]   Brian Hollingworth (in *Maria Edgeworth's Irish Writing: Language, History, Politics.* New York: St. Martin's, 1997), uses internal evidence in the novel to deduce that the islands, assumed by many critics to be situated off of the wild coast of Connaught, actually lie in a lake just outside the pale.

[16]   Edgeworth, Maria, *Ormond: A Tale* (1817). London: Macmillan, 1895, 38. All subsequent references to the novel will be to this edition. For another discussion of the hero's name as a multivalent signifier see Hollingworth. For connections to Irish history in the Henriad see Ayers, Edwards, Murphy, Niell et al.

[17]   Robert Tracy notes that in both *Castle Rackrent* and *Ennui* the estate ends up in Gaelic Irish hands, and the plots of both novels "suggest[] that some other vaguely-defined legitimacy is needed ... an unhyphenated Irish identity" (Tracy, 1985, 6).

[18]   *Nobody's Story: The Vanishing Acts of Women Writers in the Marketplace, 1670–1820.* Berkeley: University of California Press, 1994, 300.

[19]   It is also significant that most of Ormond's fortune came to him on the death of his "mahogany" half-sister and was originally amassed by his father in India. The implementation of the social order implied by the novel's comic resolution is thus heavily dependent upon

of both Corny and Ulick, who squandered their fortunes in different ways. He furthermore has legitimized his possession of it by acquiring a practical education. This education is comprised of two chief components: domestic discipline, in which Harry is schooled by his mother-in-law to be, Lady Annaly, and responsible and progressive landlordism. He acquires lessons in Smithian economics and benevolent paternalism from Sir Herbert Annaly, brother of his true love, who then conveniently dies and leaves his estates to Florence Annaly and her husband (Ormond). Corny thus represents one of the three models for the Irish ruling class that Ormond is to observe and choose among (the other two being Ulick O'Shane and Sir Herbert), and the irony in the passage quoted above provides an early signal of Corny's inadequacy in this regard.[20]

King Corny seemingly inhabits his island by choice, allowing him to avoid the encroachments of civilization. The remote and wild setting of the Black Islands recalls that of the Castle of Inismore in *The Wild Irish Girl*, but Edgeworth, unlike Lady Morgan, offers no narratorial comment to explain Corny's presence there. *Ormond* thus merely elides the historical displacements of the Gaelic Irish onto the most remote and least profitable lands in Ireland. The setting also anticipates those of the imperial romances of later in the century, perfect for a boy's adventure, and accords with Corny's mercurial temperament, by turns generous and spiteful, humorous and choleric, flippant and sentimental. His changeability and impracticality code him as childlike (as are virtually all of the other Gaelic characters in this work).[21] He continually acts rashly, and he often contradicts himself, as when Corny tells Ormond that he is passionate, and "like[s him]self the better for it." Ormond replies that Corny had just told him that he often repents being passionate. "Oh! Never mind what I said *just now* – mind what I'm saying now" (original italics).[22] There is much humor in the descriptions of Corny and his "kingdom," but the overall message that this feudal Gaelic domain is a wellspring of anti-domesticity is inescapable. Ormond must strenuously resist the incitements of his host and those of Corny's "courtiers" to join them in their excessive daily drinking (perhaps significantly Corny's chief courtier is a Roman Catholic priest),

---

the resources of the British Empire. The classic discussion of the "submerged" presence of Empire as the unacknowledged source of British wealth and power in the 19th-century novel is Edward Said's *Culture and Imperialism*.

[20]   Maurice Colgan offers a brief but useful discussion of how the three landlords and their practices provide Edgeworthian models of possible legitimacy to the Anglo-Irish ruling class: "If the Protestant Ascendancy are prepared to be efficient and honest politically and economically, and drop their anti-Catholic prejudices ... [t]heir own good qualities will legitmize their status" ("After *Rackrent*: Ascendancy Nationalism in Maria Edgeworth's Later Irish Novels," in *Studies in Anglo-Irish Literature*, ed. Heinz Kozok. Bonn: Bouvier Verlag Herbert Grundmann, 1982, 42).

[21]   Corny's temperament - impetuous, sentimental, and childish – anticipates the traits Matthew Arnold would later identify as characteristic of the Celtic "race" in his influential treatise on national cultural identity, *Saxon and Celt*.

[22]   *Ormond*, 67–8.

almost breaking Corny's heart at his "ingratitude." But Ormond stands firm, and Corny impetuously and generously gives him a large portion of his daughter's land on the assumption she will marry well – hoping in fact that she will marry Ormond himself.[23] Although he successfully withstands the call to drink, Ormond is unable to resist the other enticements of the Black Islands, and Corny diverts Ormond from his project of disciplinary reading and sturdy Protestant self-improvement in favor of hunting, fishing, looking for bird's nests, and various other boyish pursuits.

Corny's imprudence and improvidence reveal him to be an undesirable role model for Ormond, a relic of the premodern (and not a little ridiculous) Ireland that has been superseded by metropolitan British culture. Ormond rejects the anti-domesticity of the Black Islands, but his affection for Corny makes him slower in recognizing Corny's economic and managerial shortcomings. These too are central to Edgeworth's message and are detailed in terms that directly invoke Adam Smith. Some commentators read Corny's many "accomplishments," such as his homeopathic medical skills, as positive representations of a type of homely efficiency.[24] Katie Trumpener argues that "Edgeworth's ... Irish novels [subsequent to *Castle Rackrent*] shift subtly in their attitude towards nationalism," and that *Ormond* "includes a sympathetic meditation on the traditional culture preserved in the boggy isolation of the Black Islands."[25] However, beyond the comic irony of Corny's boasting about his doctoring skills as he is unable to rise from his bed with the gout,[26] lies a serious Smithian critique of the home manufacturing economy of the Black Islands, and this critique is one of the first important elements of Ormond's education:

> [Ormond] began to doubt whether it were worthy of a king, or a gentleman, to be his own shoemaker, hatter, and tailor; whether it were not better managed in society, where these things are performed by different tradesmen; still the things were wonderful, considering who made them, and under what disadvantages they were made; but Harry having now seen and compared Corny's violin with other violins, and having discovered that so much better could be had for money, with so much less trouble, his admiration had a little decreased.[27]

Ormond's affection for Corny eventually is transformed from admiration into patronizing tolerance. Thematically, Harry's acquisition of land from Corny without marrying the daughter constitutes an appropriation of Gaelic Ireland's cultural past, here represented in the Black Islands, to complement the achievement of merit enacted in the comic resolution of the novel. Significantly, the historical

---

[23]   Ibid., 41–5.

[24]   See Hollingworth, Colgan et.al.

[25]   *Bardic Nationalism: The Romantic Novel and the British Empire.* Princeton: Princeton University Press, 1997, 62.

[26]   *Ormond*, 46–7.

[27]   Ibid., 51–2.

epoch in which this historical novel is set is kept rather murky, but it becomes evident late in the novel that the action takes place at about the year 1780.[28] This period immediately precedes the brief assumption in 1782 of autonomous political power by the Irish Parliament that ended with the Act of Union of January 1,1801, an era which was for Edgeworth the Golden Age of Irish history. Also suggesting Ormond's emergence from Irish prehistory is the fact that Ormond's sojourn in the Black Islands is represented in the romance register, as a cultural stage which is superseded by modern history. Clearly Harry's development as a character is suspended during his time spent in Corny's bailiwick, only to resume under the tutelage of the Annalys, which is depicted in "historical time."[29] Ormond's social, political, and economic emergence from Irish "prehistory," then, allows Edgeworth to reimagine *Castle Rackrent* with a comic ending.[30]

"The Pistol Accidentally Went Off": *Ormond* and Familial Politics

Ormond's social education takes the form of a disciplinary domesticity, which is presented much more thoroughly throughout the novel than his economic regime, a consideration which signals Edgeworth's chief concern. Part of Harry's domestic discipline is self-acquired, possibly through the good Anglo-Irish genes he acquired from his parents. His father, an English army captain, made, according to the narrator, "an unfortunate marriage; that is, a marriage without a fortune"[31] to a woman whose origins are not commented upon. The social ostracism of Ormond's father upon his marriage suggests that Harry's mother may have been Catholic (although Corny and others note that Ormond is a Protestant). But *Ormond*'s obscurity on this point (and outright rejection, in the Peggy Sheridan episode, of union between the Gaelic and Anglo-Irish in the marriage plot) reduces Gaelic participation in the legitimate rule of Ireland to an idealized transmission of the Gaelic cultural legacy to the Anglo-Irish. Corny's hopes for the eventual marriage of his daughter Dora to Ormond, and his early death which prevents him from seeing the arrangement through to its consummation, suggest that according to Edgeworth the feudal Gaelic ruling class should have recognized the inevitability and desirability, under the circumstances, of the transmission of their cultural

---

[28]   For an authoritative discussion of the historical setting of *Ormond* see Hollingworth.

[29]   Considerations of space prohibit an adequate discussion here of the "romantic" Ireland depicted in *Ormond*, and in any case the utilization of this register in other Irish novels has received considerable attention. See especially Trumpener (1997) and Leerssen (1998) for discussions of the representation of Ireland in what Bakhtin describes as "adventure time," outside of history.

[30]   Many of Edgeworth's readers have drawn attention to the significance of this era in her philosophy and fiction, known to the Anglo-Irish as the period of "the Protestant Nation." See especially Butler, and Flanagan, 69–79.

[31]   *Ormond*, 10.

legacy to the Ascendancy, provided that the Anglo-Irish prove themselves worthy.[32] Ormond's life story is Edgeworth's blueprint for Anglo-Irish attainment of this merit, and with it legitimacy. Ormond, the product of the pure love of the mother who dies in his infancy and father who thereupon departs with the British army for India, is left at nurse in an Irish cabin before being adopted by Ulick O'Shane.[33] When Ulick recognizes that Ormond represents a threat to his scheme of marrying off his son Marcus to Florence Annaly, he avails himself of an opportunity to send Ormond to live with Corny.

In the Black Islands, as at Ulick's home, the chief threat to Ormond's development is the unsuitable education he receives there, and the central component of his "proper" education is the acquisition of domestic discipline. As with his rejection of drunken revelry, Ormond is momentarily beset by an inner conflict and then "manfully" repudiates rogue male sexuality. The conflict arises when a young Catholic peasant girl shows a romantic interest in him. Ormond's undirected reading (*Tom Jones*) and neglected moral development have left him vulnerable to temptation, and he contemplates a relationship which the narrator informs us would both be beneath him and ruin the girl: "Harry Ormond could not think of her as a wife, but he was ... with his head full of *Tom Jones*, prone to run into danger himself, and rashly ready to hurry on an innocent girl to her destruction."[34] The girl, Peggy Sheridan, turns out to be the beloved of his faithful Gaelic sidekick Moriarity Carroll. Ormond has adopted a paternalistic relationship towards Carroll out of remorse after almost fatally shooting him.[35] He renounces the affair before it can begin in order to do the right thing, not by the girl so much as by Carroll.

This impulse to overcome his passions was first awakened in Harry as a result of his feelings of guilt over shooting Carroll may be read as symbolically encoding the Peggy Sheridan episode. Ormond's unrestrained male aggressiveness leads to his literal wounding of Carroll upon their first meeting. Ormond leaves a party at Ulick's estate under the influence of alcohol in order to search for Ulick's son Marcus, whose mother worries that he is in danger from the Irish peasantry:

---

[32]   Dora is in a sense Edgeworth's version of the wild Irish girl. Brought up, like Glorvina, by a Gaelic chief in an obscure, romantic setting, she, unlike Glorvina, is uncultured, materialistic and immoral. After her marriage she tries to tempt Ormond into an adulterous affair when he encounters her on a visit to the Continent, where she lives and aspires to join the *haut monde*.

[33]   Cf. Glenthorn. Both Tracy's (1985) and Gallagher's arguments about Anglo-Irish legitimacy in *Ennui* are relevant here.

[34]   *Ormond*, 74.

[35]   Carroll's attachment to Ormond is another similarity in Edgeworth's representation of Gaelic Ireland to imperial romance (often called "boys fiction"), in which the trope of the faithful native servant was a staple from Crusoe's Friday through the tales of Kipling, Haggard, and Buchan. Carroll becomes eternally grateful and installs himself as Ormond's lifelong servant when he learns it is Harry, idol of all the Gaelic peasantry in the novel, who shoots him "accidentally" in a conflict between Carroll and Ulick's son Marcus.

"the gates [to the estate] ought to be locked! There are disturbances in the country."[36] Ormond encounters Marcus in an altercation with Carroll, and is himself drawn in: "Marcus ... said all the Carrolls were bad people – rebels. Moriarity defied him to prove *that* – and added some expressions about tyranny, which enraged Ormond."[37] The description of the event (as are references to it and Ormond's reaction to it later in the novel) at this point becomes laced with sexual imagery:

> Ormond ... was thrown into a passion and lifted his whip ... Moriarity seized hold
> of the whip ... Ormond then snatched a pistol from his holster, telling Moriarity
> he would shoot him if he did not let the whip go. Moriarity, who was in a passion
> himself, struggled, still holding the whip. Ormond cocked the pistol, and before
> he was aware he had done so, the pistol accidentally went off, the ball entered
> Moriarity's breast.[38]

That a Gaelic Irish peasant's "expressions about tyranny" are what incense Harry is notable because it reveals the stake he apparently already claims in the ruling class. But upon observing the outcome to which his inability to govern his explosive passions has led him, Ormond immediately sobers up and prays for forgiveness. Lady Annaly observes him kneeling in prayer at Carroll's bedside and tells him she wishes to assist in his reformation: "Be not ashamed, young gentleman ... that I should have witnessed feelings that do you honor ... I knew your father many years ago ... and as his son, I might feel interest for you ... I have on some occasions, when we met in Dublin, seen traits of goodness in you."[39] Lady Annaly here justifies her willingness to assist Ormond with two reasons that for Edgeworth are central and connected: his own potential for merit, signified by his repentance, and his alignment with her own class. The assistance Lady Annaly offers Ormond is in acquiring domestic discipline. She furthermore implies Edgeworth's view that the acquisition of this discipline is fundamental to Ormond's, and by extension Ireland's happiness: "[F]ate is an unmeaning commonplace ... far the greatest part of our happiness or misery depends upon ourselves."[40]

Ormond forthwith decides to repudiate ungoverned passion: "From this period of his life, in consequence of the great and painful impression which had been suddenly made upon his mind, and from a few words of sense and kindness, spoken to him at a time when his heart and mind were happily ready to receive them, we may date the commencement of our hero's reformation and improvement."[41] He makes a list of "Harry Ormond's good resolutions," and receives a list of "improving" books from Lady Annaly (including Richardson's *Sir Charles Grandison*, whose hero replaces Tom Jones as Ormond's literary role model)

---

[36] *Ormond*, 15.
[37] Ibid., 16.
[38] Ibid., 16–17.
[39] Ibid., 30, 33.
[40] Ibid., 33.
[41] Ibid., 34.

along with an invitation to visit her at her son Sir Herbert's estate. The Peggy Sheridan episode, like the Carroll shooting marked by passions and struggle on both sides, is the first test of this resolve, and the closest he comes to abandoning it. Ormond promises to secure Moriarity's future, and is more than "steady in his promise" to do so. His first act in securing that future is to "bestow" upon Carroll the girl he himself has virtuously renounced: "[Ormond was] generous, actively, perseveringly generous, in his conduct to him. With open heart, open purse, public overture, and private negotiation with the parents of Peggy Sheridan, he at last succeeded in accomplishing Moriarity's marriage."[42] That the marriage can only be accomplished through Ormond's agency infantalizes the Gaelic Irish. The tidy resolution of the Peggy Sheridan sequence is the novel's first overt statement that the "happiness" of the Gaelic population can only be accomplished by a benevolently disposed Ascendancy.

However, the narrator makes clear that good resolve is not enough to prepare Ormond to regulate his desires in an acceptable way:

> Ormond's biographer may well be allowed to make the most of his persevering generosity on this occasion, because no other scrap of good can be found to make anything in his favor, for several months to come. Whether Tom Jones was still too much, and Lady Annaly too little in his head, whether it was that King Corny's example and precepts were not always edifying – whether this young man had been prepared by previous errors of example and education – or whether he fell into mischief, because he had nothing else to do in these Black Islands, certain it is, that from the operation of some or all of these causes conjointly, he deteriorated sadly. He took to "vagrant courses" in which the muse forbears to follow him.[43]

This passage provides the key to Edgeworth's project. Ormond must not only resolve to do better, he must unlearn the "previous errors of example and education" of Tom Jones, Ulick, and Corny and be re-educated by the Annalys in order to fit himself as a legitimate ruler of Ireland. Thus ends the opening section of the novel, which serves as the statement of the problem: Ireland, developmentally childish as a nation, must emerge from a culture which has been superseded by that of the modern imperial state. This modern transnational culture in which Ireland must take its place derives its authority from and is structured upon the model of a benevolently patriarchal family which regulates desire and underwrites social, political and imperial order.

Ormond conforms to a disciplined male sexuality in the wake of Moriarity Carroll's shooting as a result of his social and political education under the guidance of the Annalys. His education comprises the long series of events in the novel which thematizes domesticity as the underpinning of the social order. Edgeworth imagines an autonomous Ireland within the larger British social body

---

[42]   Ibid., 79.

[43]   Ibid., 79.

ruled by a benevolently paternalistic Anglo-Irish Ascendancy that is in "harmonious alignment" with the mostly Catholic, mostly peasant Gaelic majority. Anne K. Mellor has demonstrated that in Edgeworth's novels the vision of a larger social reconciliation is "troped ... as the marriage of the Anglo-Irish [hero] with the Irish [heroine] ... [and] the happy bourgeois family becomes the model for colonizer-colonized relationships."[44] Mellor is correct in regard to the domestic ideal evident here, but as was previously demonstrated in case of the Anglo-Irish Grace Nugent, the colonized Gaelic Irish are not figured even as the (unequal) partners of the Union. As in *The Absentee*, the comic resolution of *Ormond* is a marriage between two members of the Ascendancy, with the Gaelic Irish figured as their dependants. This quasi parent-child relationship, of unmistakable significance as evidenced by its repetition in Edgeworth's final two Irish novels, betrays the fundamental disparity of power in her imagined Union. In a discussion of *The Absentee*, Mary Jean Corbett also argues that "the marriage plot ... functions as an imperial plot as well, constructing Ireland as an ever unequal partner in the family of Great Britain." Corbett aptly characterizes the marriage plot in *The Absentee* as a "familial plot," and her arguments about that novel apply to Ormond as well:

> [*The Absentee* employs] less the marriage plot ... than what we might call the familial plot...For in order to achieve narratively and ideologically the "harmonious alignment" between unequal partners with which the novel concludes, Edgeworth must also reform the families from which these would-be rulers of Ireland spring: she must establish legitimate modes of normative behavior for women and men.[45]

While Edgeworth's fears of sociosexual impropriety were largely focused on female characters in *The Absentee*, including Grace Nugent's mother, Grace's rival, Isabella, and Lady Dashfort, in *Ormond* anxieties about the regulation of desire are directly focused on the male hero.

In *Ormond*, undisciplined anti-domesticity also seeps down and infects the peasantry and middling classes from a very specific upper rank of Irish society, embodied in the character of Ulick O'Shane. Ulick provides an example of what Burke called "the disease of power and wealth," and is counterbalanced by the normative example of proper domestic and social discipline in the Annaly family. Ulick is thoroughly worldly and corrupt, and although he is Gaelic (and Corny O'Shane's cousin) he has renounced Catholicism in order to attain his positions of power and influence.[46] On Ormond's return to Ulick's home after Corny's death,

---

[44]   Mellor, Anne K. *Romanticism and Gender*. New York: Routledge, 1993, 80.

[45]   Corbett, Mary Jean. "Public Affections and Familial Politics: Burke, Edgeworth, and the "Common Naturalization" of Great Britain," *English Literary History* 61 (1994), 877.

[46]   In Edgeworth's Irish novels characters who "recant" are portrayed in a consistently negative manner, usually as both acquisitive and immoral. In fairness to Edgeworth many Gaelic Irish also disdained those who renounced the faith, if for different reasons, despite the fact that professing Catholicism meant exclusion from the circuits of power in Ireland's political, social or economic life. *Cf.* the Rackrents, Mrs. Rafferty in *The Absentee*, etc.

Ulick attempts to introduce Ormond into his own social and political circles in order to retain influence over him, and to this end he also brings him into contact with a succession of grasping females who are looking for husbands[47] reminiscent of the Isabella Dashfort sequence in *The Absentee*. Ormond meets a benevolent Protestant cleric, whose home also provides a model of the normative domesticity Ormond wishes to emulate. Under Dr. Cambray's influence he repudiates the marriage market and once again secures access to the Annalys, an Anglo-Irish family who do not associate with the Irish Protestants of Ulick's circle, many of whom, unlike the Annalys, also have Gaelic origins and have renounced Catholicism. The Annalys and Ulick occupy different strata within the social hierarchy of *Ormond*, which Edgeworth is careful to keep distinct. Through some acquaintances of the Annalys Harry learns of Ulick's reputation for corruption and "jobbing," by which Ulick has amassed his considerable wealth and power. At a house party of one of these acquaintances, Ormond is tutored in the nuanced but rigid class system when he hears Ulick's reputation condemned by another guest. This section of the novel provides Edgeworth's lengthy and detailed critique of the opportunistic Gaelic Irish who repudiate the Catholic Church in order to gain entry into Ireland's ruling and commercial classes. It also locates the origin of the "disease" of Irish anti-domesticity directly in this sub-stratum of the Irish class structure.[48]

Edgeworth's strongest condemnation of Irish rule is represented in the domestic plot. The policies and practices as a landlord of Ulick and others like him directly undermine the domestic discipline of the Gaelic peasantry, and in *Ormond*'s Burkean scheme the social, economic, and political problems of Ireland are the immediate consequences of this anti-domesticity. Edgeworth directly compares Ulick's land management policies to those of Sir Herbert Annaly in order to illustrate what she considers the real state of the Irish economy by contrasting it with the ideal. Ormond visits an estate of which Sir Herbert came into possession upon the death of a landlord whose practices gave rise to dissipation, idleness, and crime in the tenantry:

> This estate stretched along the sea-shore – the tenants whom [Sir Herbert, upon taking possession of the property] found living near the coast were an idle, profligate, desperate set of people ... in the habit of *making their rents* by nefarious practices. The best of the set were merely idle fishermen ... – the others were illicit distillers – smugglers – and miscreants who lived by *waifs and strays*; in short by the pillage of vessels along the coast.[49] (original italics)

In the description of Sir Herbert's quick improvements to the tenants' conditions, administered personally in contrast to Ulick's absenteeism (he lives in Dublin), Edgeworth exemplifies her ideal among the three alternative social models she provides. To ensure that the point is not missed, her hero directly states which of these is the only acceptable alternative under which Ireland should be ruled:

---

[47]   *Ormond*, 194–5.
[48]   Ibid, 209 ff.
[49]   Ibid., 233.

> [Ormond] liked to compare the three modes in which King Corny, [Ulick], and
> Sir Herbert managed [their domains]. Sir Herbert governed neither by threats,
> punishments, abuse, nor tyranny; nor yet did he govern by promises nor bribery,
> *favour and protection*, like Sir Ulick ... He treated them neither as slaves, subject
> to his will; nor as dupes ... He treated them as reasonable beings, whom he wished
> to improve, that he might make them and himself happy.[50] (original italics)

Edgeworth's imagining of possible Irish social and economic arrangements,
limited as it is to these three models, of course excludes any possibility of the
peasantry assuming title to the land it has lived on for countless generations; their
"happiness" is made or marred by the measure of benevolence with which their
current Anglo-Irish master rules over them. No program for reforming the system
is proposed; rather she prescribes that all members of the Ascendancy adopt Sir
Herbert's benevolent policies on an individualized basis.

Ulick not only provides the bad management with which Edgeworth contrasts
Sir Herbert's enlightened program, his antidomestic regime actually subverts
the reforms she would adopt. Ulick's landlording policies are therefore linked
thematically with Moriarity's requiring Harry to "secure his future," because both
imply Irish success and happiness, within a strictly limited sphere, depend on the
paternalism of the ethnically English rulers. Ulick bought the large tract of land
adjacent to the one recently improved by Sir Herbert "on the speculation that he
could set it at very high rent to [the former tenants as well as those from the adjacent
estate whom Sir Herbert has dispossessed on grounds of their unsuitability as his
own tenants – belying Ormond's claim that in their treatment they were not subject
to Sir Herbert's will], of whose *ways and means* of paying it [Ulick] chose to
remain in ignorance."[51] Nor does Ulick make any effort to improve their condition
or develop the productivity of his lands. The result is that Sir Herbert's efforts at
improving the tenantry's morals, by means of building a lighthouse and a sailcloth
manufactory in addition to assisting them by teaching modern, profitable farming
techniques, are undermined at every turn by Ulick's tenants.

A shipwreck scene encapsulates the entire breakdown of familial discipline
that results from the example and policies of Ulick and those like him. Edgeworth
suggests the episode is typical: "Whenever a vessel in distress was seen off the
coast, there was a constant struggle between the two parties who had opposite
interests – the one to save, the other to destroy."[52] The ship is plundered, and
Ormond, who had risked his life to preserve the lives of the sailors, is outraged and
pursues the thieves. The women and children of Ulick's estate thwart his heroic
efforts, however, and by this means Edgeworth represents the anti-domesticity
stemming from Ulick's rule as both the result of, and means of reproducing, a moral
contagion which is the primary threat to Ireland's future. It is worth examining this
passage in detail, because the moral disease Edgeworth depicts here, translated

---

[50]   Ibid., 235.

[51]   Ibid., 233–5.

[52]   Ibid., 235.

from Burke's "disease of power and wealth," will become an important element in British representations of Irishness henceforth:

> Ormond spent nearly three hours searching [for the ship's stolen cargo in] a number of wretched cabins, from which the male inhabitants had fled ... leaving the women and children to make what excuses and tell what lies they could ... While he listened to the piteous story of a woman, about a husband who had broken a leg *sarving* [serving] the masons at Sir Herbert's lighthouse and was *lying* at the hospital, and *not expected* [to survive], the husband was lying all the time with both his legs safe and sound in a potato furrow within a few yards of the house. And *the child* of another eloquent matron was running off with a pair of silver-mounted pistols taken from the wreck, which he was instructed to hide in a bog-hole.[53] (original italics)

There are several elements that demand comment in this tableau of Ormond confronting the dissembling mothers while their husbands and children escape with the household goods of disaster victims for whom Harry is heroically trying to "secure the future." The cravenness of the men is patent, running away and hiding behind their women from the "real man" whom they dare not face. At best Edgeworth infantilizes them if their flight is read as a "game" of outwitting their adult pursuer; either way they lack "manliness" – an important concern in British cultural nationalism of the period, as evidenced, among other places, in Burke's *Reflections*, by his many passing references to "manly" liberty, religion, etc. indicate.[54]

But more toxic than this from the standpoint of its cultural influence is the portrait of the Irish women and mothers, particularly when juxtaposed with that of Florence Aannaly. The "piteous' woman whose husband is hiding nearby in the potato furrow is not only lying to cover his crime of theft, but telling a fable as to him being injured at work, with perhaps an implicit hint of her manipulativeness (an injury from work being likely to claim Ormond's sympathy), with the strong implication that she approves and abets the husband's malingering as well as his criminality. Still more striking to the contemporary (English) reader would be the deviancy of the mothers who instruct their children to participate in this lawlessness. Edgeworth ironically refers to an "eloquent" matron, evoking an image of the woman's shrill histrionics as she creates a diversion in order for the men and children to escape, which bespeaks the profound distance of the Edgeworthian Gaelic Irishwoman from the cultural domestic ideals not only of moral rectitude but also of proper womanly modesty and demureness. But that she instructs *the child*, likewise Edgeworth's italics effectively convey the vehemence of her opprobrium of such a mother to carry out the crime suggests a society that is sunk in barbarism and degeneracy. Another mother, lying in bed with two small children, conceals "[t]he goods which they had carried off ... in the straw of the

---

[53] Ibid., 258.
[54] Burke, *Reflections*, 89, 95 and *passim*.

very bed on which [she] was lying."[55] In this image, the sanctified patriarchal marriage bed is defiled by the woman's utter moral abandonment, with the children lying in attendance and absorbing the lesson. Ormond, unable to comprehend such pervasive depravity, is completely taken in by the stories of these and other women and children until he is disabused by a Catholic informer. Edgeworth delineates a culture with women and children thoroughly involved in the crime and degradation of rootless and rapacious men, which represents the antithesis of normative British domesticity and order. Moreover, because the degeneracy that is shown to develop through the Gaelic Irish family structure continually encroaches on Sir Herbert's estates despite his most strenuous efforts, Edgeworth in this novel is figuring Irishness as a moral contagion. The conceptualization will be utilized in works ranging from novels by Thackeray to works of political reform by Friedrich Engels.

Curing "The Condition of Irishness"

To offset this thoroughgoing anti-domesticity, Edgeworth offers the idealized Annaly family. The marriage plot of Ormond and Florence Annaly encodes the restoration of balance to the social order, and Edgeworth suggests that it is through a reformed domesticity that economic and political order will be harmoniously resolved as well. The domestic ideals expressed in the character of Florence Annaly are portrayed as the means by which sectarian strife, and by extension the social, political and economic problems which in Ireland are intimately bound up with it, may be overcome. At the center of this plot is an episode in which Edgeworth represents her ideals for education, domesticity, and social, political and economic harmony being achieved. The Annaly household is portrayed as the domestic ideal, achieved, as the narrator asserts, through persistent discipline:

> The charm of *domestic politeness*, in the everyday manners of this mother, son, and daughter, towards each other, as well as towards their guests, Ormond saw and felt it irresistibly ... The external polish ... was very different from the varnish which is usually hastily applied to hide imperfections ... This polish was of the substance itself, to be obtained only by long use; but once acquired, lasting forever; not only beautiful but serviceable.[56] (original italics)

With the polish being of the substance itself, Edgeworth strongly implies a *racial* dimension to her project – the Anglo-Saxon race is *substantively* different from the Celtic. This is borne out when the Annalys are visited by a neighborhood busybody, whom Ormond recognizes from the days before her marriage as the personal servant of Ulick's wife. Mrs. McCrule, formerly Miss Black, an Englishwoman by birth, is "much alarmed and scandalized at seeing Catholic and Protestant children

---

[55] Ibid., 259.

[56] *Ormond*, 232.

mixing so much together [at Dr. Cambray's school]."[57] She comes with a friend, Mrs. McGregor, to tell Lady Annaly that she wishes the Annalys to oppose a local charitable organization's sponsorship of a promising young scholar from the Black Islands in an apprenticeship. In a scene which encodes comic sexual panic, Mrs. McCrule asserts that allowing the candidate, "little" Tommy Dunshaughlin, access to Ireland's commercial economy represents the economic undoing of the Protestant Ascendancy: "The danger, my dear Lady Annaly – the danger, my dear Miss Annaly – oh! The danger is imminent. We shall all be positively undone, ma'am; and Ireland – oh! I wish I was once safe in England again."[58] Lady Annaly discounts any such danger by insisting that domestic discipline can be inculcated in Catholics as well as Protestants at a non-sectarian school: "[A]s my friend the excellent Bishop of _____ said in Parliament, 'If you can not make them good Protestants, make them good Catholics.'"[59] Since this novel was written ten years before Catholic Emancipation, at a time when the passage of such an act looked virtually impossible, making the Irish good Catholics can have only one meaning – that of social control. Catholics were prohibited by law from participating in the rule of Ireland, so any schooling Tommy would receive alongside Protestants would be useful in the example he was provided to emulate, but would not empower him politically or socially.

Edgeworth does not only assert that domestic discipline will bring about social order, however. She represents Florence's domesticity, and the cultural authority which she derives from it[60] as the means by which the more enlightened, but still exclusionary position of the Annalys and Ormond win the debate with Mrs. McCrule's faction. When Ormond scoffs at Mrs. McCrule's assertion that Little Tommy's case will be the "ruin" of Ireland, "Florence, who saw his condition, had the kindness to draw off Mrs. McCrule's attention by asking her to partake of some excellent goose pie. This promised to suspend discussion for a time, and to unite all parties in one common sympathy."[61] Here Florence uses feminine nurturance to reconcile the opposing parties, and Edgeworth employs the domestic harmony thus created as a metaphor for Ascendancy unity in matters concerning the rule of Ireland: "When Florence saw that the *consommé*, to which she delicately helped her, was not thrown away upon Mrs. McCrule, and that the union of goose and turkey in this Christmas dainty was much admired by this good lady, she attempted playfully to pass a reflexion on the happy effect that might to some tastes result from unions in party matters."[62] Florence's application of the feminine strategies

---

[57]   Ibid., 242.

[58]   Ibid., 245.

[59]   Ibid., 249.

[60]   That is, the authority to reproduce the social order and preside over its morality, which we know from the case of Grace Nugent is only conferred – by the men – upon chaste and subservient women.

[61]   *Ormond*, 248.

[62]   Ibid., 248.

of conciliation and gentleness are only temporarily effective, however, partially because Ormond assumes a harsh masculine authoritativeness in order to rebuke Mrs. McCrule: "Florence was very busy replenishing Mrs. McGregor's plate, and Ormond haughtily told Mrs. McCrule that ... as to the rest, she was at liberty to say or hint whatever she pleased, but that, for her own sake, he would recommend it to her that she be sure of her facts."[63] Reacting to Ormond's aggressiveness, Mrs. McCrule hardens her position and warns Florence that if she persists in her opposition to Mrs. McCrule, "people I know will draw inferences."[64] Mrs. McCrule has perceived Ormond and Florence exchanging significant glances, and she thus implies that she, a notorious gossip, will make it known that Florence is supporting Tommy's cause in an effort to win Ormond's favor. In defending her virtue as pure and not shrinking from her duty even if that means it might be impugned, Florence asserts a cultural authority similar to that which Edgeworth invokes in the writing of her Irish novels to advance the cause she deems righteous: "Florence coloring not a little, but with calm dignity and spirit, which Mrs. McCrule did not expect from her usual gentleness and softness of manner, replied, that 'no inference which might be drawn from her conduct by any persons on earth, should prevent her from acting as she thought right, and taking that part which she thought just.'"[65] Edgeworth makes clear that Florence acts not out of devotion to some abstract principle, however, but instead is "excessively interested for the child."[66]

It is imperative in elaborating Edgeworth's cultural ideal that Florence's motives be self-abnegating, and the point is further advanced by the fact that Florence is supporting the interests of a child who otherwise would be mired in the slough of contagious anti-domesticity that is the Black Islands without her help. Her efforts on his behalf are on some levels analogous with Edgeworth's writing of Irish novels. Florence, like Edgeworth, claims the authority to press Little Tommy's cause in the public sphere because it is a matter of importance in which her personal interest intersects with the public interest:

> [S]he might safely avow this interest – it was in the cause of one who is innocent, and who had been oppressed. As Mrs. McCrule was so vindictively busy, going about, daily, among the lady patronesses, preparing for the great battle ... it was necessary that Lady and Miss Annaly should exert themselves at least to make the truth known to their friends.[67]

Significantly, when the vote on Little Tommy's fate is taken and decided in his favor, Florence returns to an appropriately demure role of privately encouraging Tommy while retiring from the public scene. Likewise, after publishing this novel Edgeworth also retreated from the masculine world of politics. *Ormond* is

---

[63]   Ibid., 250.
[64]   Ibid., 251.
[65]   Ibid.
[66]   Ibid., 252.
[67]   Ibid., 254.

Maria Edgeworth's final Irish novel, and the one in which she most thoroughly puts forth her position on matters of the place of Ireland in British culture, the co-existence of Catholics and Protestants, and the centrality of Burkean domesticity to a balanced social, economic and political order.[68] She would leave the debate to others, but not without having considerably influenced popular notions of proper womanhood and proper management of the Irish "condition." In her novel *Florence McCarthy*, Lady Morgan tries directly to counteract *Ormond*'s influence and that of other commentators on issues of gender and cultural nationalism. Despite the nobility of her cause and the passion with which she advanced it, Lady Morgan's success in challenging Edgeworth's authority was less than spectacular among critics, and her egalitarian views concerning the Irish and women failed to sway the culture at large in the short term. Edgeworth's influence in transforming Burke's formulation of "the disease of power and wealth" into "the condition of Irishness" thus played a significant role in hindering the creation of a British social order closer in accord with more modern ideas of fairness and equality.

---

[68]   Edgeworth's withdrawal from writing Irish novels was probably connected to the death of her father, which occurred while she was writing *Ormond*. Marilyn Butler and others have demonstrated that Edgeworth sought her father's approval when expressing her political opinions in her novels (see esp. Butler).

Chapter 4
Transcending Ascendancy:
Florence McCarthy

Contesting Edgeworth

In her novel *Florence McCarthy* (1818), Lady Morgan mounts a challenge on numerous levels to the social vision expressed in *Ormond*. She contests Edgeworth's familial politics as inadequate both as a political and gender model, based as it is upon unequal and therefore corrupting power relationships. Lady Morgan also rejects the Burkean ideal of a patriarchy regulating desire throughout society by its authority and example in order to secure economic, political, and social harmony. *Florence McCarthy* furthermore highlights the Irish social structure's intrinsic obstacles and disincentives which make the Anglo-Irish ruling elite's voluntary and individualized rehabilitation unlikely. Unlike Edgeworth, Lady Morgan views Ireland's problems as systemic and instead imagines a non-hyphenated Irish identity in which the Ascendancy shares equal power with the Catholic nobility, and women share power with men. Patriarchal gender relations are explicitly renounced. *Florence McCarthy* also burlesques Ascendancy schemes of economic and educational reform of the type so prominent in *Ormond*, and moreover depicts the Anglo-Irish land-owning class as concerned with little that goes on in Ireland so long as their rents are collected. This disconnection from the land they rule has given rise to a system of corrupt official middlemen who often manipulate the owners for their own ends, which are to wield the real political and economic power to their own material benefit and the further suffering of the Irish peasantry. Lady Morgan also expands and complicates Edgeworthian ideals of domesticity and the role of women in the public sphere. Gender relations in turn inform her political vision, as the centrality of her title character to Ireland's social, economic, and political restoration make clear. It is through Florence McCarthy's public, not domestic agency, that social balance is achieved.

Like *Ormond*, *Florence McCarthy* allegorizes the achievement of social harmony by means of a marriage plot involving the title character. Lady Morgan's hero has inherited the name of illustrious male ancestors; but she is a woman, and there are several important implications in this detail, particularly when viewed in relation to both of *Ormond*'s central male and female characters, as well as to Lady Morgan's prototypical Irish heroine Glorvina. Ina Ferris has pointed out that on visiting Ireland the protagonist of *The Wild Irish Girl*:

> encounters in the hinterland ... the pure time of origin or authenticity that makes visible the nation ... where the symbolic heroine, Glorvina ... reveals to the English hero "the pure, national, natural character of an Irishwoman." Where

The Wild Irish Girl moved directly to an origin, dissolving nation into nature, later tales like *Florence McCarthy* ... provide no center or "heart" of the nation from which to tell its story ... [but] writ[e] the nation as shadowy and mobile – a persistence (or perhaps resistance?) through time but not an identity. The changed nature of the heroine – who continues to represent the Irish motherland – makes this especially clear.[1]

Ferris might also point out here that Lady Morgan's heroine represents an *entire* nation, not merely one narrow and circumscribed social stratum of that nation. Lady Morgan, in choosing a woman to represent the nation, aligns her heroine with traditional figurations of colonized peoples and territories, including one in particular whom her heroine recalls – a shadowy and mobile figure who represents the Irish motherland in Irish folk legend, Kathleen ni Houlihan. [2] The changed nature of the heroine of *Florence McCarthy* is moreover changeable – but not in a childish sense as is Cornelius O'Shane. She bears a resemblance to Glorvina in her talent and seductiveness, but complicates the Lady Morganian heroine as well. She captivates several suitors while assuming different identities throughout the novel. She charms one for love, but the others she enchants in order to further the interests of the Irish people. Like Kathleen ni Houlihan, her first appearance in the novel is as a crone.[3] The multiple identities she assumes are all revealed as guises of the beautiful and mysterious young Florence McCarthy at the denouement.

Like the central female character in *Ormond* who shares her first name, Florence McCarthy claims the authority to engage issues in the public sphere. Her efforts are not authorized by her domesticity, however, nor are her methods limited to traditionally feminine strategies. Like Lady Morgan, Lady Clancare (the identity Florence assumes over the greatest part of the novel) writes professionally in order to advance Ireland's cause. For this activity she gains the contempt of most of the novel's Ascendancy characters who assume she is merely seeking celebrity. But when asked by a fatuous hanger-on of the largest Anglo-Irish landowner in the district why she writes at all, she explains to him she must support herself by her writing: "'[I must write books] [s]imply ... to live – you may perhaps add

---

[1]   "Writing on the Border: The National Tale, Female Writing, and the Public Sphere," 92.

[2]   Sir Walter Raleigh provided a now infamous prototypical figuration of the colonized nation as a virginal female ripe for exploitation when he described Guiana as "a country that hath yet her maiden-head" (quoted in Neill, Michael. "Broken English and Broken Irish: Nation, Language, and the Optic Power in Shakespeare's Histories," *Shakespeare Quarterly* 45:1 [Spring 1994], 21). Kathleen ni Houlihan is a shape-shifting figure, celebrated in folk tales and aislings, who first appears as a crone and is revealed to be a beautiful young woman representing Irish nationhood. For a discussion of Kathleen ni Houlihan and the aisling tradition see Innes.

[3]   Florence McCarthy's first appearance in the novel is in the guise of Mrs. Magillicudy, a hag who mysteriously continues to reappear and leads the two central male characters (General Fitzwalter and Lord Fitzadelm) to Florence McCarthy's domain.

quelle nécessité; and perhaps also,' she added significantly, 'you are right.'"[4] The very fact that she, a Gaelic noblewoman, must support herself comments upon the inadequacy of the patriarchal Ascendancy to securely enfold all members of society into a protective web, let alone afford all members of society an opportunity to express themselves in meaningful and fulfilling ways. The peasantry on Lady Clancare's estates, forced to work subsistence-level tracts of land by colonial policy which bars them from many other means of livelihood, are also impoverished.[5] Lady Clancare claims that she thus exerts herself in her writing not to romanticize Ireland's past, as her Ascendancy critics charge (and as Lady Morgan's critics charged against her), but rather for the same reasons she engages in her other work – to improve the present lot of all Ireland's inhabitants:

> [T]he present state of this poor country interests me more than its ancient greatness, real or fabled; and I should rather see my neighbors ... succeed in reclaiming that mountain, to the right of easement ... or improve in the rush and straw work I am endeavouring to teach their idle, helpless, naked children, than establish that ... Ireland was the seat of arts and letters, when the rest of the world was ... buried in utter darkness.[6]

Lady Clancare's character shares important similarities with Lady Morgan in a way which recalls Florence Annaly's parallels to Maria Edgeworth, but again, with important complications. As owner and manager of her estate she necessarily operates in the public sphere, overseeing its day-to-day activities and working to solve all of its problems. In other words, she performs a role only imagined in Edgeworth's Irish novels as being filled by an Ascendancy male. Perhaps even more importantly, Lady Clancare's efforts as a landlord are analogous to both her own writing and Lady Morgan's as well. Ina Ferris argues that "[Lady Morgan] perceived her writing as a public act, an intervention in and performance for the public domain in which the stake was public opinion."[7] Lady Morgan's heroine persistently intervenes and performs in the public sphere, and when she voices the aims of her own fictional practice she draws attention to the ways in which her project parallels that of Lady Morgan – ways quite beyond Florence Annaly's deployment of feminine agency for the purpose of restoring Ascendancy intra-party unity:

---

[4]   *Florence McCarthy* (1818). New York: D. & J. Sadlier (n.d.), 516. All references to the novel are to this edition.

[5]   Like Glorvina, Florence McCarthy is also the descendant of Catholic nobility displaced from larger estates situated on more desirable land. This novel, like *The Wild Irish Girl* but in sharp contrast to *Ormond*, goes into great detail about the historical vicissitudes which have left the Gaelic aristocracy in its present condition, mostly through the character of the local genealogist, Terrence Og O'Leary.

[6]   *Florence McCarthy*, 429.

[7]   "Writing on the Border: The National Tale, Female Writing, and the Public Sphere," 87–8.

With Ireland in my heart, and epitomizing something of her humor and her sufferings in my own character and story, I do trade upon the materials she offers me and, turning my patriotism into pounds, shillings and pence, endeavor, at the same moment, to serve her, and support myself ... I have yielded to still loving the world ... noble by chance, an author by necessity, and a woman.[8]

Lady Morgan, in the prefaces to many of her works, defends her project and claims cultural authority as an author and a woman to pursue it in direct response to critics. Lady Clancare likewise deflects charges of unfeminine ambition, and ascribes complaints about her work to two causes: the wounded dignity of vainglorious persons who imagine that they are being caricatured in her novels, and the threatened security of her real targets, those wishing to uphold the masculinist power structure. Lady Clancare ironically claims that to avoid making enemies she must write novels and not plays, because to write plays she would have to draw characters *realistically*:

[S]hould I ever abandon my high strain of romance ... and hold the mirror up to life, you would all fancy you detect in it your own reflections, and each "Would cry, that was leveled at me" ... [E]ven vanity will find out resemblances where malice could not trace similitude. There, indeed, my patience quite fails me. Conscious vice, conscious absurdity, and apprehensive eccentricity, when combined with masculine energies and decided volitions, may be excused for indulging in such fanciful appropriations.[9]

Lady Morgan, through Lady Clancare, ironically excuses the "fanciful appropriations" of those who identify with a willful retention of the conscious vice and absurdity of an inequitable and here explicitly gendered distribution of power – in effect saying "if the shoe fits, wear it." There is a further irony in Lady Clancare's apologia, consisting in the fact that Lady Morgan herself did indeed attempt to "hold the mirror up to life," and succeeded to the extent that she was often charged by some critics that she insinuated herself into fashionable society in order to find suitable characters to caricature, and that her novels were in large part *romans à clefs*.[10] The irony is hard to miss – *Florence McCarthy* has an important character modeled on the Tory politician and literary critic John Wilson Croker.[11]

---

[8]   *Florence McCarthy*, 437, 441–2. Many commentators have remarked upon Lady Morgan's various heroines being thinly veiled embodiments of the author herself. See especially Stevenson, Campbell, Ferris 1993, and Chapter 2 above.

[9]   Ibid., 515–16.

[10]   See Stevenson and Campbell for discussions of the various characters in her novels and whom they resemble in real life as well as the critical response to this aspect of her fiction.

[11]   The irony was also clearly evident to its intended targets. In a letter from Sir Robert Peel, then Chief Secretary for Ireland, to Croker dated November 22, 1817, Peel informs Croker that "you are to be the hero of some novel of which [Lady Morgan] is about to be delivered" (Jennings, 99). Although he is not actually the hero, Croker's character plays a significant role in the work.

Lady Clancare is a multi-faceted heroine who expands traditionally feminine attributes beyond an Edgworthian domesticity into public virtues. One of the most important instances of her public activity also incorporates a refutation of Edgeworth's portrayal of Irish anti-domesticity as stemming from the diseased Gaelic-Irish substratum of the Protestant ruling classes. When she administers medical treatment to some of her tenants who have contracted typhus, a dreaded contagious disease in the early nineteenth century, she explains why she exposes herself to the disease in the course of her duties to General Fitzwalter, who finds her one day directing the normal operations of her estate outside a tenant's cabin,: "[I]f I did not come, four wretches who lie there [within the cabin], dying for want of proper care, would perish ... I induced them to settle in this swampy tract, and feel myself in part answerable for their existence."[12] Lady Clancare then links the physical contagion to a moral contagion among the Irish poor. But while moral contagion is characterized in *Ormond* as a result of unregulated desire, Lady Morgan attributes both physical and moral disease to material causes: "The fever which sweeps away the poor people is, in my mind, the pure result of their poverty and its concomitants, filth and starvation. Their moral and physical ills are closely linked, and arise out of the same cause."[13] The cause Lady Clancare refers to is British colonial policy in Ireland as implemented by the ruling Ascendancy. Thus in this sequence Lady Morgan specifically challenges Edgeworth's strategy of depicting Irish moral contagion as something that seeps down through a diseased segment of the aristocracy – namely, the Gaelic-Irish middling classes represented in *Ormond* by Ulick O'Shane. Ironically, however, the linkage between physical and moral disease Lady Morgan points to (a linkage not made in *Ormond*) is one that would be picked up in later representations of the Irish that characterize Irish anti-domesticity as the cause of a multitude of social woes. Lady Morgan, on the other hand, attributes these woes to British colonial policy.[14]

Lady Morgan furthermore characterizes the cause as Anglo-Irish misrule, which colonial policy not only fails to provide checks upon, but worse, protects and sustains. The exposition of cause, effect, and solution provides the crux of her political message. *Florence McCarthy* mounts a sustained challenge to *Ormond*'s familial politics in the form of an attack upon the *structure* of Irish society. Viewed in this way, no paternalistic schemes such as Edgeworth's proposed educational efforts which seek to regulate the desire of the lower orders, or public works projects like Sir Herbert's lighthouse, no matter how benevolent in intention, can possibly restore social and economic harmony to Ireland. The picture Lady Morgan paints is of a large peasant population forced to send most of the production from its already

---

12   *Florence McCarthy*, 486.

13   Ibid., 486.

14   The argument as to whether Irish anti-domesticity is a cause of social problems or effect of the social and economic system would continue in this period and its immediate aftermath, and the role it played in the realms of British urban and social reform is discussed in Chapters 5 and 6. Like Edgeworth, James Kay ascribes an intrinsic Irish immorality to anti-domesticity, while Friedrich Engels attributes such evils as drunkenness and prostitution to the economic order, in an argument that echoes Lady Morgan's.

meager resources to the Big House to pay the exorbitant rents required to sustain a class of landowners who were born, educated, and mostly reside in England, often in capricious idleness. Lady Morgan argues that the ruling Ascendancy ignores the political and economic consequences of British colonial policy because to do so serves the material interests of both the owners and their agents. The ruling class furthermore characterizes the resulting disaffection of the Gaelic Irish as "rebellion" in order to forestall any meaningful political dialogue, because to effectually solve the social and economic problems of Ireland would require that the Ascendancy voluntarily renounce many of its privileges. Reform within the Ascendancy of the type idealized in *Ormond* is therefore wholly inadequate to effect social regeneration.

Anglo-Irish society is itself represented as multifarious and layered, and the obstacles to its reformation are portrayed as systemic. Ferris has pointed out that in her national tales subsequent to *The Wild Irish Girl* Lady Morgan complicates the representation of the Gaelic Irish: "In *The O'Briens and the O'Flahertys*, for instance, Dublin itself uncovers several different kinds of Irishness, while the countryside proves to contain, not a pure Gaelic core, but various layers with different histories."[15] This point holds true for *Florence McCarthy* as well, and significantly, in this novel the Anglo-Irish subculture is also depicted as layered. This constitutes Lady Morgan's response to the reductive portrayal *in Ormond* of the ruling Protestant classes as essentially comprised of two distinct strata: the "English" Ascendancy and the social-climbing, acquisitive, and morally bankrupt class of Gaelic Irish who have "recanted" their Catholicism. In one of the most prominent strands of the plot, General Fitzwalter has returned in disguise to Ireland after fighting various "American wars of liberation" on a ship named after himself, *El Librador*, and the authorities attempt to imprison him. The Fitzwalter character is loosely based upon Lord Edward Fitzgerald and represents an Anglo-Irish element sympathetic to the United Irishmen.[16] Lady Morgan's inclusion of the United Ireland movement in her social vision is significant, because the movement represents a non-sectarian nationalism which nevertheless has been anathematized by the British crown as well as the Patriot party (which dominated Ireland's Parliament in the latter half of the 18th century, and to which Edgeworth's father belonged). In addition to Fitzwalter and Darby Crawley's family (all of whom hold positions of power and influence including the most powerful, his son "Counsellor Con," the Croker character), other important Anglo-Irish characters include Lady Dunore's son, the young, vain and feckless Lord Fitzadelm (who nevertheless regenerates by novel's end and accepts the dispensation which restores his inheritance to its rightful owner, his cousin Fitzwalter), a Patriot politician named Mr. Daly who has resigned in disgust after passage of the Union,[17] and various sycophants of Lady Dunore.

---

[15]   "Writing on the Border: The National Tale, Female Writing, and the Public Sphere," 96.

[16]   For discussions of this connection see Stevenson and Campbell.

[17]   Edgeworth's father Richard similarly resigned from Parliament and the Patriot party after the scandalous passage of the Act of Union.

Lady Morgan represents the top echelon of society as an entity which protects its interests by either marginalizing or attainting members of the lower strata of the ruling classes who reject the status quo, in effect relegating them to the same status as the dispossessed Gaelic nobility. At the top of *Florence McCarthy*'s social system is Lady Dunore. She is represented as a typical Anglo-Irish absentee landowner (she has come to Ireland to relieve an also typical case of ennui – cf. Edgeworth), and as such provides a strong refutation of Edgeworth's familial politics. Enormously wealthy from the income she derives from her Irish estate, born and bred in England, and a cynosure of London society wholly as a result of her wealth, she has little incentive to reform in the manner of Harry Ormond.[18] Her castle is described as representative of the prevailing order, whose owners are subtly acknowledged to be usually either recipients of the property from the British Crown (patentees) or "English"-Irish absentees:

> The castle ... remained in *statu quo*, antique, superb, and desolate, such as may be found in every province in Ireland – the ancient residence of Irish chiefs, the quondam possession of English lords of the pale, the property of more recent patentees, or the inheritance of English-Irish absentees, known only by name to the tenants they have never visited.[19]

Lady Morgan characterizes the alienating system which places Lady Dunore in power (over a peasantry for whom she does little to hide her revulsion) as responsible for the neglect of the town near her castle and all the surrounding area, none of which she has hitherto seen. She has no contact with her tenantry, and leaves the management of her estates to the Crawleys. To relieve her ennui, she takes up various causes and persons to provide her with momentary excitements born of continuous change. She interests herself briefly in politics (until she learns it consists of much tedious work) by attempting to influence the local election and place her son in Parliament (in her rotten borough, of course), takes up Bible study with Darby Crawley's sycophantic sister, and stages an amateur theatrical in her drawing room. All of the activities of Lady Dunore and her court are presented with great humor and irony, while at the same time any (necessarily short-lived) benevolence on the part of the present occupant of the Big House is depicted as an inadequate solution to a systemic problem.[20]

---

[18] Implicit also in Lady Morgan's argument are the restrictions placed on Catholic ownership of land and colonial policies which prohibit many types of agricultural commerce and export. Under these policies the reformed farming practices Edgeworth prescribes through Sir Herbert would provide only very limited benefits, and still less to Catholics.

[19] *Florence McCarthy*, 151.

[20] Ironically, Benjamin Disraeli would later make a similar argument, applied to the case of the English countryside, in *Sybil*, in which the practices of a dissolute and absentee aristocracy are compared unfavorably with the management of their surrounding lands by monks prior to Henry VIII's dissolution of the abbeys. Disraeli idealizes the commitment to and continuity of stewardship and sense of community that the monks provided as opposed to the modern arrangement under which tenants were at the mercy of the whims of the current occupant of the "Big House."

"Neither in Command nor Supplication"

The idealized solution Lady Morgan proposes is an integrated Anglo- and Gaelic-Irish aristocracy and a removal of the legal and social restrictions placed upon the preponderantly Catholic and Gaelic population of Ireland. She suggests that an aristocracy which embraces members who share the same language, religion and culture with the peasantry would implement a more benevolent paternalism, and moreover, this elite should include the Irish common people in the nation's economic life. The various schemes Lady Dunore and her cohort hatch to reform the peasantry are characterized as distractions, whether intentionally devised as such or not, from the real problem. Whereas Edgeworth's central theme is the reformation of Ascendancy familial politics through the individual efforts of the landlords, Lady Morgan emphasizes the direct connection between economic relief and social stability, while belittling what she characterizes as the triviality of the vast majority of reform efforts:

> It is ... curious enough to see people troubling their heads about elections and evangelical schools, and private theatricals and chapels, and bible societies and things, when the people to be represented are starving; the people to be edified, amused, and instructed, are literally perishing for want. Give them something to eat first, and then instruct them; teach them to labor, then to read ... for after all, the first law of nature is to exist. People must live, in order to live piously.[21]

In Lady Morgan's figuration, social regeneration would ramify throughout this more closely-knit Irish society by means of a reform which Lady Morgan strongly implies but does not state directly – Catholic Emancipation. The local senachy,[22] Terrence Og O'Leary, voices for Lady Morgan the prevailing Gaelic view of Irish history. He explains that the poverty of the peasants is a direct effect of the isolation of the peasants from the ruling classes, who are separated by a class of middlemen or agents, in this novel represented by the Crawley family. With no access to the material resources of the country, the tenantry must furthermore pay exorbitant rents and tithes to maintain the tiered social system:

> [W]ith all the labour and pains and industry of the craturs [creatures], let them work night and day, and let them have ever such good friends to back them, it's hard for them to get before the world ..[because they are] beholding to them Crawley pirates, bad luck to them, and their likes, who, by polling and pilling the poor to make their own fortunes, and carrying on many cautelous practices, ruin the land.[23]

---

[21]   *Florence McCarthy*, 457.

[22]   In Gaelic Ireland, senachy was the hereditary position of court genealogist to the local chief. O'Leary, a hedge schoolmaster and amateur antiquarian, considers himself senachy to the McCarthys.

[23]   *Florence McCarthy*, 503.

Only Protestants could, among other advantages, hold political, administrative, or legal office in Ireland, and thus agents like Crawley, far removed socially from the ruling classes, at the same time belong to a social class distinct both culturally and economically from the majority of the population.[24] The political system which "ruins the land," in O'Leary's phrase, is, as he further indicates, embodied in *Florence McCarthy* by the Crawley family. The Crawleys represent both the primary obstacle to the peasantry's attainment of adequate subsistence and the refusal of the ruling classes to redress the situation in a meaningful way. They purposely oppress the peasants and cunningly exploit the rulers in order to solidify their own position of power and increase their own wealth, while Lady Dunore and her circle utilize the Crawleys for the purpose of performing the dirty work required to maintain their own position. The interaction between the Crawley family and the family of Lady Dunore in *Florence McCarthy* thus encapsulates the history of Anglo-Irish rule.

Lady Dunore came to her title and property through the connivance of her now deceased husband and Darby Crawley to cheat her nephew by marriage, General Fitzwalter, out of the marquisate. She only becomes aware of this fact, however, when Darby visits her late at night to inform her that her son must withdraw his bid for a seat in the British Parliament lest "a violent opposition" to the Dunore interest expose the corruption and bribery with which the Crawleys have attempted to secure his election. He instead proposes that his son Counselor Con (the Croker character) run for the seat, a maneuver which will consolidate his own family's power and influence. Lady Dunore defers to his political acumen when Darby cunningly appeals to Lady Dunore's vanity and sense of caste by suggesting that his son will "just keep the seat open for the real member [her son] till the desolution [sic, i.e. "dissolution" (of Parliament)], ... for all the world as your ladyship's footman keeps your box for you at the theater till you arrive yourself."[25] She even more wholeheartedly embraces his assistance when Darby explains that Lady Dunore will need friends like Con in the House to counteract Fitzwalter's claim to the property: "[Fitzwalter's] uncle [Lady Dunore's late husband] and his father connived to put him out of the way to raise money ... at one time his uncle thought to bastardize him ... this attempt failed ... after his brother's death he had the boy kidnapped [by Crawley's agents, and sold into slavery] ... and then trumped up a story of his drowning."[26] The Crawleys managed to quell the legal challenges and hush up the story for the family, and in so doing gained power over Lady Dunore's husband and hence the district which he rarely visited. Upon the General's

---

[24] The movement to remove the Catholic "disabilities" described here was widely popular in Ireland but vehemently opposed in England by most of the population and politicians save some Whigs and Radicals. It finally succeeded, however, with Daniel O'Connell's election to the British Parliament in defiance of the law and the subsequent passage of the Catholic Emancipation Act in 1828.

[25] *Florence McCarthy*, 529–30.

[26] Ibid., 533.

incognito return to Ireland, the Crawleys carry out the dirty work of disposing of Fitzwalter by accusing him of fomenting rebellion. They are in a position to do so because, the absence of the landowners being combined with the Catholic disabilities, they administer both the estate and the local government. Counselor Con, as head of the local militia, furthermore accuses the rebellious peasants who are disaffected by the exorbitant rents they must pay and the government's attempts to imprison their leader.[27] While the machinery of Lady Morgan's plot is cumbersome, the implications are clear enough. The ruling classes are beholden to the middlemen, who protect their dubious claims to their property and the great wealth they derive from it. The middlemen are in turn able to consolidate their own position, and any opposition to the status quo is characterized as violent rebellion, which is then suppressed by force. With Counselor Con's assumption of the seat in Parliament, the Crawleys' power is also shown to have grown incrementally over the generations, Con's grandfather having taken, according to O'Leary, "some of the property of the late Earl of Clancare in trust for him during the painals [penals], sir, and refused to restore it after the repail [sic], which was the first step he got in the world."[28]

Lady Morgan's central argument is that no country ruled by such a fractured and alienating system can be integrated successfully into a nominally United Kingdom. O'Leary attributes Irish political disaffection, as well as sectarian disunity, not to a moral contagion emanating from a degenerate aristocracy, but the patriarchal ruling class's religious, social and political exclusion of the Gaelic Irish from the body politic: "The result of this misrule and oppression of ages, of this religious disqualification ... is to extinguish what you call the Irish spirit ... when three-fourths of the people are, as it were, branded on the forehead like the descendants of Cain, and wandering in foreign lands, because they profess the faith of their forefathers."[29]

Lady Morgan imagines the restoration of social harmony through the direct inclusion of the Gaelic Irish into the British social body. The marriage plot of *Florence McCarthy* allegorizes a full integration of Irish society by imagining the union of the Gaelic Lady Clancare with the Anglo-Irish General Fitzwalter. As noted in a previous chapter, Lady Morgan's Irish novels call attention to the many assimilations that had taken place over the course of Irish history; Fitzwalter's Anglo-Norman name also subtly attests to this. The marriage ceremony between Fitzwalter and Lady Clancare is itself a celebration of reconciliation and inclusiveness.

---

[27]   The leader is Padreen Gar, who in a heavy-handed touch of political symbolism turns out to be the bastard son of Fitzwalter's father. Gar's "rebelliousness" is moreover portrayed as sincere attempts to attain economic justice, though it is characterized by the Crawleys as political agitation promoting violence against the law-abiding productive classes.

[28]   *Florence McCarthy*, 329.

[29]   Ibid., 503–4.

[B]efore the high altar, at whose feet reposed the ashes of the great McCarthy-More, the young descendant and inheritor of his title and name gave her hand to the representative of his hereditary enemies. The ceremony was performed by the Reverend Denis O'Sullivan, titular Dean of Dunore, assisted by the parish priest. The Protestant rector, who was to repeat the rites according to the forms of the Protestant Church (the parties being of different persuasions), also attended at Lady Clancare's particular request.[30]

Lady Morgan's program attempts to imagine a national cultural identity other than as a type of ethnically pure hegemony augmented by cultural appropriation, as in Edgeworth. Instead, she imagines the creation of a modern Ireland as a part of Great Britain by promoting a more enduring nationalism. Benedict Anderson has argued that successful modern nations are founded on a nationalism that "has to be understood by aligning it, not with self-consciously held political ideologies, but with the large cultural systems that preceded it, out of which – as well as against which – it came into being."[31] In other words, Lady Morgan seems to have understood, as Edgeworth had not, that in order for Ireland to become and remain an integral part of a cohesive United Kingdom, it was essential to construct a cultural nationalism in which what Anderson characterizes as the "contingencies and fatalities" of Irish history acquire a meaning that allows *all* Irish people to enter modernity by embracing and being embraced by the Union, rather than merely consign the vast majority to remain dependent on a type of more indulgent feudal masters. In Anderson's terms, Irish national cultural identity must be imagined as arising out of the multifarious cultural systems which preceded it, producing at once an ancient and coherent identity that has furthermore left in the past its struggles for cultural supremacy among competing tribal and ethnic groups.[32] Lady Morgan attempts to accomplish this in the marriage between Fitzwalter and Lady Clancare, which figures the inclusion of all the cultural strands into a new, non-hyphenated Irish identity.

Their marital partnership is furthermore depicted as a rejection of patriarchy. Fitzwalter is engaged to Florence McCarthy (whom he only met briefly, and does not now recognize as Lady Clancare) as a result of a promise he made to her dying father while serving under him in South America: "His death, which was the purchase of my life, imposed on me an obligation I would have requited to his daughter."[33] But the bargain Fitzwalter makes is for his assumption of paternal protection, "soothing a father's death-bed anxieties for the fate of his friendless child ... answering all his paternal solicitudes, by offering to give his child the only

---

[30]   Ibid., 558.

[31]   *Imagined Communities*, 12. Edgeworth seems to have agreed with this point; hence, the Ascendancy appropriation of Gaelic culture in her novels.

[32]   See *Imagined Communities*, Chapter 2, "Cultural Roots."

[33]   *Florence McCarthy*, 432.

protection a man [of Fitzwalter's] age could afford a woman of hers"[34] However, military exigencies interrupt the marriage as it is about to take place between them on the altar, Fitzwalter is taken prisoner, and Florence McCarthy enters a convent. Upon encountering her in Ireland and being seduced by the supposed Lady Clancare's talent and generosity (in much the same way as Horatio was seduced by Glorvina), Fitzwalter regrets the commitment to Florence McCarthy, whom he perceives as unequal to and dependent upon him. He explains however to Lady Clancare, whom he truly loves, that his feelings of obligation to Florence prevent his marrying anyone else. Lady Clancare continues to conceal her true identity in order to retain temporary influence over Lady Dunore and the Crawleys.

When she finally reveals who she is and marries, Lady Clancare retains her important role in the public sphere. She wields social and political power greater than that of Fitzwalter, as is demonstrated when Fitzwalter is arrested on trumped-up charges of sedition at Con Crawley's instigation in order to prevent Fitzwalter from claiming the Dunore estates. The peasants form a mob and threaten to forcefully extricate Fitzwalter from custody, and his efforts to control them are unsuccessful: "In a momentary pause, Fitzwalter (sternly, as one accustomed to command) ... endeavored to address the mob, and induce them to quietly return to their work or their homes; [he was] only answered by shrill and wild shouts, which convinced [him] of the inefficiency of [his] efforts."[35] The situation threatens to degenerate into mob violence until Lady Clancare intervenes:

> [A] general engagement was about to take place; but the voice and interference of Lady Clancare produced an effect, as unexpected as singular. She addressed them in Irish – it was evidently neither in command nor supplication. Whatever she said produced bursts of laughter and applause; every eye, flashing humor and derision, was turned on the constables and their satellites. A new impulse seemed to be given to the susceptible auditory she addressed. Rage was turned to contempt; anticipated triumph shone in every eye. They drew back, suffered the military to close around the carriage, dropped their missiles, and followed in regular order the track of the carriages, as they now proceeded to the Castle of Dunore.[36]

Lady Clancare's control of the crowd has several implications for the restoration of balance to the social order. Although traditionally the inferior partner in marriage, the woman in Lady Morgan's imagined Union is the equal of Fitzwalter who retains

---

[34]   Ibid., 491. The age discrepancy might seem to be Lady Morgan's tacit admission of Ireland's developmental backwardness as a nation, a backwardness figured as irremediable in the Edgeworthian marriage plot where the Gaelic Irish are figured as the dependent children of the partnership. Lady Morgan strongly refutes such a conclusion, however, in her portrayal of Lady Clancare as, if anything, the stronger and more effective member of the partnership.

[35]   Ibid., 560.

[36]   Ibid., 560–61.

her authority with the Irish people. Her auditory is "susceptible" and willing to follow "in regular order," renouncing political violence, because they recognize that gross injustice, which she and they alike contemn now with good Irish humor, will be addressed in good faith by a sympathetic leadership which has been more closely integrated with the general population. A leadership which is comprised of both Catholic and Protestant, Gaelic and Anglo Irish members will afford all segments of the Irish population access to justice, whether it be political as in the case of General Fitzwalter and Padreen Gar, or economic and social justice for the masses. Lady Clancare is an authority figure who recognizes and will address the material causes for their suffering while assuming neither a masculinized position of command nor femininized attitude of supplication. Her relationship with the people is direct and immediate, signaled by the fact that she speaks to them in Irish. No alienating, corrupting system of agents stands between rulers and ruled. With her representations of relationships on all levels, be it parties to the Union, men and women, the Gaelic- and Anglo- Irish, the Catholic and Protestant churches, or rulers and the ruled, Lady Morgan has completely overturned the rigidly exclusionary scheme of *Ormond.* Ironically, Maria Edgeworth, the avowed opponent of romance, had obscured the hegemonic political implications of her narrative by utilizing the tropes of melodrama, depicting the public concerns of social control as interiorized conflicts within an Ascendancy marriage plot. Lady Lady Morgan's novel, on the other hand, argues for a solution much more in line with modern Western ideals (and these too are inclusive in *Florence McCarthy* – of social justice, political equality, economic justice, gender equality, and human rights in general, which are all explicitly engaged in the plot) – in a work that overtly announces its alignment with romance. Most critics have long considered Edgeworth's artistry superior to Lady Morgan's. Edgeworth's politics remained triumphant for quite some time too. It was not until well into the twentieth century that Western society as a whole began to embrace the idea that, as Lady Morgan pointed out in *Florence McCarthy*, true social harmony and justice can only consist in partnerships not reduced to the polarities of command and supplication.

Chapter 5
Policing "The Chief Nests of Disease and Broils"

Introduction

Britain's social arrangements and hierarchies were contested not only in the province of fiction, as attested by the Irish novels of Lady Morgan and Edgeworth, but also in the discourses of social reform. The migration of some of the figurations of Irishness (such as, for example, it being a marker of moral contagion) across discursive boundaries demonstrates the influence of the novel in and of itself, and I now wish to examine some examples of these boundary-crossings both to examine some of the particularities of that influence, and to trace the evolution of the memes in question over time. If anything, Irishness figured even more prominently as a signifier in the political debates over the management of British industrial expansion in the aftermath of Lady Morgan and Edgeworth's "dialogue."

Modern conventional wisdom holds that Irish emigration was largely a product of the Great Famine, and most sociological studies of the Irish in Britain concentrate on the years around and immediately following 1845-6, years of massive Irish influx into Britain. However, Irish immigration, while not as heavy as at mid-century, occurred in significant numbers and was steady throughout earlier decades of the 1800s.[1] In this chapter and the next I will attempt to show that trends in representing Irishness characteristic of Edgeworth's novels informed to a great degree what were considered at the time objective analyses of urban and social problems, owing in no small degree to the increased presence of displaced Irish in British cities. I will moreover attempt to show that, along with this development, the figure of the Irish woman became increasingly important in conceptualizing British national identity in political discourse and, in subsequent chapters, in fiction and the public press.

Much recent historiography concerned with Irish immigrants in Britain in the first half of the nineteenth century suggests a widespread perception in the host society that Irish crime constituted a great danger to the safety and security of British citizens.[2] Roger Swift voices what seems to be the consensus among

---

[1]   See O'Tuathaigh, M.A.G. "The Irish in Nineteenth-Century Britain: Problems of Integration," in *The Irish in the Victorian City*, eds R. Swift and S. Gilley. London: Pinter, 1985, 13–36.

[2]   See for example Frances Finnegan, *Poverty and Prejudice: A Study of Irish Immigrants in York 1840–75*. Cork: Cork University Press, 1982; Clem.Richardson, "The Irish in Victorian Bradford," in *The Bradford Antiquary* ix, 294–316; and Roger Swift, "Another Stafford Street Row: Law, Order, and the Irish in Mid-Victorian Wolverhampton,"

historians at the turn of the twenty-first century about British popular attitudes in the early nineteenth century: "Indeed, while crime and disorder were popularly perceived to be Irish traits, it was also held that the Irish were more criminal than other sections of the host society and, as such, represented a challenge on the part of the 'dangerous classes' in which the Irish bulked large, to authority and order in nineteenth-century Britain."[3] In other words, the fact that the Irish were disproportionately represented in crime statistics throughout the century has been adduced to argue that the Irish "bulked large" for the Victorians in the "criminal classes" and thus were perceived to play a large part in making their rapidly expanding cities dangerous. Modern historians like Swift seek to correct what they characterize as a Victorian misperception of Irish criminality as wide-ranging and general by pointing out that much Irish crime was petty, arising out of necessity and the brutalized living conditions to which the Irish were subjected.[4]

The Irish were indeed viewed as a threat to the British social body, but there was nothing like a general or widespread fear among the English of being robbed or assaulted by an Irish criminal. Instead, the threat that Irish criminality posed was seen as limited and of a specific character. In fact, the Irish were not associated with crime in general, but rather with disorder arising from what was perceived as

---

Immigrants and Minorities 3:1 (March 1984), 5–29. Other historians have argued that some Britons perceived Irish crime and degeneracy as natural by-products of Catholicism, and thus sought to minimize the "racial" aspects of anti-Irish prejudice. For instance, Sheridan Gilley argues that since the Irish did not constitute a "race" they were not the object of racial but religious prejudice (Gilley, "English Attitudes to the Irish in England 1789–1900," in *Immigrants and Minorities in British Society*, ed. Colin Holmes. London: 1978, 81–110). Graham Davis claims in a similar vein that Irish immigrants were more widely dispersed than many contemporary observers suggested, and that rather than suffering from racial bias the Irish only shared the same stigma that English Catholics bore, as well as that of poverty, which they shared with the English lower classes ("Little Irelands" in *The Irish in Britain 1815–1939*, eds Roger Swift and Sheridan Gilley. London: Pinter, 1989, 105). These arguments cannot be addressed within the scope of this study, but L. Perry Curtis discusses the slipperiness of the term "race" as used by the Victorians and their predecessors and effectively refutes what he describes as the historical revisionism of reducing anti-Irish Victorian British attitudes to sectarianism by Gilley and others (*Apes and Angels*, Washington, D.C.: The Smithsonian Institution, 1997, 109–16). While sectarianism surely colored some of the perceptions described in this chapter (and as Linda Colley has demonstrated in *Britons: Forging the Nation 1707–1837*. New Haven: Yale University Press, 1992, Protestantism was a significant factor in British cultural nationalism), the works under investigation here make no references to religion.

  [3]   Swift, 1984 op. cit., 164.

  [4]   One of the most widely cited recent accounts of English perceptions of Irish immigrants is O'Tuathaigh. The term "Victorian" is used here with a note of caution – although the historians cited employ the term since their studies for the most part encompass a wide sweep of the 19th century, most of the documents I will be focusing on were produced in the period immediately preceding Victoria's 1838 accession to the throne.

their primitive state of civilization. Parliamentary Committee reports of the 1830s[5] represent Irish criminality according to patterns recognizable in contemporary ethnography as well.[6] The Irish are consistently portrayed in the testimony of "expert" witnesses throughout these reports as an inferior people who resist law and order and whose unrestrained licentiousness is a product of primitive, childish intemperance and improvidence. This characterization accords with popular British fictional representations of the Irish from not only the first half of the nineteenth century, as evidenced in Edgeworth's Irish novels, but later as well in Thackerayan characters from Barry Lyndon to Captain Costigan. A general conclusion of the Parliamentary reports under consideration here is that the riotous violence of the Irish, who are characterized as an inferior alien tribe lacking the social and family structures which would enable their assimilation into the United Kingdom, poses problems for the police forces precisely because those forces were developed to maintain order within a more civilized society.[7] At the same time, the Irish are represented as incapable by nature of the types of crime that require skill and planning, which are characterized by the witnesses and authors of these reports as the kinds of crimes which pose a real danger to British society. Therefore, Irish criminality is portrayed as both a product and a marker of Irish inferiority.[8]

The threat to the British public posed by the Irish, that is to say, was not perceived to be that of a "dangerous class" committing criminal depredations on the host society. Irish offenses were overwhelmingly characterized as "petty," and it was recognized that the violence in Irish districts was mostly confined within the Irish community itself in brawls, or directed at the police who tried to impose order on them. The accounts of the authorities in the Parliamentary reports of the 1830s tended, if anything, to *minimize* the danger that the British citizenry might become victimized by Irish criminals, and this in spite of the large numbers of

---

[5]   My central focus here will be the reports of the Select Committee on Drunkenness (1834), the Select Committee on the State of the Irish Poor in Great Britain (1836), and the Royal Commission to Inquire into the Best Means for Establishing an Efficient Constabulary Force in the Counties of England and Wales (1839), in all of which the Irish received considerable attention. Hereafter these Reports will be referred to by the year in which they were produced.

[6]   For the definitive account of the development of British ethnography in this period, see George Stocking, *Victorian Anthropology*. New York: Free Press, 1987. Early British ethnology ascribed the "unrestrained licentiousness" of "primitive" cultures to a degenerate inability to master their instinctive needs.

[7]   The characterization would remain consistent in the discourses of British social science, appearing in definitive works from Edwin Chadwick's Parliamentary *Sanitary Report* (1842) to Mayhew's *London Labour and the London Poor* (1861–62).

[8]   My claim that Irish crime was regarded as relatively harmless is not entirely new. L. Perry Curtis argues in *Apes and Angels* that there was "a gradual but unmistakable transformation of Paddy, the stereotypical Irish Celt of the mid-nineteenth century, from a drunken and relatively harmless peasant into a dangerous ape-man" (Curtis, xxxi and passim). But this dangerousness was not perceived until the rise of Fenianism.

Irish arrested in some cities in any given year.[9] Rather, British fears were largely centered on the idea of the Irish contaminating the English working class with the degenerated morals evidenced in the type of criminality peculiar to the Irish. While Edgeworth had raised the specter of this moral contagion in *Ormond*, in the Parliamentary Reports of the 1830s the suggestion is insistent and sustained. Lady Morgan, responding to *Ormond* in *Florence McCarthy*, characterizes Irish crime as produced by British economic and social injustice, which is also the cause of their wretched living conditions. In the Reports of the 1830s, on the other hand, Irish degeneracy is portrayed as a product of the squalid material conditions in which they live, conditions described as "natural" to them.

Moreover, in these reports Irish criminality is explicitly linked with Irish deviance from the emerging British national cultural norm of bourgeois domesticity. Indeed, in contrast to earlier reports documenting Irish criminality, in the Parliamentary reports of the 1830s Irish female criminality assumes a central role in the characterization of the Irish threat, as constitutive of what might be termed Irish anti-domesticity. These Parliamentary reports represent Irish cultural alterity as that which both negatively defines normative British domesticity and threatens to contaminate it. Calling for greater police powers as a means of containing Irish degeneracy within British cities, the reports cited "expert" witnesses who linked Irish criminality both metaphorically and metonymically with contagion. Like the cholera which ravaged British cities in the 1830s and 40s, disorder and crime were said to breed in the pestilential rookeries of the overcrowded Irish neighborhoods, and like cholera they threatened to infect the English lower classes who came into contact with them. Eventually, by extension, moral degeneracy threatened to spread in ever-widening circles throughout British society unless contained by newly empowered, professionalized police forces, who like the increasingly professionalized medical practitioners of the period, were seen as engaged in containing contagious diseases.[10] The Parliamentary reports can thus be characterized more as ideological exercises than empirical studies, and have important implications in any consideration of the representation of the Irish in British public discourse in the early nineteenth-century.

Widespread cultural beliefs are reinforced in various domains of public discourse, and thus they all play a crucial role in the construction of the imagined

---

[9]   A table provided by William Parlour, Superintendent of Liverpool Police, in an appendix to the 1836 *Parliamentary Report* records "the number of persons apprehended by the Liverpool police" amounting to 4258 Irish arrested in 1832, and 5217 in 1833 (1836, 493). Despite these high numbers, accounts of Irish assaults on the English populace are virtually nonexistent in all of the reports.

[10]   The classic account of emergent professionalized discourses which in discrete but parallel ways sought to contain criminal, medical, sexual and social deviancy is Michel Foucault's *Discipline and Punish*. See also Mary Poovey's *Making a Social Body*. Chicago: University of Chicago Press, 1996; and Martin Wiener's *Reconstructing the Criminal: Culture, Law, and Policy in England 1830–1914*. Cambridge: Cambridge University Press,1990 (esp. pp. 26–45) for persuasive accounts of the convergence of discursive domains in the containment of criminal and moral deviance in 19th-century Britain.

community of Britain. The present chapter does not attempt to present any all-encompassing conclusions about the attitudes of either the British public or its government towards Irish immigrants by examining a limited number of official and quasi-official reform documents. Rather, like *Apes and Angels*, this study seeks "to identify and explain a few of the more striking features of that cluster of attitudes and assumptions"[11] which made up the image of the Irish poor in these reports and in this sense complements Curtis's work. The present argument is divided into three parts. The first details how Irish criminality was perceived as a sign of Irish inferiority. The second demonstrates that these works portrayed the threat Irish criminality posed to Britain not as a danger to life and property, but rather as the epiphenomenon of a "disease" which would contaminate the morals of the British working class. The third section argues that the authors of these urban reform documents of the 1830s, developing a rhetorical strategy that differed significantly from earlier works of reform, depicted the anti-domesticity of Irish women as the engine of moral contagion, and thus the basis of the real threat to the social order.[12] As suggested above, these reports do not only utilize the trope of anti-domesticity which is so central to novels such as *The Absentee* and *Ormond*. Perhaps more importantly, they develop and elaborate quite thoroughly the motif of moral contagion, which will become in turn what makes Thackeray's Emily Costigan so dangerous to Arthur Pendennis. In other words, the changed nature of the Irish threat in British social discourse parallels that in British fiction.

Inferior Irish Criminality

In order to contain the threat of "contagious" Irish degeneracy, it was necessary to "cellularize" them. The Irish are consistently described in reports of the Parliamentary Select Committees as childlike, reckless and improvident, and characterized as racially inferior both implicitly and explicitly.[13] In the 1836 *Report on the State of the Irish Poor in Great Britain*, Michael Whitty, Superintendent of

---

[11]   *Apes and Angels*, xxxii.

[12]   The representation of domesticity as the foundation of middle-class social order in the literature of urban reform parallels the trend demonstrated by Nancy Armstrong in the novels, conduct books, and educational treatises of the period. Armstrong, adapting Foucault, argues in *Desire and Domestic Fiction* that the political power of the newly emerging middle class, which was becoming dominant at precisely this time, was based in large part on domestic surveillance: "[The domestic woman] was inscribed with values that addressed a whole range of competing interest groups and, through her, these groups gained authority over domestic relations and personal life. In this way, furthermore, they established the need for the kind of surveillance upon which modern institutions are based" (Armstrong, 19).

[13]   Cf. Corny O'Shane and the other Gaelic Irish in *Ormond*. The representation of the Irish in these reports reflects trends in Britain on the stage, and in novels, political cartoons and elsewhere in this period and throughout the nineteenth century. For two authoritative accounts of these trends see Curtis, and Hadfield and Maley in Bradshaw et al.

the Liverpool Night Watch, claims that "nine-tenths of the Irish settled in England did not come over from necessity, but in a spirit of wild adventure."[14] The author of the 1836 *Report*, George Cornewall Lewis, clearly ascribes this "spirit of adventure" to cultural primitivism: "The Irish retain their ancient habits ... [and] so rarely advance themselves from the poorer to upper or middling ranks."[15]

Further evidence of Irish primitivism is offered in what the contemporary witnesses consistently characterize as a kind of inferior criminality that most often arises out of drunkenness. Crimes against property (other than damage resulting from rows) are rare among the Irish, according to Cornewall Lewis: "The Irish in the large towns of Lancashire and Scotland commit more crimes than an equal number of natives, but their crimes in general are not of a very dangerous character, being for the most part brutal assaults committed in a state of drunkenness."[16] The assertion that brutal assaults are not considered "of a very dangerous character" may at first seem surprising, until one realizes that it is correct insofar as they presented little danger to the larger British society, since the victims were most often themselves Irish. The testimony of William Jeffrey, Superintendent of Police of Gorbals a town near Glasgow, is typical of the Committee's many witnesses from the police forces of the provincial towns: "[T]he Irish fight both in streets and houses ... [but] the rows are chiefly among themselves."[17]

The causes assigned by the experts to these rows are not the brutalized living conditions of the Irish, however, but petty rivalries. The effect produced is a trivialization of the social problems in Irish neighborhoods, and the tone of the witnesses is often contemptuous. George Redfern, prison-keeper and deputy constable of Birmingham, testifies that "the Irish ... fight with one another in public houses and in the streets ... frequently on the merits of their respective counties."[18] Testifying before the 1839 Royal *Commission to Inquire into the Best Means for Establishing an Efficient Constabulary Force* in the Counties of England and Wales, Edward Davies, Superintendent of the Manchester Watch, also draws attention to the mostly "Irish on Irish" nature of these crimes: "Parties of men come mad drunk out of these [houses in Irish districts where illicit whiskey is sold], armed with pokers and staves, and patrol the streets in order to assault any person whom they meet, but especially Irish from other provinces."[19] It becomes clear in this

---

[14]   1836 *Report*, 431. While such an assertion would not now be given serious consideration, at the time it apparently was, not least because in addition to his expert status as Superintendent of the Watch, Whitty was an Irish Catholic. His testimony was also read verbatim into the *Report of the Royal Commission to Inquire into the Best Means for Establishing an Efficient Constabulary Force* in 1839; Whitty therefore was influential in the organization of the provincial police forces.

[15]   1836 *Report*, 441. *Cf* Thackeray's article in *Punch* of August 1848 in which he claims that Irish primitivism precludes their joining "the march of history" (Chapter 7).

[16]   Ibid., 446.

[17]   Ibid., 447.

[18]   Ibid., 447.

[19]   Ibid., 88–9.

context that Irish criminality did not constitute the activities of a "dangerous class" in British popular perceptions, but instead was regarded as something like a low-grade fever which, though it bore monitoring, did not produce alarm.

Rather, Irish violence is explicitly linked to Irish inferiority, both in racial terms and in the authorities' perception of the threat it posed to British society. In the 1836 *Report*, Redfern asserts that the Irish often use sticks and other primitive weapons, but that "the English never make rows of this kind. An English row is generally between two persons and they fight with their fists."[20] The reference to English brawlers' use of their fists clearly implies that they practice a less cowardly form of fighting than the Irish, one that more closely resembles the "manly" sport of boxing in which Englishmen of the period took a measure of national pride.[21] Redfern's conclusion that Irish criminality reflects their cultural inferiority to the English conforms with interpretations offered by other witnesses before other Select Committees.

In testimony before the *Select Committee on Drunkenness* (1834), for example, Benjamin Braidley, Boroughreeve of Manchester, also makes an unflattering comparison between the Irish and the English in regard to the effects of drink upon them: "The Irish, I think, drink spirits more than the English, as a body; and we notice this difference: If there be a company of English drinking in a beer shop, they are very good friends if they get drunk together, but if it be a party of Irish drinking whiskey or spirits, they will quarrel or fight before they reach home."[22] Moreover, direct comparisons like these between English and Irish predilections for violence, in which Irish racial inferiority is implicit, give way in later reports to statements in which British superiority is made explicit. The association of the Irish with crimes of violence leads the authors of the 1839 *Constabulary Report* to take a perverse national pride in the crimes they now associate with the English:

> We find that ... crimes of violence ... are in a course of gradual diminution. It is true, however, that crimes of fraud have increased perhaps in a greater proportion. But this substitution may itself be an improvement. Crimes committed by means of violence are characteristic of a barbarous age and of a people subject to the domination of blind passion. Crimes of fraud are characteristic of a state less barbarous.[23]

---

[20] Ibid., 447.

[21] For a contemporary literary source in which boxing is represented as a source of English national pride, see George Borrow's novel *Lavengro*. Although published in 1851, the Preface to the 1st edition asserts that "[t]he time [of the novel's events] embraces nearly the first quarter of the present century." A more recent account of boxing's prominent place in British cultural nationalism of the period is Albert Borowitz's *The Thurtell-Hunt Murder Case* (Baton Rouge: Louisiana State University Press, 1987), which details the circumstances of a crime perpetrated by an unscrupulous boxing promoter and his cronies in 1823.

[22] 1834 *Report*, 383.

[23] 1839 *Report*, 40.

Irish inferiority in these accounts also extends beyond a mere predisposition for street brawls. In fact, the Irish are described as criminally primitive, in that they are incapable of committing sophisticated crimes like fraud, the kind which Cornewall Lewis presumably classifies as dangerous. Michael Whitty, the Superintendent of the Liverpool Watch, directly attributes the dearth of Irish criminals among those represented in theft statistics to Gaelic primitivism: "[T]he majority of the professional thieves of Liverpool are from London and Yorkshire, as the craft probably requires as much skill and dexterity as many of the mechanical trades ... The Irish are contented with stealing small articles, and this they practice to a considerable extent."[24] In other words, the low level of "skill and dexterity" to which their racial inferiority limits them reduces Irish thieves to practicing a socially insignificant petty larceny. This assessment fits neatly with another cultural stereotype – that of Irish drunkenness, which was held on dubious grounds to far exceed that of the English working class.[25] In earlier reports, drunkenness was cited as a factor in Irish participation in dangerous crimes, as the testimony of one witness before the 1817 *Report on the Police of the Metropolis* makes clear: "The effects of liquor upon the Irish in every scene of depredation and murder, needs only to be adverted to; it is certain that the abuse of this stimulus foments and keeps alive the most atrocious and appalling crimes."[26]

By the 1830s, however, Irish degeneracy was characterized as leading only in rare instances to dangerous crimes, at least in "mainland" Britain. Cornewall Lewis explicitly denies the danger of Irish crime to a "superior" population of English or Scots: "[C]rimes against the person ... murders, nightly attacks on houses, beatings, vindictive rapes, which unhappily are frequent amongst the Irish in their own country, scarcely ever occur among them in Great Britain."[27] An overwhelming majority of Cornewall Lewis's police witnesses substantiate this assertion, as well as his conclusion that in any case, these crimes are largely perpetrated against Irish victims and thus do not constitute a significant danger to the home society. In the new valuation, drunkenness was precisely what kept the Irish threat to the English social body relatively insignificant. Colonel (later Sir) Charles Rowan, the first commissioner of the London Metropolitan Police, asserts the general principle that drinking to excess renders a would-be criminal incapable of carrying out all but the most primitive of crimes: "Drunkenness is not an auxiliary to other crimes save assaults"[28] Rowan and other witnesses furthermore associated the lack of

---

[24]   1836 *Report*, 448.

[25]   This stereotype was widespread, but by no means universal. Roger Swift cites a Birmingham clergyman who claimed that the Irish "have more reputation for drunkenness than they deserve because they are so noisy and brawling" ("Crime and the Irish in Nineteenth-Century Britain," 167).

[26]   1817 *Report*, Minutes of Evidence, Q 45.

[27]   1836 *Report*, 446. The assertion that these serious crimes are "unhappily frequent" in Ireland is at odds with the reality, according to modern historians (see esp. R.F. Foster, *Modern Ireland 1600–1972*. London: Penguin, 1988). Trollope engages exaggerations of this type some years later in a series of letters to *The Examiner* (see below, Chapter 8).

[28]   1834 *Report of the Select Committee on Drunkenness*, vol VIII, 354.

Irish involvement in major crimes explicitly with drunkenness, reinforcing the 1834 Select Committee's construction of a strictly limited (in terms of its social threat) Irish criminality.

Although they now characterize Irish crime as relatively harmless, Whitty and Rowan express what was in the 1830s a culturally received perception of Irish inferiority, one which had been utilized in a plea for police reform by novelist Henry Fielding from his position as Magistrate of the City and Liberty of Westminster almost a century before. In a discussion of the large number of vagrants in the Irish lodging-houses of what was then the outskirts of London, Fielding decries "the Destruction of all Morality, Decency, and Modesty; [and] Swearing, Whoredom, and Drunkenness ... is eternally carrying on." He then employs a touch of irony to assert that, as bad as Irish crime is, the British can be thankful that the Irish are indeed inferior, or as he puts it, deficient in "capacity":

> Among other Mischiefs attending this wretched Nuisance, the great Increase of Thieves must necessarily be one. The Wonder in fact is, that we have not a thousand more Robbers than we have; indeed, that all these wretches are not Thieves, must give us either a very high Idea of their Honesty, or a very mean one of their Capacity and Courage.[29]

Although the officers of the nineteenth century have begun to employ a professionalized language unfamiliar to their predecessors of the eighteenth, as instantiated in Rowan's assertion that cultural stereotypes are not "auxiliary" to other types of crime, the underlying message of inferiority is the same. What is different is the move to create various cadres of professionalized forces of containment of the newly classified types of social threats. It is from this perspective of classification that the police forces will take their place alongside other emerging professionalized groups such as social scientists in the mold of Thomas Malthus, political economists, sanitary reformers, medical professionals etc.

The reports of the 1830s make clear that the Irish posed problems for the police precisely because those forces hitherto had only to deal with "civilized" populations. The reports of the 1830s assert that the provincial police forces would still be adequate for the enforcement of the law amongst the English were it not for the influx of hordes of Irish savages. The Irish are portrayed as so primitive that they have not developed bonds of sympathy among themselves or the society at large,[30] and their atavism is placed in sharp relief against English cultural advancement and characterized as a new type of social threat:

---

[29]   Fielding, Henry. *An Enquiry Into the Causes of the Late Increase of Robbers, &c.* (1751). Middletown, CT: Wesleyan University Press, 1988, 143–4.

[30]   For a discussion of the early (i.e., late 18th-early 19th-century) anthropological view of a more highly developed sympathy as a marker of racial superiority, see Stocking. This perspective finds a parallel in literature. In the genres of the eighteenth-century romance, one of the hallmarks of the gothic novel is the elevated sympathy of the hero and heroine, in which is coded their superiority over the (often southern European, Catholic) villain.

The defective state of the police in the large provincial towns of England had not been found to produce any serious inconvenience on account of the habits of obedience to the law which the people have formed and the mutual assistance which, in emergencies, they afford to one another. But when large bodies of Irish, of less orderly habits, and far more prone to use violence in fits of intoxication, settled permanently in these towns, the existing police force, which was sufficient to repress crime and disorders among a purely English population, has been found, under these circumstances, to be inadequate to the regular enforcement of the law.[31]

In this configuration, primitivism, disorder, and the Irish are equated. The central idea being advanced here is that the containment of the type of criminality which arises from racial inferiority requires a new kind of professional apparatus devised on scientific principles. This thesis is afforded more cultural weight by the testimony of Dr James Kay (later Kay-Shuttleworth), Poor Law Commissioner of Manchester, who reinforces the same points Cornewall Lewis makes but couches them in the language of the newly emerging discourse of social science:

[T]he Irish population is placed under regulations devised for the government of one much more advanced in the social scale ... so that expedients which might be efficient in restraining vice and preventing crime among a purely English population fail to produce these results in towns in which the Irish exist in great numbers.[32]

The Migratory Thesis

The Irish districts in British cities were portrayed in the testimony of Kay and others as requiring a type of paramilitary force (like the Royal Constabulary which already existed in Ireland) that could subdue an inferior alien nation unaccustomed to the rights and responsibilities of civilization. Furthermore, the references to a "purely English population" in both Cornewall Lewis and Kay's arguments make clear that the threat the authorities feared from the Irish was not that of a large population of depredators loosed upon the peaceful natives of Britain, but rather the contagion of Irish depravity and degeneracy seeping out to infect first the British laboring poor who lived in the same or contiguous neighborhoods, and eventually spreading throughout society. Cornewall Lewis explicitly states the absence of any real danger in Irish criminality, while asserting at the same time that the state of Irish morality is a matter of real concern for British authorities: "The number and character of crimes committed by Irish settlers in Great Britain further requires consideration, as throwing much light on their moral habits ... but their crimes in general are not of a very dangerous character."[33] Rather, the 1836 report, and by extension the 1839 *Constabulary Report*, which incorporates large

---

[31]   1836 *Report*, 466.

[32]   Ibid.

[33]   Ibid., 446.

sections of the 1836 report verbatim, suggests that the purpose of containing the Irish is to immunize the native population against the threat of the debasement of English "character" through Irish moral contagion. Roger Swift has pointed out that "[t]he Commission on the Constabulary Force of 1839 put forward the view that much crime was the product of migratory criminals in general and vagrants in particular ... [T]he migratory thesis ... was a powerful force behind [nineteenth-century] perceptions of criminality and, within this context, the Irish were particularly vulnerable"[34] The migratory thesis was developed in the domain of medical science; the spread of infectious diseases like typhus and cholera from one district to another was attributed in large part to migrant laborers and vagrants, and the Irish were perceived to constitute a large proportion of both these groups.[35] Its persuasiveness in that context explains its use, sometimes by the very same authorities, in the discourse of urban reform.

The Parliamentary reports of the 1830s invoke the migratory thesis to link the Irish with a variety of social ills, including infectious diseases, increased poor rates, low wages for industrial workers, and depraved morality.[36] In part, this rhetorical strategy was developed out of a long-standing tradition associating the Irish with vagrancy and the debasement of the value of all things English. As early as 1751, Henry Fielding, while noting a disproportionate number of Irish in British crime statistics, ominously warned of both "immediate and remote" consequences of their presence:

> [W]hen we consider the Number of these Wretches, which ... amounts to a great many Thousands, it is a Nuisance which will appear to be big with every moral and political Mischief. Of these ... every Species of Debauchery, and the Loss of so many Lives to the Public, are obvious and immediate Consequences. There are some more remote, which, however, need not be mentioned to the Discerning.[37]

---

[34] "Crime and the Irish in Nineteenth-Century Britain," 174. Swift also notes that recent historical research has shed doubt on the migratory thesis, but I am arguing here that at the time it was mobilized rhetorically to link the Irish with contagion, both of infectious diseases and depraved morality. For an influential argument casting doubt on the migratory thesis see Emsley, pp. 48–77.

[35] See, for instance, James Kay's *The Moral and Physical Condition of the Working Classes ... in Manchester* (1832), or the *Sanitary Report* (PP, 1842) of Edwin Chadwick, who also co-authored the 1839 *Constabulary Report*. Kay's work is examined more specifically in the next chapter.

[36] Mary Poovey argues (in *Making a Social Body*, Chapter 3) that in his report on the 1832 outbreak of cholera to the Poor Law Commission of Manchester, Kay rhetorically links the Irish, low industrial wages, degenerate morality and disease in order to argue for, among other things, the removal of the Irish poor from British industrial cities. Many of the same rhetorical strategies and logic are mobilized by Cornewall Lewis, the authors of the 1839 *Constabulary* and 1842 *Sanitary Reports*, and others in works of reform of this period.

[37] Fielding, op. cit., 144.

One remote consequence that Fielding hints at here is the spread of venereal disease. While he thus implicitly links the Irish with the spread of disease, he has not yet metaphorically linked physical contagion to the contamination of English morals from Irish criminality, however, as do Kay and others in the 1830s.

The explicit linkage of moral contagion and physical disease might be said to have developed out of their frequent close juxtaposition in earlier contexts, and gradually become overt. For instance, the connection between Irish criminality and contagion is somewhat more pronounced than it had been in Fielding's comments in a discussion of Irish vagrants in the 1816 *Report on Mendicity in the Metropolis* (which accompanied the 1817 *Report* on the metropolitan police). These reports, it will be remembered, appeared at virtually the same time as Edgeworth's *Ormond*. The author of the 1816 report conjectures that recent estimates that one-third of London's criminal vagrants were Irish are far too conservative: "Of the number of beggars, Mr Martin stated thirteen years ago that of 15,000, 5300 were Irish, but the committee ... will show the probability of this number being considerably more."[38] Irish beggars are accused of adopting the appearance of distress only in order to further their criminal ends, and moreover of organizing their efforts: "Beggars scarrify their feet in order to make the blood come ... tear their clothes for an appearance of distress; forty to fifty sleep in a house, and are locked in lest they carry something away, and let out in the morning all at once. They assemble in the morning to agree on which route each shall take."[39] Here the Irish are depicted as swarming vermin, and so degenerate that they are unable to trust even each other, while engaged in organized, but petty crime. Significantly, the criminality of vagrants and the risk of disease are closely juxtaposed in this report:

> Street beggars, with few exceptions, are utterly worthless and incorrigible ...
> One class of paupers is so numerous as to render it desirable ... to make a special statement to the House respecting them. We allude to the natives of Ireland ...
> In a court in Marylebone parish containing only 24 small houses, 700 of these poor people were found in a situation likely to occasion a considerable risk of contagion.[40]

The representation of the Irish as contaminators of English purity appears in more ways and with increasing frequency in discussions of crime and other urban social problems from around the turn of the nineteenth century onwards. In his 1797 book arguing for the professionalization of the police force of London, Patrick Colquhoun noted significant Irish involvement in the counterfeiting of British money. Counterfeiting was perceived as a serious concern in a time of increasing danger to national security arising from Britain's rivalry with France, particularly since in his widely influential *Wealth of Nations* (1776) Adam Smith had warned that the modern British economy was dependent on the integrity of its monetary

---

[38]   1816 *Report*, 395.

[39]   Ibid., 396.

[40]   Ibid., 396–7.

system and letters of credit. However, even though the Irish are characterized by Colquhoun as the most frequent perpetrators of a crime to which authorities felt especially vulnerable, their role is represented as much less dangerous to the British nation than the English and Jewish counterfeiters who traffic in gold coins: "The lower ranks among the Irish, and the Jews, are the chief supporters of the trade of circulating base money in London; there is said to be scarce an Irish laborer who does not exchange his week's wages for base money; taking a mixture of shillings, sixpence, and copper."[41] Unfortunately, Colquhoun provides no statistics on the proportion of Irish-born among those convicted of counterfeiting to verify these assertions. However, he notes that convictions are rare for the type of counterfeiting he associates with the Irish: "[I]f they sell plain half-pence, or what are called Irish harps ... it is doubtful whether the conviction will not fail."[42] Colquhoun is not engaged here in anything like the systematic construction of the Irish as bearers of physical, moral, and spiritual contagion in the Parliamentary reports of the 1830s. However, he does depict Irish participation in the system as corrupting and debasing it. This pattern will be specifically invoked in the 1830s, when the Irish are held responsible for the devaluation of industrial wages and the price of alcohol, both of which were seen to have deleterious effects on the morals of the British working classes.

Counterfeiting had traditionally been regarded as treason in English criminal law, but the crime ascribed chiefly to the Irish was termed, almost contemptuously, the "passing of base coin." While the language reflects the perception among the older authorities of the low-level threat it posed, the crime was nevertheless regarded as the de*base*ment of British money. In the 1830s, by way of contrast, the unlicenced manufacture and sale of alcohol was likewise regarded as the debasement of the price of liquor, but this crime was now regarded as particularly insidious by the authorities, because it ostensibly made drunkenness more common among the *English* working classes. In an appendix to the 1836 *Report on the Irish Poor in Great Britain*, the Irish are deemed by William Parlour, Superintendent of Liverpool Police, as almost wholly responsible for these crimes in his district: "Certain classes of crime are almost exclusively committed by the Irish in Liverpool, viz., illicit distilling and passing of counterfeit coin. Both are practiced by persons of the lowest class of Irish."[43] Parlour's characterization is consistent with those of other witnesses. For example, the Superintendent of the Paisley Police also asserts that "[m]ost [illicit] distilling in England [is] confined to the Irish."[44]

---

[41]   Colquhoun, *A Treatise on the Police of the Metropolis*. London: H. Fry, 1797, 119. Because both the more "serious" and the lowlier types of counterfeiting are attributed to the Jews, Jewish criminality is here, as it had long been and would remain in European culture, characteristically represented as a serious and insidious potential threat, while Irish criminality is represented in a way that is also becoming characteristic in British culture (until the rise of Fenianism), as constituting only the lowest level of threat.

[42]   *A Treatise on the Police of the Metropolis*, 124.

[43]   1836 *Report*, 493.

[44]   Ibid., 449.

In the Parliamentary reports of the 1830s, moreover, British authorities repeatedly linked the availability of cheap liquor to the spread of disorder and immorality in British cities. In the 1834 *Report on Drunkenness*, Mark Moore, who is described as "having connections to several benevolent organizations which have for their objective the improvement of different classes of society," was asked by the Committee, "What do you think has led to this low state of moral degradation [of workers at the London docks]?" His reply is typical of the testimony of many witnesses before the committee, and reflects the general conclusion of the report as well: "I should think that the low price of distilled spirits has been the principle cause of it"[45]

The debasement of the value of liquor and British money fits into a larger pattern of representation of Irish crime in the general conclusions of the reports of the Select Committees under examination here. In a section of the 1836 *Report* sub-headed "Influence of the Irish on the moral disposition of the English and Scottish working classes," Cornewall Lewis sums up the testimony of the many witnesses from the clergy, medical professions, mill-owners and police as conclusively demonstrating that the Irish immigrants are contaminating the British lower classes:

> In general this influence is stated to have been of a mischievous description; nor can it be doubted that the turbulent and irregular habits of most of the Irish, and the comfortless and uncleanly mode of living to which they are in general accustomed, tend, *by their moral contagion*, to injure the superior character of the English and Scottish poor (emphasis added).[46]

This report and others make clear that the same conditions which breed pestilential diseases also engender criminality, and moreover corrupt the "native" population. In the 1836 *Report*, Peter Gaskell, the Surgeon of the Stockport infirmary, relates a

---

[45]   1834 *Report*, 334. Although the overwhelming weight of the witnesses' evidence, as well as the conclusions of the committee, suggest that the moral degradation of the English working classes is produced in large part by the smuggling and distilling of illicit alcohol by Irish criminals, this thesis is directly contradicted by the testimony of witness Charles Saunders. Saunders informed the committee that it was a notorious practice of the *employers* of these dock workers – that of paying their employees at employer-owned taverns and forcing them to either take a large percentage of their pay in drink or lose their jobs – that was much more directly responsible for the workers' moral degradation. When asked by the committee whether the coal-whippers, a great many of whom were Irish, "would be better satisfied if they received their wages and were not required to purchase any liquor," Saunders answered, "A great deal better satisfied." This argument was taken up by the Young England faction of the Conservative Party soon afterwards, notably in Disraeli's novel *Sybil* (Book 2, Chapter 1 and *passim*). The abuses were curtailed some time later. However, Saunders's testimony seems to be wholly discounted in the conclusions of this report, perhaps because he is only a lowly "coal-whipper." The full text of Saunders's testimony appears in the 1834 *Report on Drunkenness*, 367–71.

[46]   1836 *Report*, 464.

case in which the Irish who moved into a street in his district created a "dunghill" by piling their refuse in the middle of their street rather than taking it to the dump. The Irish were eventually joined in this practice by the English residents of the district, who had given up trying to stop them. Gaskell concludes that "this case was plainly owing to defective sanitary police ... and it affords a perfect example of *an evil produced by the moral contact of the Irish*, but remediable by law" (italics added).[47] Gaskell also connects the threat of physical disease with the violent disorder so pervasively associated with the Irish: "In a lodging house where a case of cholera occurred ... 48 persons slept one night in four rooms. These lodging houses are the chief nests of disease and broils, and it appears to me that there should be some interference of the law to prevent the Irish crowding together."[48] Like the creation of the dunghill, Gaskell implies that "disease and broils" among the English working classes are the inevitable consequences "produced by the moral contact of the Irish."

The contagiousness of Irish physical and moral degeneracy is argued most insistently and systematically by Cornewall Lewis's most authoritative witness, Dr James Kay. Cornewall Lewis asserts more than once that Kay's testimony is "of much weight, and based upon much observation."[49] Kay characterizes the Irish as disease-bearing vermin in order to metaphorically link the threat of physical and moral contagion:

> When the outskirts of a rapidly increasing town ... become the seat of an Irish colony, who invariably fasten upon the ... worst and most unhealthy situations – bringing with them their uncleanly and negligent habits ... and herding in large numbers ... the whole presents an appearance of filth, neglect, confusion, discomfort, and insalubrity, which it would be in vain to seek in any English town inhabited solely by the natives of the place.[50]

The implications of contagion are obvious here in the dehumanizing of the Irish through the use of such words as "colony" and "herding," and moreover such squalor is characterized as alien to the English. Thus moral contagion, like the cholera, is ascribed to "foreign and accidental" causes. By comparing areas of Manchester suffering Irish "infestation" to areas under his observation free of these pestilential immigrants, Kay "proves" that Irish immigration contaminates the morals of the English working classes:

> The colonization of a large manufacturing town in England by a less civilized race than the natives is not without its influence on the manners of the resident population, especially in those districts where the population is mingled [sic] together ... [T]he meal and potato diet and the intoxications of the taverns [result

47   Ibid., 469.
48   Ibid.
49   Ibid., 465.
50   Ibid., 468.

from] mixing with the Irish ... In towns near Manchester not colonized by the Irish, the dwellings of the poor contain more furniture, are cleaner, and their diet is superior.[51]

Uncleanliness and intoxication – the keys to physical and moral contagion – are here explicitly coded as Irish, in whom they are inextricably linked together. The unmitigated negative "influence on the manners," unmistakably identified with domesticity and the cleaner homes and "superior" diet of the English, is described as the inevitable result of contact with the Irish.

As the testimony of medical professionals like Gaskell and Kay makes evident, the threat of Irish moral and physical contagion was understood as a general Irish debasement of a British national culture, which was constructed upon an idealized bourgeois domesticity.[52] The low wages in many industrial jobs, blamed by many witnesses in these reports on Irish competition,[53] led not only to the increased participation in the public sphere of women and children, who in many cases had to find work in order to enable their families to survive, but also to the debasement of the private sphere.[54] Thus, the Irish were blamed for conditions produced by

---

[51]   Ibid., 466.

[52]   The construction of British national cultural identity at this same historical moment around the "cult of domesticity" or "separate spheres ideology" has been well-documented, and the widening influence of women's "conduct books" in the 1830s directly coincides with the construction of Irish domestic deviancy in these Parliamentary reports. For an influential overview of separate spheres ideology, see Davidoff and Hall.

[53]   The issue of Irish "debasement" of British industrial wages is complex, and there is some testimony even in the 1836 *Report* from English laborers who suggest that mill owners encouraged Irish immigrants to replace striking English workers, thus showing that at least some members of the British working classes considered English capitalists, and not the Irish, as responsible for their low wages (see pp. 452–6). Contemporary novels of the period which explore the issue include *Sybil*, Charlotte Bronte's *Shirley* and Elizabeth Gaskell's *North and South*. The extent of the role played by British commercial interests and government in helping create the economic conditions in Ireland which engendered massive emigration is not addressed in this report. Instead, the overwhelming weight of the evidence given by the authorities in this report suggests that the Irish were responsible for devaluing British laborers' wages.

[54]   Although the authors of the various reports as well as the witnesses before the Committees of the 1830s uniformly characterize the streets in Irish neighborhoods as nests of vice and crime, modern historians reject this assessment as an oversimplification. Although the presence of women and children in the public sphere violated British notions of respectability, crowded living quarters, and not moral depravity, led to the unseemly (to some contemporary observers) incidence of Irish persons in the streets without specific purposes or destinations. Lynn Lees, for example, has pointed out that for the Irish, "streets served as extensions of cramped interiors, playgrounds for children, draping areas for laundry and meeting places for neighbors" (Lees, 82). Elizabeth Gaskell's novel *Mary Barton* portrays a young woman forced into the public sphere by the changes in living conditions occurring in an industrializing Manchester. Engels also makes frequent mention not only of working-class women being forced into the public sphere, but also "the victims of prostitution" in *Condition of the Working Classes in England*.

the new industrial order which were forcing more persons into the public sphere; moreover, the presence of Irish women and children in the public sphere was utilized as an example in these reports of cultural deviance. This construction of Irish anti-domesticity as a model of alterity against which British cultural norms were defined is perhaps the most significant difference between the Parliamentary reports of the 1830s and earlier representations of Irish criminality.

"Women Half-Naked Carrying Brickbats and Stones"

In earlier reports dealing directly with Irish immigrant criminality in British cities (those of Committees on the *Metropolitan Police* and *Mendicity* of 1816 and 1817), the dislocations of the Irish family were blamed squarely on male intemperance. The danger to English society from Irish crime is portrayed as greater in the earlier reports as well. In the 1816 *Report on the Police of the Metropolis*, Sir Daniel Williams, Magistrate of Whitechapel, attributes both Irish distress and crime in his district to male Irish workers refusing to provide for their families and instead spending their wages on liquor: "[W]hen [Irish workers] receive money for their labor they are improvident and do not apply it to the benefit of their families, but in general indulgence and intoxication, and the consequence of that is, that it breaks out sometimes into riots of some consequence."[55] Irish women are not mentioned in these early reports in any connection, which stands in sharp contrast to the reports of the 1830s.

The Parliament Select Committee reports of the 1830s are replete with examples of Irish women and children on the streets and in taverns, and represent in detail their participation in crime and disorder. The Irish are characterized by many witnesses as willing to forego "domestic conveniences" in order to pay for their dissipations, including subsisting on a diet wholly confined to the potato. In the 1836 *Report*, a Dr Duncan of Liverpool testifies that [t]he Irish always inhabit the cheapest lodgings they can find ... The Irish seem to be as contented amidst dirt and filth and close and confined air as in clean and airy situations."[56] Dr Kay makes the connection between physical and moral contagion in these situations explicit: "In general ... the house of an Irishman is that of a person in a lower state of civilization ... not only in his domestic conveniences, but in the moral relations which should subsist between himself and members of his family."[57] Here Kay seems to be assigning responsibility for this "lower state of civilization" to the male head of the household, but he quickly shifts the blame for this state of disorder from the Irish male to the female. Irish squalor is a product of the "unthrifty and dissolute character of the woman."[58] Notions of English domesticity and respectability are entirely alien to the Irish, according to Kay: "The Irish often

---

[55] 1816 *Report*, 100.
[56] 1836 *Report*, 437.
[57] Ibid., 437–8.
[58] Ibid., 439.

take the entire family to the tavern ... Hence Irish women are more drunken and dissolute than English and Scottish women."[59] The 1836 *Report* suggests that the absence of domesticity among the Irish is both produced by and evidenced in an abnormal criminality among Irish women:

> In general there is much less crime among women than men. The state of our penal colonies bears witness to this fact, where there are about four men to one woman; but in Glasgow bridewell, in March 1833, there were more Irish females than males; among the Scotch and English, males outnumbered females.[60]

While the author of this report allows that the greater number of Irish women than men incarcerated might prove to be an anomaly "if the numbers for a series of years could be known,"[61] the implication that Irish women are deviant is quite clear.

The extent of Irish female degeneracy is portrayed as widespread, and the reports suggest that it results at least in part from their presence in the public sphere. Whitty, Superintendent of the Liverpool Watch, claims that he "never knew an Irish row in which women were not engaged."[62] John Watson, Superintendent of Glasgow Police, affirms that "of persons taken up for being drunk and disorderly, more than half are Irish men and women."[63] In the 1839 *Constabulary Report*, Edward Davies, Superintendent of the Manchester Watch, is quoted at length about the difficulties the poorly organized Watch encounters in executing warrants and evictions in the Irish neighborhoods: "[I]n order to apprehend one Irishman, we are forced to take from ten to twenty, or even more, watchmen. The whole neighbourhood turn out with weapons; even women, half-naked, carrying brickbats and stones ... In these rows the women ... are as much engaged as the men."[64] The overall picture constructed by the reports of the 1830s of the savagery of Irish women clearly represents the virtual opposite of the idealized British woman's modesty and submissiveness.

Another product of this female criminal deviance, according to the reports of the 1830s, is the abnormal amount of juvenile crime attributed to the Irish. In fact, the police witnesses consistently claim that Irish women train their children to engage in crime. The chief difference between the characterization of juvenile crime in the metropolitan police reports of 1816 and 1817 and that in the reports of the 1830s is that in the later reports juvenile crime is explicitly linked to the deviancy of Irish women, whereas in the earlier reports it was generally ascribed to the improvidence of the men. In the 1816 *Report*, for instance, Sir Daniel Williams observes that "there is an increase of offenders among the juvenile branch [of Irish] which is considerable, and they are frequently trained up to such pursuits by

---

[59]   Ibid.

[60]   Ibid., 439.

[61]   Ibid., 439.

[62]   Ibid., 447.

[63]   Ibid.

[64]   1839 *Report*, 88.

their relatives and connections."[65] Williams makes no specific mention of deviant Irish mothers; on the contrary, he attributes both Irish "distress" and crime to "the general indulgence and intoxication" of Irish working men.[66] In the 1836 *Report on the State of the Irish Poor*, on the other hand, Whitty, of the Liverpool Watch, asserts that "[Irish] pilfering habits are acquired at an early age and are generated by the vagrant and mendicant life which the parents, and *especially the mothers*, too often follow" (emphasis added).[67] The characterization of Irish mothers as primarily responsible for the abnormal criminality of Irish youth, though not substantiated with any hard evidence, is consistent with the portrayal of Irish women as half-naked savages. It is also consistent with Edgeworth's portrayal of Irish children being bred to a life of crime in *Ormond*; unlike Edgeworth, however, the authors and witnesses of these reports' condemnation of Irish mothers is more explicit, sustained, and direct.

Whitty's testimony is also consistent with the evidence of ten more witnesses associated with various police organizations who are cited immediately after him, creating what would seem to be irrefutable substantiation of Whitty's evidence. However, the tendentiousness of the 1836 *Report on the Irish Poor* is revealed in this very consistency. Both the conclusions of Cornewall Lewis and testimony of the witnesses whose opinions dominate this report suggest bias, not least because the reliability of the evidence characterized as authoritative here would be regarded today as totally unacceptable. Among the questionable evidence presented to corroborate Whitty is the testimony of J.S. Thomas, Deputy Constable of the Township of Manchester, who claims that Irish mothers send their children out to steal and do not allow them back into the family home unless they have managed to produce at least sixpence. Thomas's "evidence" is comprised not of statistical data produced in his district in Manchester, nor does it contain any recorded statements of Irish juvenile offenders or even the police who have arrested them. Rather, his testimony consists of generalized statements about juvenile crime observed in *London*: "This practice prevailed to a great extent among the Irish of St Giles and the purlieus of Drury Lane; it rarely occurred among the English. I consider the Irish very negligent of the morals, cleanliness, and care of their children."[68] By whom the "practice" which gave rise to his opinion of Irish morals was observed is not stated – that is to say, it is not clear whether Thomas's testimony is based on his own observations in some (possibly previous) official capacity, or made while visiting London as a tourist, or gathered from hearsay. The conclusions of the 1836 *Report*, which are entirely consistent with those of this purported expert witness, thus seem to rely upon conjecture and prejudice. As a result, British government policy towards the Irish poor remained insensible of the causes and insensitive to the effects of Irish poverty; moreover, the organization of the Constabulary forces

---

65   1816 *Report*, 100.
66   Ibid.
67   1836 *Report*, 448.
68   Ibid., 448.

in many provincial cities in Great Britain was greatly influenced by what I am arguing was a systematic and tendentious representation of Irish criminality.

The purposes of the concerted rhetorical strategy in the Parliamentary reports of the 1830s are evident: to terminate Irish immigration into Great Britain, and to empower a police force with the means of effectively containing the Irish who remain. Cornewall Lewis's opening remarks in the 1836 report directly announce the first goal:

> It is stated that Irish immigrants have exercised a pernicious influence on the English and Scottish working classes, by lowering their wages and debasing their moral character, and that certain measures ought to be introduced into Ireland with a view of preventing the emigration of the poor into Great Britain.[69]

The "facts" collected in this report were evidently intended to leave little doubt that the influence of the Irish was indeed "pernicious," although the report seems to answer less certainly the question of whether any change in the law was "likely to put a stop to the immigration in question."[70] For this reason the 1836 *Report* again and again urged the strengthening of the police forces in British cities, and its rhetoric was so successful that a subsequent Commission was convened in 1839 which saw fit to incorporate much of the testimony and conclusions of the earlier report. It is clear that these works of urban reform employ figurative strategies which participate in the construction of British cultural nationalism defined in significant part by an Irish Other. These rhetorical devices in turn can be seen to have migrated across discursive boundaries, and thus played an important role in more than just the shaping of casual attitudes amongst certain segments of the British reading public. The 1839 *Constabulary Report* is, after all, the foundational document of Britain's modern national police system. Later developments, including Britain's response to the Famine in Ireland in the 1840s (particularly under the Whig government of Lord John Russell), were also informed by values which attached to Irishness as a signifier. For an idea of just how pervasive these tropes were, as well as how the dominant ideology expressed through them was contested by some, we will next look more directly at the work of Dr Kay, and a book upon which he had a profound impact: Friedrich Engels' *Condition of the Working Classes in England*.

---

[69]   Ibid., 429.

[70]   Ibid., 429. The 1836 report even investigates means for the removal of Irish immigrants. A table detailing the number of Irish Poor removed from England for vagrancy is included in the appendix to the 1836 *Report* at p. 485. The procedures are described as ineffective and prohibitively expensive, but a grand total of 39,869 Irish were removed from England via the city of Liverpool at the expense of the County of Lancaster between the years 1824–31.

Chapter 6
Kay, Engels, and the Condition of the Irish

Introduction

Edwin Chadwick, one of the principal authors of the Parliamentary Commission Report that led to the famous, or infamous, amending of the Poor Laws in 1834,[1] later undertook researches into the causes of the influenza and typhus epidemics of 1837 and 1838. The result was his *Report Into the Sanitary Conditions of the Labouring Population of Great Britain* (1842). Peter Stallybrass and Allon White note a tendency in much of the literature of British urban social and political reform throughout the nineteenth century to deploy representations of filth, disease, and contagion to achieve broad rhetorical purposes, and they cite Chadwick's 1842 *Sanitary Report* as a prime example of the suggestive use of filth as a sliding signifier with which to figure clusters of urban problems:

> Chadwick connects slum to sewage, sewage to disease, and disease to moral degradation: "adverse circumstances" lead to a population which is "short-lived, improvident, reckless and intemperate" ... Chadwick traces the metonymic associations between filth and disease: the metonymic associations ... are constantly elided with and displaced by a metaphoric language in which filth stands in for the slum-dweller: the poor *are* pigs.[2]

As the Parliamentary Reports examined in the previous chapter should make evident, the figurative strategy detailed by Stallybrass and White was not pioneered by Chadwick. Mary Poovey has shown in *Making a Social Body* that Chadwick's report is preceded by a similar document that views poverty not as an individual problem, but as a social disease requiring government action, and combines with this the use of anti-Irish prejudice to make a powerful appeal for social reform in Manchester: James Kay's pamphlet *The Moral and Physical Condition of the Working Classes Employed in the Cotton Manufacture in Manchester* (1832). As I have been arguing, metaphoric associations of the Irish with disease and filth had been seeping into public discourse at least as early as Maria Edgeworth's novel *Ormond*, published in 1817, and the appearance of these figurations in other

---

[1]   The "New Poor Law" of 1834 was famously excoriated in the opening passages of Dickens's *Oliver Twist*, among other places. Among its more draconian measures were the provisions that able-bodied persons could only receive relief from the authorities through the workhouse, and that conditions in the workhouse be made very harsh to discourage people from seeking relief.

[2]   Stallybrass, Peter and Allon White. *The Politics and Poetics of Transgression.* Ithaca: Cornell University Press, 1986, 131.

discursive domains allows us to trace the development of the use of Irishness as a signifier.[3] In its turn, Kay's work was extremely influential. Not only does Chadwick pick up some of the rhetorical tropes and organizational devices which Kay's treatise disseminated, but other reformers working in seemingly unrelated fields do so as well. Indeed, after the Reform Act of 1832, the rhetorical strategy Kay employed appears in various works of social reform, utilized to construct varyingly inclusive models of normative British cultural nationalism centered, as was Kay's, on a newly politicized middle class.[4]

In this chapter I wish to incorporate some of Poovey's insights into an argument that is at once both broader and more direct. Poovey asserts that Kay "focus[es] his analysis not on economic or political relations but on the site of the workers' most intimate relations – the domestic sphere."[5] However, Kay, a Unitarian and Utilitarian, addresses his arguments to like-minded members of the ruling class, many of whom shared his affiliations, including Edwin Chadwick,[6] precisely for the purposes of maintaining social control and increasing the working class's productivity. Many years later, Kay would admit that as a young doctor he had come to view his medical mission as inadequate to meeting the demands of the problems in Manchester's poorer districts:

> I came to know how almost useless were the resources of my [medical] art to contend with the consequences of formidable social evils ... Parallel, therefore, with my scientific reading I began to make myself acquainted with the best works on political and social science, and obtained more and more insight into the grave questions affecting the relations of capital and labour, and the distribution

---

[3]   Actually, charges that the Irish were contaminating English purity appear earlier, in documents such as Patrick Colquhoun's *A Treatise on the Police of the Metropolis* (1797, in this case with low-level counterfeiters debasing British currency) and Parliamentary reports contemporaneous with the publication of Edgeworth's novel (see above). Kay, following Edgeworth, initiates the *systematic* construction in political discourse of the Irish as bearers of physical, moral, and spiritual contagion in the 1830s, however.

[4]   The characterization would remain consistent in the discourses of British social science, appearing in definitive works from Edwin Chadwick's Parliamentary *Sanitary Report* (1842) to Henry Mayhew's *London Labour and the London Poor* (1861–62). For examples of Kay's considerable influence, see especially the *Royal Commission to Inquire into the Best Means for Establishing an Efficient Constabulary Force in the Counties of England and Wales* (1839), the *Select Committee on Drunkenness* (1834), and the *Select Committee on the State of the Irish Poor in Great Britain* (1836), all discussed in the previous chapter. Poovey also asserts that Kay influenced the reforming MP Viscount Ashley, an aristocratic Tory, among others (63).

[5]   Poovey, Mary. *Making a Social Body*. Chicago: University of Chicago Press, 1996, 62. Hereafter identified as Poovey.

[6]   In addition to Chadwick, other Mancunain civic leaders who like Kay were associated with the Unitarian Cross Street Chapel as well as with housing, sanitation, or urban reform include Samuel and William Rathbone Glen, Thomas Southwood Smith, and the novelist Elizabeth Gaskell, whose husband was also a prominent citizen (Uglow, 89).

of wealth, as well as the inseparable connection between the mental and moral condition of the people and their physical well-being.[7]

Implicit in this statement is a fear of social upheaval, which is stated explicitly in his *Moral and Physical Condition*, as when he notes that "[t]he wealth and splendour, the refinement and luxury of the superior classes, might provoke the wild inroads of a marauding force [namely, the working class]" if they were not taught in addition to the offerings of the Mechanics' Institutions the "ascertained truths of political science" and "*correct* political information (emphasis in original)."[8] Already in 1832 the gravity of the problems affecting relations between capital and labor occupy much of Kay's attention, and he emphasizes that this tension must be reduced to prevent any radical social dislocations, like those recently occurring in France that were still so fresh in British public memory. In so doing, Kay makes clear that the dissolution of the home and family is *primarily* an economic threat. It is the production of wealth that Kay regards as the key antidote to social ills, and the Irish immigrants threaten to sap the Manchester working classes' ability to produce wealth efficiently.

The prominence of the economic arguments in *Moral and Physical Condition* took on an unquestionable centrality in a work whose English title bears a striking similarity to Kay's pamphlet, and which overtly draws on that work only to turn its economic argument completely inside-out. Friedrich Engels' *The Condition of the Working Classes in England* (1844)[9] utilizes much of Kay's research as well as his rhetorical strategies, and in it Engels repeatedly acknowledges Kay's influence. Given the thrust of Kay's arguments (noticeable in his writings on educational reform as well), it is hardly surprising that Engels would take them on. But scant critical attention has been paid to this aspect of the relationship between these works, perhaps because *Moral and Physical Condition* was seen primarily as a document of sanitary reform until Poovey examined the ways in which it constructs cultural nationalism.[10] Engels hopes to bring about economic change through political means and uses many of Kay's observations to argue for its necessity, while Kay obscures the political ramifications of the domestic ideal's role in upholding the social and economic status quo. We know of course

---

[7]   Quoted in Smith, Frank. *The Life and Work of Dr James Kay-Shuttleworth*. London: John Murray, 1923, 13–14. Kay's autobiography was composed in 1877.

[8]   Kay, James. *The Moral and Physical Condition of the Working Classes Engaged in the Cotton Manufacture in Manchester* (1832). Shannon: Irish University Press, 1971, 71, 72. Hereafter this work will simply be referred to as Kay.

[9]   Engels, Friedrich. *The Condition of the Working Class in England (1844)*. London: Penguin, 1987, 51. All subsequent references to this work will be specified as Engels.

[10]   Many commentators have noted, however, that Engels does acknowledge Kay's work and cites it often. Poovey quotes many of the same passages I invoke here, but her purpose is to establish that Kay's social vision is constructed upon a domestic ideal, and while she notes some of Kay's claims about the economic system her emphasis is upon the cultural implications of his argument.

that the bourgeoisie was triumphant throughout the nineteenth century (despite considerable sympathy for and popularity of the Chartists and other radical groups) and that the dominant forms of British cultural nationalism, with which this book is concerned, centered on a middle-class domestic ideal that often utilized the figure of the Irish woman as the antithesis of the British "angel of the hearth." Engels, however, utilizes Kay's argument to assert to the contrary that a society formed around capitalist ideals destroys the domestic virtues of the working classes and is directly responsible for the social ills Kay regarded as the cause of the problem. (Engels regarded all working-class women, including prostitutes, as victims of a plight produced by the economic system Kay defends.) Engels, then, responds to Kay so directly because he recognizes that Kay, while wishing to mitigate some of the more brutal effects of industrial expansion, promotes the exclusion of Irish immigrants within the system of *laissez-faire* capitalism and the existing power structure as the *economic* cure to England's social disease.

Poovey points out that in Kay's report the Irish are figured as carriers of social and physical disease, against which the English social body can only immunize itself by adopting a middle-class domestic ideal in which good morals and good hygiene are enacted and from which the "accidental and foreign" sources of disease – namely, the Irish – must be removed. But Kay's equating of Irishness with disease serves the rhetorical purpose of maintaining social control and maximum profitability while leaving the economic and power structures of the society intact. The workers were to be adequately fed and their sufferings ameliorated, but the hierarchical social strata were regarded by *laissez-faire* Utilitarians, even those performing noble public service as did Kay, as rooted in nature.[11] Engels retains Kay's Irishness = disease formula, but for Engels, the influx of Irish workers into Britain will hasten the social crisis produced by the economic system, bringing about an alliance of the working classes and ending the "war of each against all." In other words, whereas Kay uses the threat of foreign contagion to promote a *nationalist* cultural ideal which privileges middle-class domesticity to empower and enrich the bourgeoisie, Engels deploys Irishness to advocate for the working classes to ally themselves against the property-owning classes in his *internationalist* agenda.

---

[11]   I argue elsewhere that Kay and other Utilitarian reformers sought to contain and control the problems not only of disease but also vice and disorder (as specifically referred to in Kay's title, but also the subject of frequent digressions in Chadwick's report) by isolating them within a community described by its labor function, and that this view was in keeping with Adam Smith's argument that the working poor must be treated differently from those individuals (the middle and upper classes) capable of "specular" morality. See "Gaskell's *Pieta*: Spectacle, Death, and the Victorian City," (forthcoming). See also Mary Elizabeth Hotz's "Taught by Death What Life Should Be: Elizabeth Gaskell's Representation of Death in *North and South,*" *Studies in the Novel* 32:2 (Summer 2000), 165–85, which discusses some aspects of that novel in relation to Political Economy.

"Banish the Jealous Suspicion with Which One Order Regards Another"

Before proceeding to examine Engels's argument, it will be necessary to summarize and comment on several points in Poovey's analysis in order to clarify Kay's position. Poovey argues that in his *Moral and Physical Condition* Kay rhetorically links physical, social, and moral ills with cholera, metonymically figuring these both as the devastation visited upon the working class in the new industrial system and as the threat the poor pose to the rest of the social body, i.e. the middle and upper classes. Furthermore, Poovey argues, by representing England's social problems in "a single conceptual cluster" as a kind of disease, Kay can "present the unruly poor as victims in need of aid rather than agents who should be punished. This is especially important to Kay's argument because class conflict – and class consciousness – would undermine his image of a single, harmonious body."[12] Poovey's analysis here is for the most part insightful; her last point is a trifle misleading, however. While Kay undoubtedly wishes to prevent class conflict, he by no means attempts to obliterate class consciousness. His arguments on the contrary *naturalize* class divisions, and by laying responsibility for the working class's social woes on the Irish, Kay is able to sidestep the economic system's role in creating the divisions in the first place.

Kay argues for the repeal of the Corn Laws in order to permit free trade. This, he suggests, would reduce the pressure on profits in the manufacturing trades which leads to the importation of cheap labor from Ireland, and simultaneously reduce tensions between the working and middle classes within England resulting from the influx of immigrants and the resulting competition for wages. Poovey asserts that Kay's metaphorical use of cholera enables an analogous logic by which the "social ills" resulting from industrial wage competition are said, like cholera, to have a "foreign and accidental" origin. Kay identifies the cause of English social problems with the Irish immigrants, who in his account are debasing the health of the English social body by introducing destructive and abnormal domestic relations into Manchester. Kay's Malthusian scheme is worth quoting at length, because here and elsewhere in the report, the emphasis is on Irish moral contagion reducing worker productivity:

> The evils affecting the working classes, so far from being the necessary results of the commercial system, furnish evidence of a disease which impairs its energies if it does not threaten its vitality ... The colonization of the Irish ... has proved one chief source of the demoralization, and consequent physical depression of the people. The effects of this immigration, even when regarded as a simple economic question, do not merely include an equation of the comparative cheapness of labour; its influence on civilization and morals, as they tend to affect the production of wealth, cannot be neglected. Want of cleanliness, of forethought and economy, are found in almost invariable alliance with dissipation, reckless habits, and disease. The population gradually becomes

---

[12] Poovey, op. cit., 58–9.

less efficient as the producers of wealth – morally so from idleness – politically worthless as having few desires to satisfy, and noxious as dissipators of capital accumulated.(emphasis in original)[13]

Kay goes on to specify the type of moral contagion stemming from Irish anti-domesticity and the dangers it poses to British prosperity. Not only does he warn of reduced productivity stemming from licentiousness, but he raises the specter of the creation of a large welfare state, with the simultaneous reduction of the working class to a subhuman level:

> A debilitated race would be rapidly multiplied. Morality would afford no check to the increase of the population: crime and disease would be its only obstacles – the licentiousness which indulges its capricious appetite, till it exhausts its power – and the disease which, at the same moment, punishes crime and sweeps away a hecatomb of its victims. A dense mass, impotent alike of great moral or physical efforts, would accumulate; children would be born to parents incapable of obtaining the necessaries of life, who would thus acquire, through the mistaken humanity of the law, a new claim for support from the property of the public ... Such a race is useful only as a mass of animal organization, which consumes the smallest amount of wages ... They are only necessary to a state of commerce *inconsistent* with such a reward for labour as is calculated to maintain a state of civilization. (italics in original) [14]

Kay's solution, as Poovey points out (while also noting the dehumanization of the Irish in this passage by the phrase "mass of animal organization"), is the purification of the working class by removal of the Irish. He envisions productivity enhanced to ever-higher levels, making Britain's global trade ever more lucrative, but warns that any attempt to tamper with the system would be destructive morally, socially, and economically:

> With a virtuous population, engaged in free trade, the existence of redundant labour would be an evil of brief duration, rarely experienced ... Ingenuity and industry would draw tribute from the whole world more than adequate to supply the ever-increasing demands of a civilized nation ... Under these circumstances, every part of the system appears necessary to the preservation of the whole ... the conditions of the working classes cannot be much improved, until the burdens and restrictions of the commercial system are abolished (original emphasis)[15]

Poovey notes that Kay argues the working poor, who have been contaminated with these social ills through their contact with the Irish, must be immunized by their integration into the national social body, and furthermore, this social body is identifiable by its relationship both to property ownership and moral virtue – in other words, to bourgeois domesticity. She further asserts that "after [Catholic emancipation] in 1829, the diacritical mark of Britishness (not Englishness)

---

[13]   Kay, 63–4.

[14]   Ibid., 64–5, 65–6.

[15]   Ibid., 64.

became a certain level of property ownership. If a man met the *L*10 qualification, even if he were Catholic, he belonged to the kingdom of Great Britain in a way that he did not if he failed to meet it."[16] Nevertheless, the "contagious example" of domestic (and especially reproductive) improvidence of the Irish would exclude any member of the English working class who had been infected by it:

> [The] new mark of [national] difference ... must be reinforced if it is to work as effectively as the old ... Kay links certain *attitudes* toward property with certain domestic behaviors, which he has already linked to the Irish. By implication, of course, this grounds British respectability not in class but in "nature" – the natural morality of sexual self-control, cleanliness, forethought, and health – all of which are implicitly the domain of women.[17]

In other words, the social disease Kay identifies with the Irish could be cured "by equating national well-being with the economic health of a newly politicized, respectable middle class."[18]

However, Kay does not identify the workers with the "middle" class. He repeatedly refers to the working, laboring, or operative class, but at no time does he envision a leveling of society through property ownership; rather, he encourages the inculcation of virtue, and particularly religion, as a means of reducing tensions and "jealousies" between the various classes of people, the hierarchies among which he also regards as natural. Furthermore, he asserts that natural sympathy between the classes has been destroyed by the legal entitlements of the Poor Law, and made the recipients of relief ungrateful:

> Charity once extended an invisible chain of sympathy between the higher and lower ranks of society, which has been destroyed by the luckless pseudophilanthropy of the law ... The bar of the overseer is crowded with sturdy applicants for a legalized relief who regard the distributor of this bounty as their stern and merciless oppressor, instructed by the compassionless rich to reduce to the lowest possible amount the alms which the law wrings from their reluctant hands. This disruption of the natural ties has created a wide gulf between the higher and lower orders of the community, across which the scowl of hatred banishes the smile of charity and love.[19]

Kay deplores the fact that "sturdy," that is to say, able-bodied applicants are overcrowding the offices where government-mandated handouts are given the poor, and implies that the shiftlessness and ingratitude he describes are the inevitable results of tampering with the natural order. This is of a piece with what he regards as the general slide into immorality resulting from contact with

---

[16] Poovey, 68.
[17] Ibid., 69.
[18] Ibid., 72.
[19] Kay, 54.

the Irish, and can be quantified by Kay the statistician[20] by the drop in church attendance as well: "[M]orality is exceedingly debased, and ... [t]hat religious observances are exceedingly neglected [among the operative population] we have had constant opportunities of ascertaining ... With rare exceptions, the adults of the vast population of 84,147 contained in Districts Nos. 1, 2, 3, 4, spend Sunday either in supine sloth, in sensuality, or in listless inactivity."[21] Yet like Edmund Burke, who saw social hierarchies ranging from the patriarchal family all the way up to and including the monarchy as rooted in nature and divine law, Kay asserts that improvements in morality and religious observance will lead to a lessening of conflict between the classes, not the obliteration of class formations: "With pure religion and undefiled, flourish frugality, forethought, and industry – the social charities which are the links of kindred, neighbours, and societies – and the amenities of life, which *banish the jealous suspicion with which one order regards another*" (italics added).[22]

Kay, a noted educational reformer (indeed his greater fame came later as Kay-Shuttleworth and owed to his contributions to that field), prescribes in *Moral and Physical Condition* an educational program for the working classes, but it is not to raise them out of their station, but rather to maintain social order within it: "The poor man['s] ... education should comprise such branches of general knowledge as would prove sources of rational amusement, and would thus elevate his tastes above a companionship in licentious pleasures."[23] While he advocates for some relief from economic stress such as lower food prices (through repeal of the Corn Laws), Kay is insistent that the class divisions remain in place. Furthermore, a paternalistic relationship between the higher and lower classes would enable the inculcation of domesticity and at the same time provide opportunity for disciplinary oversight:

> Those portions of the exact sciences which are concerned with his occupation, should be familiarly explained to him ... Much good would result from a more general and cordial association of the higher and lower orders ... [A Liverpool charitable society's members] visit the people in their houses – sympathize with their distresses, and minister to the wants of the necessitous; but above all, they acquire by their charity, the right of inquiring into their arrangements – of instructing them in domestic economy – of recommending sobriety, cleanliness, forethought, and method. Every capitalist might contribute much to the happiness of those in his employ, by similar exercise of enlightened charity.[24]

Here then is Kay's *laissez-faire* project laid out in clear terms: an end to government interference in business and markets (with the relaxation of restrictions on trade

---

[20]   Kay was a founding member of the Manchester Statistical Society.

[21]   Kay, 58.

[22]   Ibid., 58.

[23]   Ibid., 71.

[24]   Ibid., 71, 72–3.

and repeal of the Corn Laws) and an end to government welfare programs, turning charity back over to benevolent associations and faith-based organizations. Such a program would allow profits to increase, wages to stay relatively low, and *surveillance* over the workers into the bargain. Kay produces what we would today call something along the lines of a prospectus for global development, in which all the benefits would accrue to the greater glory of the British Empire and presumably trickle down to the lower orders eventually. That Kay has these imperial visions in mind is made clear when he states that:

> we have exposed, with a faithful, though a friendly hand, the condition of the lower orders connected with the manufactures of this town ... A system which promotes the advance of civilization, and diffuses it all over the world – which promises to maintain the peace of nations, by establishing a permanent international law, founded in the benefits of commercial association, cannot be inconsistent with the happiness of the *great mass of the people* (italics in original).[25]

The Two Nations: Working Class and Bourgeoisie

In *The Condition of the Working Class in England*, Engels recognizes the implications of Kay's argument, but inverts what Kay posits as causes and effects. He begins by first invoking an English "golden age" in which the productive members of society grew up in social, political, and moral harmony:

> What the moral and intellectual character of this class was may be guessed ... [W]eavers stood upon the moral and intellectual plane of the yeomen ... They were "respectable" people, good husbands and fathers, led moral lives because they had no temptations to be immoral ... The young people grew up in idyllic simplicity and intimacy.[26]

Engels deploys the idea of this mythic past, in which yeomen and "workers" belong to "separate but equal" classes although they stand upon the same moral and intellectual plane, to provide a contrast against the horrors of industrial modernity. At the same time he ironically undercuts the notion of a golden age by ascribing a virtually subhuman consciousness to these pre-industrial workers: "[I]ntellectually, they were dead; lived only for their petty, private interest ... They were comfortable in their silent vegetation; and but for the industrial revolution they would have never emerged from this existence, which, cosily romantic as it was, was nevertheless not worthy of human beings."[27]

---

[25]   Quoted in Marcus, Steven. *Engels, Manchester and the Working Class.* New York: Random House, 1974, 54.

[26]   Engels, 51.

[27]   Ibid., 52.

Here Engels subtly inscribes the seeds of the social woes attendant on the current economic system, and by extension the patriarchal domestic ideal, in the class-based social order that predated the industrial age. If the weavers and other artisans living their pre-industrial rural and village lives were intellectually dead and existing in a state of "silent vegetation," the sacred social order of Burke has been undermined, even when ironically admitted to be "cosily romantic" as it was. Engels's irony is double-edged – he has deromanticized pre-industrial life by portraying it as culturally bankrupt, while making its romanticization by Burke and others overt. He then proceeds to deromanticize contemporary social arrangements as well. With the coming of industrialism, he observes, comes the "unfeeling isolation of each in his private interest," which leads to "social war, the war of each against all ... openly declared."[28]

Although his project is to strip the romance from the current cultural narrative, Engels provides his own happy ending for the one with which he would replace it. He subtly invokes a "fortunate fall" from the golden age, and claims that contact with the Irish will hasten the death of the English proletariat's cultural nationalism, enabling them to be "born again" into the "salvation" of revolutionary consciousness. This enables the young and still optimistic Engels to argue the inevitability of a future, detailed in the chapter entitled "Results," in which contact with the anti-domestic Irish precipitates the Socialist society. He constructs a pattern in which the introduction of the "degrading" influence of the Irish immigrants produces a "race wholly apart," whose "drunkenness and sensual pleasure" leads to the breakdown of the traditional English domestic values and practices among the working classes; this anti-domesticity in its turn produces crime, which further leads to the "war of each against all" and the proletarian class versus the "blind" property-owning class. For Engels, invoking the Bible and *Hamlet*, this struggle will culminate in the triumph of socialism "whether the bourgeoisie has eyes for it or not, and will surprise the property-holding class one day with things not dreamed of in its philosophy."[29]

Irish immorality epitomizes the degradation of the industrial order for Engels. Moreover, following Kay, he asserts that their drunkenness and sensuality is contaminating the English proletarians who are exposed to them: "Here [in the parish of St Giles, in London] live the poorest of the poor, the worst paid workers with thieves and the victims of prostitution indiscriminately huddled together, the majority Irish, or of Irish extraction, and those who have not yet sunk in the whirlpool of moral ruin which surrounds them, sinking deeper daily."[30] The whirlpool explicitly draws in all who come in contact with it, Irish and English alike. In contrast to Kay, however, Engels attributes the plight of the Irish to the forces of capitalism which forced them to emigrate to Britain in the first place, and forced women from the home and hearth side into the public sphere of the

---

[28]   Ibid., 69.

[29]   Ibid., 157.

[30]   Ibid., 71.

workplace, and, much worse, into prostitution. Here his argument partially reflects that of Carlyle's *Chartism* (1839), in which the Briton Engels most admired unleashed bitter, satiric invective against British policy in Ireland, claiming that the influx of the "hordes" of Irishmen reduced to savagery and coming to London to beg was a clear case of England reaping "fifteen generations of wrong," which England must either rectify or be doomed to suffer the same fate as the Irish. Carlyle also referred to the Irish as a "disease" now caught by England.[31] Engels too insists that Irish immigration is degrading the English working class in a way analogous with physical contagion: "[Irish immigration has] degraded the English workers, removed them from civilization, and aggravated the hardship of their lot ... For the course of the social disease from which England is suffering is the same as the course of a physical disease."[32]

Engels surpasses even Kay's rhetorical excess when he describes the course of the disease, warning that it threatens to drag the English very near to the boundary between human and animal. Just as Stallybrass and White had noticed in Chadwick, the associations of the Irish with animals slide back and forth between metonymical and metaphorical, until the Irish ultimately become virtually conflated with pigs. The poor districts of Manchester are described as filthy, with "debris, and offal heaps, ... [and a] multitude of pigs walking about in the alleys ... the industrial epoch ... has conjured hither from the agricultural districts and from Ireland; the industrial epoch alone enables the owners of these cattlesheds to rent them for high prices to human beings."[33] In direct contrast to Kay, once again, Engels specifically ascribes the process of degradation to the economic system. The link between the Irish and animals is strengthened a few pages later when Engels describes Manchester's Little Ireland neighborhood:

> A horde of women and children swarm about here, as filthy as the swine that thrive upon the garbage heaps and in the puddles ... The race that lives in these ruinous cottages ... in measureless stench, in this atmosphere penned in as with a purpose, this race must have reached the lowest stages of humanity. This is the impression ... this district forces upon the beholder.[34]

In this section of his book, Engels' repeated references to the large families of the Irish imply both his condemnation of the overcrowding that their licentiousness and "breeding habits" have produced, and the racial inferiority which activates such improvidence. In the passage quoted above, moreover, the animalized women and children are "swarming" about in public view (echoing Kay's description of the Irish who "colonize" certain districts of Manchester), and occupying traditionally male public space. He then quotes Dr Kay as asserting that "a number of cellars once filled up with earth have now been emptied and are now occupied once more

---

[31] Carlyle, Thomas. *Chartism* (1839). New York: James B. Millar, 1885, 24–6, 29.
[32] Engels, 149.
[33] Ibid., 91–2.
[34] Ibid., 98.

by Irish people."[35] This too implies the subhumanity of the Irish, who like rodents burrow underground to find shelter.

Engels' rhetorical purposes for emphasizing Irish anti-domesticity soon become apparent – they are debasing the Englishman's ability to earn a living in what is proclaimed by the bourgeoisie as a "British" empire, but which Engels argues is in fact a transnational economic entity that furthers the interests of the bourgeoisie at the expense of the proletariat. In his chapter on "Competition," Engels describes the effect of this "foreign" competition on English wages:

> [O]ne needs more than another, one is accustomed to more comfort than another; the Englishman who is still somewhat civilized needs more than the Irishman who goes in rags, eats potatoes, and sleeps in a pig-sty. But that does not hinder the Irishman's competing with the Englishman, and gradually forcing the rate of wages, and with it the Englishman's level of civilization, down to the Irishman's level.[36]

Engels specifies the level of civilization to which contact with the Irish has brought the English worker, the hallmarks of which are irreligiousness and wallowing in the only pleasures they can afford, sensuality and drunkenness. After describing the anti-domestic habits of the Irish, he turns his attention to the English:

> [L]et us here consider the results of the influences cited above ... [A]mong the masses there prevails almost universally a total indifference to religion ... And like the rest of the conditions under which he lives, his want of religious and other culture contributes to keep the working man more unconstrained, freer from inherited stable tenets and cut-and-dried opinions, than the bourgeois who is saturated with the class prejudices poured into him from his earliest youth.[37]

Engels here cites religion as a "stable tenet" which might produce social control, but at the same time implies the neglect of all facets of human development other than grinding toil which working-class life produces (a point he and Marx will emphasize in *Das Kapital*). He makes explicit the system's total neglect of the workers' physical, mental and social needs when he discusses drunkenness and debauchery: "Next to intemperance in the enjoyment of intoxicating liquors, one of the principal faults of English working men is sexual license ... But is that

---

[35]   Ibid.

[36]   Engels, 112. Cf. Kay: "The system of cottier farming, the demoralization and barbarism of the people, and the general use of the potato as the chief source of food have encouraged the population in Ireland more rapidly than the *available* means of subsistence have been increased ... The paucity of the amount of means and comforts *necessary for the mere support of life*, is not known by a more civilized population, and this secret has been taught the labourers of this country by the Irish. As competition and the restrictions and burdens of trade diminished the profits of capital, and consequently reduced the price of labour, the contagious example of ignorance and a barbarous disregard of forethought and economy, exhibited by the Irish, spread" (quoted in Poovey, 63–4).

[37]   Engels, 150–51.

to be wondered at? When a class can purchase few and only the most sensual pleasures by its wearying toil, must it not give itself over blindly and madly to those pleasures?"[38] By this reasoning, Engels places fault for English as with Irish anti-domesticity squarely onto the social and economic system: "Thus the social order makes family life almost impossible for the worker."[39] The system, in effect, both produces and reproduces anti-domesticity: "Neglect of all domestic duties, neglect of the children, is only too common among the English working people, and only too vigorously fostered by the existing institutions of society. And children growing up in this savage way, amidst these demoralizing influences, are expected to turn out goody-goody and moral in the end!"[40]

The picture of anti-domesticity that Engels draws is used to set the next stage of his argument, that crime and disorder result from it, and must lead to the war of each versus all, which in turn will culminate in conflict between the bourgeoisie and the proletariat. He cites statistics on arrests for criminal offences beginning in 1805 and shows a sevenfold rise in them over the period ending in 1842. He then compares statistics of, among other things, "offences against property," compiled ten years earlier by Peter Gaskell, another Manchester Unitarian reformer, which leads him to conclude that Britain's crime rate outstrips that of the Netherlands by about a factor of ten, and that crime has increased significantly since Gaskell's numbers were collected.

Citing these figures allows Engels to quantify the degradation of the working classes in a manner similar to Kay. For Engels, though, this thorough contamination of the English workers has completed the alienation of the English proletariat from the elites, who he argues belong to a transnational culture (as evidenced in their commercial interests etc.). As a result of the contact with Irish immigrants, he argues, "the [English] working class has gradually became [sic] a race wholly apart from the English bourgeoisie ... The workers speak other dialects, have other thoughts and ideals, other customs and moral principles, a different religion and politics than those of the bourgeoisie. Thus they are two radically dissimilar nations, as unlike as difference of race could make them."[41] The accuracy of Engels's observation (although perhaps not what he attributes as the cause – i.e., contact with the Irish) is attested to in an unexpected source. Benjamin Disraeli, about as radically opposed politically to Engels as it was possible to be, famously stated in the very same year (1845) through one of the characters in his novel *Sybil, or The Two Nations*, ideas almost identical to those expressed in *The Condition*:

> "Two nations; between whom there is no intercourse and no sympathy; who are as ignorant of each other's habits, thoughts, and feelings, as if they were dwellers in different zones, or inhabitants of different planets; who are formed by different breeding, are fed by different food, are ordered by different manners, and are not governed by the same laws."

---

[38] Ibid., 153.

[39] Ibid., 154.

[40] Ibid.

[41] Ibid., 150.

"You speak of" – said Egremont, hesitatingly.
"The Rich and the Poor." [42]

Engels predicts their "social disease" will ravage the English working class so badly as to completely sever them from the capital-owning classes: "Irish immigration ... has ... degraded the English workers, removed them from civilization ... but, on the other hand, it has thereby deepened the chasm between workers and bourgeoisie and hastened the approaching crisis."[43] In other words, Engels identifies the bourgeoisie as an international entity with no real stake in a national cultural identity other than to exploit the nationalist loyalties of the producing classes. It is precisely the international commercial reach of the ownership class that separates it culturally from the working class: "The bourgeoisie has more in common with every other nation of the earth than with the workers in whose midst it lives."[44]

Engels herewith posits a pseudo-racial category – working class – to construct for it as he had for the owners an international cultural identity which defines itself in opposition to its "other" – bourgeois. But what of the debasement of the working class, which by Engels' own admission is proceeding apace in the slums of Manchester? Here Engels' rhetoric takes Kay's contagion metaphor a step further, using it to suggest that the disease which the Irish represent has provoked a quasi-medical crisis. In Engels' new figuration, the medical crisis is analogous to a spiritual crisis; the "fortunate fall" of industrial capitalism makes possible the salvation of socialist revolution: "And as the English nation cannot succumb under the final crisis, but must come forth from it, born again, rejuvenated, we can but rejoice over everything which accelerates the course of the disease."[45]

Although intense ideological and political struggles took place over the cure for what became known as the "condition of England," in Carlyle's famous phrase, one thing is clear from the "dialogue" between Kay and Engels: Irishness itself was metaphorized as a "condition." Culturally, this move was so pervasive that it presented itself to Engels as the most powerful rhetorical means with which to advance his socialist views in *Germany*.[46] Despite his attempts to use his opponents'

---

[42]   Disraeli, Benjamin. *Sybil, or The Two Nations* (1845). Ware, Hertfordshire: Wordsworth Classics, 1995, 58. While of course Disraeli's ideas differed from Engels' in regard to what to do about the problem, his novel, in which he lays out his program for "Young England," has remarkable similarities to *Condition*, including condemnations of "capitalists," satirical sketches of characters from the nobility mouthing the doctrines of Malthus (although these as well as the "capitalists"are portrayed as misguided individuals; like Edgeworth he does not condemn the system), moving accounts of the plight of hand-loom weavers and others, and oblique references to the problems of immigration.

[43]   Engels, 149.

[44]   Ibid., 150.

[45]   Ibid., 149.

[46]   As is widely known, *The Condition of the Working Classes in England* was not published in England until 1892 (the first English language edition was published in the U.S. in 1886). Engels appended a dedication to the first edition written in English to "the English Workingman," and copies of the book were given to English readers in hopes that

own arguments against them, however, Engels in effect "lost" the culture war to a triumphant bourgeoisie. The elaboration of this middle-class identity became central to British cultural nationalism, and, as in Kay, Irishness played an important part in defining it. The increasing prominence of the figure of the Irish woman as the focal point of Irish alterity in the definition of Britishness, so noticeable in Kay's work, was also evident in popular novels and literary criticism, and to some of these we will turn in the next chapter.

the book would be noticed by influential British commentators such as Carlyle. But its argument is made to warn German workers of the coming crisis by examining the most advanced industrial system of the time, that of Great Britain.

Chapter 7
British National Identity and Irish Anti-Domesticity in Pre-Famine British Literature and Criticism

Introduction

As the preceding chapters have shown, the meme of Irish moral contagion crossed and re-crossed discursive boundaries among the republic of letters and the discourses of political and social reform. I wish now to study the role that other aspects of the writing of Ireland played in the elaboration of a new middle-class cultural ideal in works of literature and criticism, an ideal that would come to dominate popular perceptions of British national identity. In a previous chapter I noted that in Edgeworth's Irish novels the aristocracy is imagined as evolving into what resembles a meritocracy (that in some ways Kay might be said to personify), which seems to represent an intermediate cultural formation between Burke's aristocratic ideal and the bourgeoisie Nancy Armstrong focuses upon. This transformation itself, as well as the role Irish anti-domesticity played throughout this evolution, is observable in some of the work of John Wilson Croker and William Makepeace Thackeray. Croker associates himself with a professionalized middling class; however, it is apparent from his letters and papers as well as numerous remarks and references in his criticism, that early in the century he still adheres to a notion of its inferior position within a hierarchy headed by the titled aristocracy. Within this hierarchy gentlemen of letters assumed a place which in the 1810s and 20s, when Croker was at the height of his influence, was based more upon their political than their literary function, as John Klancher has noted: "No discourse was so immediately identified with power as that of the great party quarterlies, the *Edinburgh Review* and the *Quarterly Review*."[1] Thackeray, by contrast, in his journalism and fiction of the 1830s and early 1840s, portrays a dominant middle class and an idle aristocracy that is either effete, corrupt, or both. The ruling class is composed of professionals and only gentry insofar as they practice professions such as politics. The work of these two writers might therefore be said to exemplify a shift taking place in the society at large. We'll begin with a look at some of Croker's literary criticism, moving then to Thackeray's early career, first considering some of his reviews and criticism, and concluding the chapter with a close examination of the novel *Barry Lyndon*.

---

[1]   Klancher, Jon. *The Making of the English Reading Audiences, 1790–1832.* Madison: University of Wisconsin Press, 1987, 69.

Class Hysteria: Croker

The Anglo-Irish Croker, in addition to holding an important position as editor of the *Quarterly Review*, was a member of Parliament, first Secretary of the Admiralty, a fellow of the Royal Society, a founder of the Athenaeum Club, a respected critic of the French Revolution,[2] and a confidante of the great Tory leader Robert Peel. He thus was a figure of considerable power and influence not only in the literary establishment but also in Britain's ruling party. The vituperativeness and scurrility of Croker's work in *The Quarterly Review*, a Tory journal founded in response to the immediate popularity and influence of the Whig *Edinburgh Review*, is well documented. His scathing assessment of Keats's *Endymion* was notorious, but a more frequent target of his venom was Lady Morgan, in whose social vision the professional class of Anglo-Irish middlemen, to which Croker belonged, was responsible for many of Ireland's woes.[3] Croker's attacks on Lady Morgan center on the premise that her gender, and much more so her anti-domesticity, debar her from inclusion within the emerging professional-gentry class, in which journalists and novelists, as well as actors and artists, were just beginning to find a place.[4]

The Quarterly Review, which began publication in 1809 under the direction of Croker and William Gifford, unleashed a blistering attack in its opening number on Lady Morgan's *Woman: Or Ida of Athens*, and found frequent occasion to disparage both the author and her work for years to come. The most notorious of the *Quarterly*'s attacks on Lady Morgan came in Croker's review of her travel book *France* (1816), and it is worth examining this review[5] in some detail, since in addition to containing some of his most notorious aspersions upon her[6] the review comments upon many of her other works, including her Irish novels *The Wild Irish Girl* and *O'Donnell*.

---

[2]   For a useful overview of Croker's literary career, see Peter F. Morgan's *Literary Critics and Reviewers in Early 19th-Century Britain.* London: Croom Helm, 1983.

[3]   In response to Croker's venomous attacks, Lady Morgan based a pivotal character in *Florence McCarthy* on Croker in order to dialogize his ideological positions (see above, Chapter 4). (Croker is also the putative model for the character Wenham in Thackeray's *Vanity Fair* and Mr Rigby in Disraeli's novel *Coningsby.*) As noted above in Chapter 1, Ina Ferris has argued persuasively that reviewers such as Croker saw the restoration to reviewers in the male-dominated republic of letters of the cultural authority that had been "usurped" by female authors as a large part of the mission of the *Quarterly* and other reviews. See also Ferris (1991), Chapter 1.

[4]   See Klancher, Ferris 1991, Chapter 1 et al.

[5]   In *Quarterly Review* (henceforth *QR*) 17:23, April 1817.

[6]   Including his famous epithet "this audacious worm" (284). His attack was denounced as "unmanly" by commentators from all sides of the political spectrum, including Macaulay, whose review in the *Edinburgh Review* of Croker's edition of Boswell's *Johnson* contains a notorious diatribe against him, and others who disagreed with Lady Morgan's political positions.

Novelists, as well as critics, were hitherto regarded as engaged in the less than dignified realm of commerce, and Croker in his critique of Lady Morgan seeks to associate her with trade. In his review of *Ida of Athens*, Croker had utilized some of the more familiar charges brought against the romance genre to dismiss Lady Morgan's novel: excessive sensibility, overwrought style, and pretension. But while he dismisses the writing as "merely foolish," he warns that her "sentiments" are "mischievous in tendency, and profligate in principle; licentious and irreverent in the highest degree."[7] These charges he regards as more serious; such unfeminine sentiments, he makes clear both here and in the review of *France*, are potentially subversive of the social order. In a superior, even supercilious tone, Croker reports on the first full page of the review of *France* that the *Quarterly* has gained Lady Morgan's attention, but that she has failed to benefit from its instruction:

> Lady Morgan remembers — with more anger than profit — the advice which we gave her in our first number on the occasion of *Ida of Athens* ... and, in the Preface [to *France*] ... informs us, that we made one of the most hastily composed and insignificant of her works a vehicle for accusing her of licentiousness, profligacy, irreverence, blasphemy, libertinism, disloyalty, and atheism.[8]

Far from denying her accusations, Croker asserts that Lady Morgan has failed to benefit from the "advice" because she purposely ignored his most important point, that an acceptable feminine domesticity is to be gained from instruction and piety:

> "To cure her" (she adds) "of these vices, we presented a nostrum of universal efficacy; and prescribed" (by the way Lady Morgan's language smells vilely of the shop since her marriage) "a simple remedy, a spelling book and a pocket dictionary, which, superadded to a little common sense, was to render her that epitome of female excellence" ... We were not so lightly impressed with the danger of her case to suppose that it might be alleviated by a spelling book and vocabulary only: there was, *as she well knows*, another BOOK ... need we add that we spoke of the Bible? (italics in original)[9]

In the opening salvos of his lengthy critique Croker thus makes clear the outlines of his position. His characterization of her language as "smelling vilely of the shop" seeks to place her in a social position beneath the one which reviewers considered themselves to occupy, but were not fully ready as yet to admit to novelists. Furthermore, his insinuating reference to her marriage, which he comments upon more fully later in the review, is a stab at her supposed social climbing and pretension. Lady Morgan's husband was knighted shortly before their marriage and it was through him that she gained her title. But at the center of Croker's argument is her anti-domesticity; the idealized British domestic woman

---

[7]   *QR* 1, 1809, 52.
[8]   *QR* 17:23, April 1817, 261.
[9]   Ibid.

is referred to here as "that epitome of female excellence." This is the "danger of the case" which impresses him so heavily.

Croker further emphasizes Lady Morgan's class liabilities by associating her not only with commerce, but Irish commerce: "[T]he sylphid Miss Owenson, the elegant Lady Morgan, is in fact a mere bookseller's drudge (we tremble as we write it!) ... And ... this large and valuable quarto volume, so pleasantly denominated *France*, was written under contract, to be delivered, like other Irish provisions, between the months of November and March."[10] Croker, though born in Ireland, has distanced himself from the Irish merchant classes entirely and here characterizes their productions as imports, although Ireland was a member of the United Kingdom since 1801. But his overall point is to establish Lady Morgan's rootlessness and promiscuity. Deirdre Lynch has pointed out that it was Croker who initiated the malicious rumor that "Lady Morgan's anti-domestic itinerancy had begun when her mother gave birth to her aboard the Dublin packet-boat, midway across the Irish Sea."[11] Croker had also made use of the "mystery" surrounding her birth to make sneering comments in regard to Lady Morgan's actual age, a tactic he reverts to in the review of *France* when he refers to her as "this young lady (such, ten years ago, we supposed her to be)."[12] The implications of these points taken together are clear: older women of the lower social classes marrying above their station disrupt the social order. We will see this theme revisited, again with an Irishwoman as its focus, in Thackeray's *Pendennis*.

 Croker makes these points more explicitly elsewhere in his review. He goes so far as to enumerate them, and then one by one detail her transgressions in each category (although he states more than once that to do full justice to her each of the charges would require volumes): "Our charges (to omit minor faults) fall readily under the heads of — Bad Taste — Bombast and Nonsense — Blunders — Ignorance of the French Language and Manners — General Ignorance — Jacobinism — Falsehood — Licentiousness, and Impiety."[13] The first five of these categories are catalogues of trivial complaints brought forth mainly to sabotage Lady Morgan's credibility. Under the heading "Blunders," for example, Croker explicitly asserts that Lady Morgan's gaucheries "savour very strongly, not of French, but Hibernian origin."[14] In other words, her own *déclassé* origins render her unable to appreciate the hierarchical French society under the monarchy, which social system Croker lauds and defends throughout the article. He dismissively notes that Lady Morgan "intimates ... that her own personal talents and celebrity obtained her admission into French society"[15] and disavows such meritocratic sentiments by suggesting instead (with his characteristic irony) that it was her husband's title and contacts

---

[10]   Ibid., 263.

[11]   Lynch, op. cit., 47.

[12]   *QR* 17:23, 262.

[13]   Ibid., 264.

[14]   Ibid., 266.

[15]   Ibid., 269.

which gained her respectability and upward mobility within the patriarchal power structure: "Lady Morgan ... obtained the reward of her improvements, in the person of Doctor Lady Morgan; and ... is become ... a respectable ... mistress of a family."[16] But he seeks to cast doubt on Lady Morgan's entree into the higher ranks of French society by directly accusing her of lying (without offering any evidence to support his claims): "The eternal exordium to all her anecdotes is 'La princesse de _____ *said to me*; la marquise de _____ *said to me*;' &c. Now we will take it upon ourselves to dispute most of these *dites à moi*. That something like them was said, or rather told to Lady Morgan, we well believe; but not by the persons represented (italics in orginal)."[17]

The focus of Croker's review is to undermine Lady Morgan's political position, and the establishment of Lady Morgan's falsehood is an important element in Croker's rhetorical strategy. Indeed, Croker directs most of his rhetorical energy toward these final three and most socially disruptive of what he deems Lady Morgan's sins, termed Jacobinism, falsehood, and licentiousness and impiety. His argument betrays familiar cultural, class, and gender anxieties and seeks to demonstrate that her political opinions are irresponsible and, worse still, dangerous. Her falsehood, as he sought to demonstrate in the passage just quoted, presents the danger of undermining the social order, according to this "avowed disciple of Burke,"[18] in part because in Burke's, and by extension Croker's scheme, feminine sociosexual impropriety is a dangerous threat to the social, political and imperial order in a society founded upon primogeniture.[19] Jacobinism encodes associations of political, social and sexual anarchy. Licentiousness and impiety are equally cancerous to the patriarchal social organism, which Burke, in *Reflections on the Revolution in France*, constructs in terms that at once naturalize it and make it sacred:

> We wished at the period of the [1688] Revolution, and do now wish, to derive all we possess as an inheritance from our forefathers. Upon that body and stock of inheritance we have taken care not to inoculate any cyon alien to the nature of the original plant.[20]

In this conception, the state's power is both modeled upon and derived from the intimate relations within the patriarchal aristocratic family. Indeed, the power of the imperial nation-state is *identified* with domesticity in Burke's phrasing when he goes on to state that: "[w]e have given to our frame of polity the image of

---

[16]   Ibid., 261.

[17]   Ibid., 281.

[18]   Lynch, 47.

[19]   For two good sources on the class and gender associations of Burke's rhetoric, see James T. Boulton's *The Language of Politics in the age of Wilkes and Burke*. London: Routledge and Kegan Paul, 1963, and Ronald Paulson's *Representations of Revolution 1789–1820*. New Haven: Yale University Press, 1983.

[20]   Burke, 27–8.

a relation in blood, binding up the constitution of our country with our dearest domestic ties."[21] It is clear that Croker's logic is structured and argued to depict Lady Morgan as a medium for just the type of "alien cyon" Burke warned about.

He accuses her (as he had in the review of *Ida of Athens*) of Jacobinism, defined for his readers as "a word which includes disloyalty and impiety."[22] He castigates her admiration for Parny, author of *Éloge à Éléonore* and *La Guerre des Dieux*, but attributes it to ignorance rather than willful corruption of the morals of her British readers: "[T]his Parny ... is the most detestably wicked and blasphemous of all the writers who ever disgraced literature! ... the *Éloge* ... [is] a system of debauchery, written in the language of the brothel ... *La Guerre des Dieux* ... is the most dreadful tissue of profaneness ever inspired to the depraved heart of man ... We will be fair ... We do not believe she could have seen or known what she was talking about."[23] In a rear-guard action to defend his own morality, Croker primly announces that "we still tremble with horror at the guilt of having read *unwittingly* even so much of the work as enables us to pronounce this character of it (emphasis in orginal)."[24] Having to his satisfaction established his own piety and propriety, he returns to Lady Morgan's lack of these fundamental attributes of approved British female domesticity. He does so in a way which suggests Lady Morgan has been corrupted by her reading, and in turn will corrupt her own female readers:

> Some of our readers may have heard the title *Les Liasions Dangereuses*. We had hoped no British female had ever seen this detested book; it seems we are mistaken. Lady Morgan sneers at the Court of Louis XVIII 'because all [copies of] *Liasions Dangereuses* are banished from it.' ... [She] goes on to say that when piety usurps their place (i.e. the place of deliberate seduction and debauchery, or as she delicately words it, of 'gallantry and the graces') it is as if chimney sweepers were to usurp the place of Cupids ... [Lady Morgan] appears equally well-read in the loose volumes of Pigault Le Brun.[25]

---

[21]   Ibid., 30.

[22]   *QR* 17:23, 279. Lady Morgan answers this charge directly in *Florence McCarthy*, published within a year of the appearance of the review of *France*, by showing how legitimate political opposition to the bribery and corruption practiced by the Ascendancy is termed "rebellion" and "Jacobinism." Darby Crawley (father of the Croker character in the novel) informs Lady Dunore that her tenants and other townspeople in her district are seeking to resist the Crawley's attempts to install Lady Dunore's handpicked candidate in Parliament: "[H]is opponent means to petition against him in Parliament, on the score of what they ... call his bribery and corruption, his trates [treats] and his presents, and other illegal practices to which he has had recourse ... the rebelly thieves! ... Nothing has been done here, that hasn't been done since the beginning of the Europayan world, at all elections; and would pass muster anywhere, only for them jacobin Whigs ... [who are] always open-mouthed against loyal men" (*Florence McCarthy*, 527). The Croker character (as leader of the local regiment) then has the opponent arrested on charges of sedition and is himself elected to Parliament.

[23]   Ibid., 275–6.

[24]   Ibid., 275–6.

[25]   Ibid., 282.

Croker asserts that such corrupt reading leads directly to immoral action. He details Lady Morgan's admiration for Madame D'Houdetot, a former lover (or, as Croker puts it, a woman who has "passed through the hands") of Voltaire, St Lambert, Rousseau, and others, in order to suggest through the use of a heavy-handed irony that Lady Morgan herself is promiscuous: "[I]t would be uncandid and unjust to take her *au pied de la lettre*, and suppose she would *really have found delight in tracing the steps of* Madame D'Houdetot (italics in original)."[26]

Having reached a high rhetorical pitch, Croker concludes his denunciation by characterizing Lady Morgan as an inversion (perversion?) of the domestic ideal elaborated by Burke. Citing a passage in which a French noblewoman regretted that some members of a previous French court were both impious and ungrateful to the king, Croker describes Lady Morgan's repudiation of the divine right of kings as blasphemous:

> To us, who have been taught to "fear God and honour the King," [Madame de Maintenon's statement] does not seem a very extraordinary, nor a very hazardous remark; but Lady Lady Morgan is of a different mind, and parodies Scripture for the purpose of turning it into ridicule — "It was the *fashion* of that *pious* day to *confound* the sovereign and the Deity, and to consider the king both '*as the law and the prophets*' within the purlieus of his own court" ... she calls [the *petits soupers* of Paris] "the Passover of family reunion," words which really have no meaning, and excite no idea but that of disgust and horror at the profanation on which this audacious worm seems to pride itself.[27]

Lady Morgan's crime here is to profane the established social order from top to bottom — from the deity and king, who represent the epitome of the patrilineal political and legal system, to its foundation, the sacred Burkean hearth at which the patriarchal French family gathers. In a postscript, Croker appends a comment upon two subsequent *Letters from Paris*, which, he charges, evidence the same admiration for social and political anarchy: "Both exhibit the same slavish awe when speaking of the usurper [Napoleon], the same impudent familiarity when noticing the lawful monarch; both profess the same admiration for all that was feeble, and treacherous, and bloody in France ... [Lady Morgan] can see nothing, can hear of nothing, but plots to overthrow the government, and bring back the golden age of their day-dreams, the reign of rebellion, plunder, and blood."[28] With the words "rebellion, plunder, and blood," Croker invokes all the political, social, and sexual anxieties which Lady Morgan had aroused in her novels and travel books in an attempt to discipline the British readers under his influence.

---

[26] Ibid., 283.

[27] Ibid., 283–4.

[28] Ibid., 285.

Happy Beef and Pudding: Thackeray's Anti-Romance

In a much less shrill way, William Makepeace Thackeray in his work also constructed an idealized British cultural nationalism centered upon domesticity, and at the beginning of his literary career was, like Croker, a journalist and critic with a personal stake in the Irish Question. His wife, the former Isabel Shawe, was Anglo-Irish, as were relatives of his step-father, William Carmichael Smith. Furthermore, Thackeray's mentor in the republic of letters was William Maginn, the colorful Anglo-Irish editor of *Fraser's Magazine*, the lively Tory journal.[29] Thackeray contributed poems, satires, and literary reviews to *Fraser's* throughout the 1830s and early 1840s, where he also published his first two novels, *Catherine* (1839–40) and *Barry Lyndon* (1843), in serial form. Maginn and *Fraser's* provided a congenial nursery in which Thackeray could cut his literary teeth and develop his anti-romanticism, publishing frequent lampoons and burlesques of Byron, Bulwer-Lytton and others.

Thackeray's journalism often concerned itself with Irish politics and literature, and one of his chief complaints against romance recalls Croker's objection to Lady Morgan's "dangerous" sentiments. Thackeray charged that the radical themes often expressed in romance cannot be contained by the gesture toward social harmony in the comic ending. In a review entitled "A Box of Novels," which appeared in *Fraser's* simultaneously with the opening chapters of *Barry Lyndon*, Thackeray ironically praises Charles Lever's most popular novel, *Harry Lorrequer*, perhaps partly because *Lorrequer* was light-hearted and extremely popular, and partly in order to prepare the reader for his later, explicit condemnation of similar novels:

> If we may be allowed to give an opinion about *Lorrequer* ... it would be to ... say the author's characteristic is ... neither more nor less than sentiment ... If Mr. [Daniel] O'Connell, like a wise rhetorician, chooses, and very properly, to flatter the [Irish] national military passion, why should not Harry Lorrequer?[30]

When he turns to a discussion of Samuel Lover's novel *Treasure Trove* in the same review, however, Thackeray undercuts this irony. In this novel Lover celebrates Irish military valor in the plot and in songs, and recreates the battle of Fontenoy

---

[29]   Maginn is widely regarded to be the model for the Captain Shandon character in *Pendennis*, a loosely autobiographical *roman d'apprentissage* which contains an extensive portrait of the London literary journals of the 1830s. Croker served as the model for the minor character Wenham in that novel (a character who reappears in *Vanity Fair*. A discussion of *Pendennis* appears below in Chapter 9). The best biographies of Thackeray, which include commentary upon these characters, are by Gordon Ray, whose work remains definitive, Catherine Peters, and Lionel Stevenson. The most comprehensive account of Maginn and *Fraser's* remains Miriam Thrall's *Rebellious Fraser's*. Maginn's anti-romanticism was evidenced in many articles and reviews, but perhaps found its fullest expression in the novel he co-wrote with John Lockhart, associated with *Blackwoods Magazine* and son-in-law of Sir Walter Scott, entitled *Whitehall, or the Days of George IV*, which burlesques many of the targets Thackeray later lampooned in *Mr. Punch's Prize Novelists*.

[30]   *Fraser's* 29, 156.

(a victory of combined Irish and French forces over the English). The novel concludes with a reaffirmation of Union: "Thanks be to God those unnatural days are past and the unholy [penal] laws that made them so are expunged. In little more than sixty years ... at Waterloo, Erin gave to Albion, not only her fiery columns, but her unconquerable chieftain"[31] Thackeray often good-naturedly lampooned Irish boasting of military prowess, but his objections to the glorification of Irish military might turned against England were serious, as he makes clear in this review when he castigates Lover for what he considers the provocative lyrics in a song of one of Lover's characters: "It is a good rattling lyric, to be sure, but is it well sung by you, Samuel Lover? ... Leave the brawling to the politicians and the newspaper ballad-mongers ... Don't let poets and men of genius join in the brutal chorus, and lead on starving savages to murder."[32] The anxieties Thackeray expresses here will become amplified by him later in the 1840s, when Irish political agitation became more strident. As the reference to "starving savages" makes clear, race-inflected considerations of class also inform Thackeray's critique. While he implicitly recognized Irish (albeit Anglo-Irish) men and women of letters such as Lover as fully integrated members of British imperial metropolitan culture, Gaelic Irish men and women are almost without exception *déclassé* in Thackeray's canon.

Another issue consistently at stake in Thackeray's early work, which was alluded to above and will be examined at more length in the discussion of *Barry Lyndon*, is the representation of Ireland in historiography and romance, and in particular historical romance. In a review of Lever's novel *St Patrick's Eve*, which appeared in the London *Morning Chronicle* of April 3, 1845, Thackeray again decries what he calls the "sentimental politics" of historical romance for what he characterizes as mystification: "Occasion is here taken ... to enter a protest against sentimental politics altogether ... You cannot have a question fairly debated [when an author] ... invent[s] incidents, motives, and characters in order that he may attack them subsequently."[33] He argues that novels such as these seek to dissociate the radical themes they engage from concrete political consequences through the evasion performed by the comic resolution, and he locates that disavowal precisely in romance's comic structure: "At the conclusion of these tales ... there somehow arrives a misty reconciliation between the poor and the rich; a prophecy is uttered of better times for the one, and better manners in the other; presages are made of happy life, happy marriage and children, happy beef and pudding for all time to come."[34]

---

[31] *Fraser's* 29, 164. "Albion's unconquerable chieftain" is the Anglo-Irish Wellington. As is evident from this passage, Lover's novel is characterized less by its humor than its chauvinistic celebration of (Anglo-) Irish military glory. Harry Lorrequer, on the other hand, might fairly be described as a military Bertie Wooster, and the novel depicts his misadventures in a strain of high comedy. Lever, who is all but forgotten today, was once praised by George Bernard Shaw as "our greatest comic novelist."

[32] *Fraser's* 29, 164–5.

[33] Reprinted in *Thackeray's Contributions to the Morning Chronicle*, ed. Gordon Ray, 72.

[34] *Thackeray's Contributions to the Morning Chronicle*, 73.

Anti-Domesticity and the Return of the Colonial Repressed: *Barry Lyndon*

Thackeray expands his project of anti-romance in his fiction, and in his novels constructs a British national identity rooted, like Burke's, in domesticity. Two of his novels written in the 1840s make extensive use of Irishness, and Irish womanhood in particular, in enunciating his social vision: *The Memoirs of Barry Lyndon, Written by Himself* (serialized in *Fraser's* throughout 1843), and *The History of Pendennis*, serialized in *Punch* in 1849–50 (with an extended hiatus in late 1849 owing to the author's grave illness). Thackeray makes clear in these novels that the Gaelic Irish, although nominally British subjects, cannot really be members of the British social body because they have not transcended history. The form in which *Barry Lyndon* is written, the picaresque novel, originated in sixteenth-century Spain as a reaction to the excesses and artificialities of medieval romance. The critical consensus regarding *Barry Lyndon* has long held that the novel continues and expands the project taken up less successfully *Catherine*, in which Thackeray unsentimentally portrays a criminal case from the eighteenth century in order to engage in a dialogue with the wildly popular sensation or "Newgate" novels of the period such as Bulwer-Lytton's *Eugene Aram* (1832), Ainsworth's *Jack Sheppard* (1837), and Dickens's *Oliver Twist* (also published serially in 1837–39).[35] By depicting his Irish hero in a novel which engages the national tales initiated by Lady Morgan and Edgeworth (a tradition adapted and transformed into the historical romance by Walter Scott), Thackeray delineates the contrast between Ireland's place (or lack thereof) in the imperial nation-state and that of the English, Scottish, and Welsh. As Ian Duncan has argued in a discussion of Scott's Waverley novels, "to be a British subject is to be middle class, to have transcended historical process in order to occupy a generic idyll of private life."[36]

The hero of *Barry Lyndon* cannot be assimilated into British metropolitan society essentially because he is premodern. In this way Thackeray's novel resembles the one Irish national tale of Maria Edgeworth which is not structured as a comedy, *Castle Rackrent*. The impoverished son of a "noble" family who makes his way in the world by adventuring, Barry is the product of the social conditions to which Ireland has been reduced, and although his "luck," charm and wit gain him much, he squanders it all and ends by writing his memoirs from the Fleet, a debtor's prison. But *Barry Lyndon* is more than just an allegorical representation of relations between Ireland and Great Britain. While some of the events of Barry's life recapitulate episodes in Irish history, perhaps more importantly, his "Life" recapitulates Irish *historiography*. In other words, Thackeray uses the supposed autobiography of an eighteenth-century Irish *debauché* to comment upon the representation of Ireland in historical romances and national tales.

---

[35]   For a brief survey of the criticism on *Catherine* and a discussion of it as a reaction to these novels see Robert Colby's essay "*Barry Lyndon* and the Irish Hero," *Nineteenth-Century Fiction* 21 (1966)], 109–30, especially pages 109–11. These early novels of Thackeray were patterned in part on the anti-romantic works, *Jonathan Wild* and *Tom Jones*, written by his literary idol, Henry Fielding.

[36]   Duncan, *Modern Romance*, op. cit., 55.

This places more at stake in *Barry Lyndon* than an unsentimental portrayal of Barry's criminality. Because much of the action of the novel takes place on the Continent, Thackeray strongly implies that in the context of a "unified" metropolitan culture of Western Europe the Irish have been excluded from the circuits of commercial and political power and reduced to trading on their charm and wit. Barry, who in many ways resembles portraits of *nineteenth-century* Irishmen in contemporary travelogues and adventure romances such as those by Charles Lever and Samuel Lover, nevertheless is primitive even in comparison with figures from an *ancien-régime* Europe on the verge an industrial revolution. He engages in many "romantic" adventures such as duels, gambling (at which he always cheats), and impetuous courtships. He believes his own nobility (he claims descent from Irish kings) entitles him to any prize he can lay hold of. Barry becomes first a soldier of fortune on the battlefields and later a fortune hunter in the gambling salons of Europe by force of circumstances. He asserts that the blackmail and coercion which characterize his "wooing" of a countess and eventually Lady Lyndon is justified by this exclusion:

> [T]hough some rigid moralist may object to its propriety ... men so poor as myself can't afford to be squeamish about their means of getting on in life. The great and rich are welcomed, smiling, up the grand staircase of the world; the poor but aspiring must clamber up the wall, or push and struggle up the back stair, or, *pardi*, crawl through any of the conduits of the house, never mind how foul and narrow, that lead to the top.[37]

Implicit in Barry's frank admission of ambition is a reference to British economic and social policies which have kept Ireland in a premodern state of existence through the creation of the "Protestant aristocracy and Catholic peasantry" that Thackeray described in *The Irish Sketch Book* (1842) and that Edgeworth had earlier so stoutly defended. At the conclusion of *The Irish Sketch Book*, Thackeray explicitly asserts it is the social structure resulting from British colonial policy, which included the penal laws, that has kept Ireland in a state resembling that of premodern European nations:

> [L]et us hope that the *middle class* ... (which our laws have hitherto forbidden the existence in Ireland, making there a population of Protestant aristocracy and Catholic peasantry), will exercise the greatest and most beneficial influence over the country ... [H]aving their interest in quiet, and alike indisposed to servility or rebellion; may not as much be hoped from the gradual formation of such a [middle] class, as from any legislative meddling (italics in original)?"[38]

---

[37] Thackeray, William Makepeace. *The Memoirs of Barry Lyndon, Written by Himself* (1844). Lincoln: University of Nebraska Press, 1962, 156. Hereafter *BL*.

[38] *The Irish Sketch Book* (1843). New York: T.Y. Crowell (n.d.), 582. In his essay "Colonial Discourse and William Makepeace Thackeray's *Irish Sketch Book*" (*Papers on Language and Literature* 29:3 [Summer 1993], 259–83), Kenneth L. Brewer argues that Thackeray displaces the coding of Irish difference from the category of race to that of class.

In some of his later, post-Famine journalism, Thackeray decries the inability of the Irish to adapt themselves to British metropolitan culture, and argues they thus must remain "outside of history," using starkly racialized terms. But in *Barry Lyndon*, as in *The Irish Sketch Book*, he clearly attributes Irish backwardness to colonial policy.

In a device familiar from the national tale, Thackeray allegorically portrays Irish history in some of the events of Barry's life. Barry's attempt to woo a local Irish girl, and failure to impress her because he is outdone by an English captain, the "originary" episode which sets Barry on his course of adventuring, is one such instance. Barry is rash and violent as he seeks to win his cousin, Nora Brady, despite the contrary wishes of her father and brothers. The men in her family have been friendly to him, but prefer Captain Quin as a suitor since he has promised to pay the father's debts. Barry challenges Quin to a duel and seemingly kills him, and to escape punishment for this crime Barry enlists in the British army. Having safely escaped to the Continent with the army, Barry meets an Irish captain who tells him of the Bradys' plot to increase the family's financial and social position by marrying the Englishman into the family: "She took on so at your going away that she was obliged to console herself with a husband. She's now Mrs. John Quin ... The ball you hit him with was not likely to hurt him. It was only made of tow. Do you think the Bradys would let you kill fifteen hundred a year out of the family?"[39] Barry refuses to believe that the Bradys can admit such a poltroon into "one of the most ancient and honourable families in the world," but Captain Fagan explains the Bradys' pragmatic reasons for doing so: "He has paid off your uncle's mortgage ... he gives Nora a coach and six ... That coward has been the making of your uncle's family. Faith! the business was well done!"[40]

Thackeray, in the tradition of *Castle Rackrent* and the national tales, here encapsulates the consolidation of power by the Protestant Ascendancy in Ireland in the history of the Bradys family.[41] The satire is double-edged, however. Nora is at best a dubious prize — she is old, ugly and treacherous. Likewise, Ireland is mired in outmoded social and economic structures, poor, and regarded as "disloyal" to its partner in Union, Great Britain (an allegorical reference to Ireland's intrigues with France, notably in 1798). Furthermore, Thackeray here as elsewhere in the novel is engaging not only the Irish past, but also representations of that past. *Barry Lyndon* directly parallels the plot structure in *The Wild Irish Girl*, the most influential of the Irish national tales. In Lady Morgan's novel, it will be recalled, Ireland is represented allegorically as a beautiful and mysterious and virginal woman. A curious Englishman who is exploring the romantically wild countryside meets

---

[39]   *BL*, 67 .

[40]   Ibid., 68.

[41]   In the sixteenth century, many Irish chieftains consolidated their local power by claiming allegiance to the British crown (and accepting the Protestant faith), thus gaining the resources from their English allies with which to subdue their rivals and live quite prosperously, but reducing Ireland to a state of political vassalage and consigning the overwhelming majority of the population to poverty.

and falls in love with her. After overcoming various obstacles to their courtship, they are united and settle in Ireland on their "joint" estate. In the Captain Quin/ Nora plot, Thackeray invokes many of the tropes of the national tale, including the gendering of the allegorical relationship. However, he satirizes these tropes as well. Nora, far from being virginal (in the sense of never having had any emotional commitments), like Voltaire's Cunegonde is old and has had many lovers, all of whom (until Barry and Captain Quin) have abandoned her. The country she lives in is brutal and squalid, not romantic and wild. Quin is not a curious and brave adventurer, but a coward who sells his commission upon his "winning" of her through a subterfuge concocted with his wife's grasping relatives.

In the marriage plot of Barry and Lady Lyndon, Thackeray complicates the symbolism even further by reversing the gendering of the relationship in the national tales and removing from it the youth and idealism of the lovers. Lady Lyndon is the younger wife of an elderly, worn-out and crippled aristocrat, which signals her own acquisitiveness, and the fact he can court her at all while her husband still lives speaks loudly of her questionable moral qualities. Barry is elevated financially by their subsequent marriage, but he promptly degrades his wife's estates by making "improvements" such as, among other things, chopping down ancient groves of trees (in an historically symbolic act of desecration). He alienates her servants and relations, openly conducts adulterous affairs, and squanders her fortune. This allegorical representation of recent Anglo-Irish relations is thus much more cynical than that of the national tales: Ireland, far from benefiting from attempts to "improve" it, is wasting Britain's precious resources, destabilizing England's social relationships at home (cf. Kay and Engels) and brazenly consorting with Britain's foreign political rivals. Moreover, Barry's degradation of not only her Irish, but more significantly her English, estates, utilizes a trope of the return of the colonial repressed which will be picked up later in novels such as *The Moonstone* and *Dracula*.

Thackeray's burlesque of the national *tale* is part of a larger project in *Barry Lyndon* and throughout Thackeray's oeuvre which might be described as anti-romance. In addition to the various courtship plots which parody those of romances, Thackeray's representation of Barry's military career engages the wildly popular adventure novels of the period, including those of Samuel Lover and Charles Lever. These tales, modeled in part on Scott's Waverly novels (which in turn owe a debt to Edgeworth and Lady Morgan), usually featured Irish heroes and glorified military prowess. Gunther Klotz has noted that Thackeray attempted to counteract the utilization of Irishness as a signifier of romance in these novels: "Irishness was a paradigm of late romantic literature which [Thackeray] ... campaigned to overcome"[42] (Klotz 95). Klotz further asserts that Thackeray himself appropriated this signifier in order to complicate contemporary uses of stereotype and the

---

[42]   Klotz, Gunther. "Thackeray's Ireland: Image and Attitude in The Irish Sketch Book and Barry Lyndon," in *Literary Interrelations: Ireland, England and the World (Vol. 3, National Images and Stereotypes)*, eds Wolfgang Zach and Henry Kosok. Tubingen: Gunter Narr Verlag, 1987, 96.

romance form itself: "The content and structure of his abominations [sic] were part of his complex endeavors to create literary images and a narrative method better suited to dealing with contemporary problems than the literary conventions and successful stories of his time." To this end Thackeray ironizes the glorification of military exploits in the portrayal of Barry's "exploits" as a mercenary soldier, such as his robberies of a superior officer as well as a local family who had sheltered him after a battle. Frederick the Great of Prussia, whom Carlyle lionized, is depicted as a greedy adventurer, and Barry matter-of-factly narrates descriptions of brutish violence on the battlefield and the systematic robbery of corpses by soldiers on both sides.

Female Strength as a Demonic Force: Irish Anti-Domesticity and the British Middle Class

Within Thackeray's fiction also is a fuller elaboration (than in his journalism) of a national identity which privileges a middle-class cultural ideal founded upon domesticity. In the 1840s he utilizes Irishness quite extensively to enunciate this ideal. *Barry Lyndon* begins with the hero's ironic assertion that "Since the days of Adam, there has been hardly a mischief done in this world but a woman has been at bottom of it ... Ever since ours was a family ... women have played a mighty part with the destinies of our race."[43] As many critics have noted, it is entirely in keeping with his character that Barry should deny responsibility for his downfall, but Thackeray establishes more here than merely the delineation of Barry's character. The opening passages of his "memoirs" devote concentrated attention to depicting the domain in which he grows up as a wellspring of anti-domesticity, reminiscent in some ways of Corny O'Shane's Black Islands in *Ormond*. But whereas in Edgeworth's novel the mother is absent, Barry's mother is present and instrumental in shaping his character.

As Catherine Peters has noted, Barry's lack of a work ethic is a marker which sets him apart from the middle-class characters of Thackeray's later novels: "The hard-work ethic which Pendennis, Clive, and Phillip all subscribe to is in the end replaced by lies, blackmail and bullying."[44] Barry acquires his aversion to working for a living from his mother, who also inculcates his snobbish, social-climbing manners. Although left penniless and deep in debt by his father, a dissolute adventurer who "supported our illustrious name with credit in London" and died at the racetrack as his "fortune was just on the point of being made," Mrs. Barry moved in with her husband's relatives at Castle Brady where she "ordered the servants to and fro ... and "English Redmond," as [Barry] was called, was treated like a little lord."[45] Her spoiling of Barry develops in him a willfulness which results in his refusing to be educated:

---

[43]   *BL*, 3.

[44]   Peters,Catherine. *Thackeray's Universe: Shifting Worlds of Imagination and Reality.* New York: Oxford University Press, 1987, 115.

[45]   *BL*, 7, 9.

In the matter of book-learning, I had always an uncommon taste for reading plays and novels, as the best part of a gentleman's polite education [but] ... [a]s for your dull grammar, and Greek and Latin and stuff, I would have none of them. This I proved pretty clearly at the age of thirteen, when my aunt Biddy Brady's legacy of 100*l.* came in to Mamma, who thought to employ the sum on my education ... But six weeks later I made my appearance again at Castle Brady ... [having] refused to submit altogether.[46]

Barry's unregulated reading recalls that of Harry Ormond, but unlike Edgeworth's hero he is not reformed by an education in disciplinary domesticity. He considers himself justified in his renunciation of learning, and cites an encounter with Dr. Johnson[47] to support this opinion:

I say this to let parents know the value of [education]; for though I have met more learned bookworms in the world, especially a great hulking, clumsy, bleary-eyed old doctor, whom they call Johnson ... yet I pretty soon silenced him in an argument ... "Sir" said I, in reply to the schoolmaster's great thundering quotation in Greek, "you fancy you know a great deal more than me, because you quote your Aristotle and your Pluto [sic]; but can you tell me which horse will win at Epsom Downs next week?"[48]

His mother acquiesces in his departure from school, and instead of educating Barry for a profession helps him develop the talents to pursue his dissolute and debauched career as an adventurer in the drawing rooms and casinos of the Continent. Barry's education ironically concentrates on typically feminine accomplishments: "Nor was my learning neglected in the ornamental parts ... I had a quick ear and a fine voice, which my mother cultivated to the best of her power, and she taught me to step a minuet gravely and gracefully, and thus laid the foundation of my future success in life."[49]

Mrs. Barry is, in short, the antithesis of normative British domesticity, and nowhere is this theme made more clear than in the description of her vanity and, even more so, in her false piety. She attends church mainly to try to ensnare Lord Bagwig, an elderly earl who Mrs. Barry hopes will soon become a widower. Barry describes her appearance and manners at church with pride:

[C]onsidering the smallness of our income, w[e] kept up a wonderful state. Of the half-dozen families that formed the congregation at Brady's Town, there was not a single person whose appearance was so respectable as that of [my

---

[46]   Ibid., 15–16.

[47]   Johnson was the *éminence grise* of anti-romance in nineteenth-century British culture. The reading of Johnson, for instance, serves as a marker of proper social regulation in contemporary novels such as Gaskell's *Cranford*, and Johnson is the idol of Becky and Amelia's ostentatiously prim and proper schoolmistress in Thackeray's own *Vanity Fair*.

[48]   *BL*, 16–17.

[49]   Ibid., 15.

mother's], who ... took care that her garments should be made so as to set off her handsome person to the greatest advantage; and indeed, I think, spent six hours out of every day in the week in cutting, trimming, and altering them to the fashion.[50]

Barry relates his mother's vain preparations straightforwardly in Thackeray's anti-romance, and beyond the irony of her very unchristian vanity, there is an additional irony in the contrast with the high-flown sentimentality in which female demureness is usually described in romance novels. Barry describes his mother's false humility and ostentatious piety with equally ingenuous candor, and her self-promotion and false piety unmistakably create the diametric opposite of the proper heroine in British novels:

> [We] march[ed] up the aisle with as much state and gravity as a Lord Lieutenant's lady and son might do ... My mother would give the responses and amens in a loud dignified voice ... [and] had a fine loud voice for singing ... you would hardly hear any other voice of the congregation ... In fact, my mother had great gifts in every way, and believed herself to be one of the most beautiful, accomplished, and meritorious persons in the world. Often and often she has talked to me and the neighbours regarding her own humility and piety, pointing them out in such a way that I would defy the most obstinate to disbelieve her.[51]

In his discussion of *Waverley*, Ian Duncan notes that "the logic of [the Victorians'] admiration [of Scott's female characters] converted the strong into the weak heroine precisely around the axis of her purity, and female strength into a demonic force."[52] Barry's mother reverses this formulation: she is a figure of female strength who raises Barry without a husband or (after their brief stay with relatives at Castle Brady) material resources, and inverts the traditional Victorian heroine's modesty and purity. As noted in a previous chapter, in *Chartism* Carlyle had warned that the Irish had been reduced to savagery owing to short-sighted British colonial policy, and as a result of this policy now were coming into England in hordes. Thackeray's novel depicts Irish anti-domesticity as a hallmark of this savagery, as well as the chief element which reproduces it.

---

[50] Ibid., 12.

[51] Ibid., 13.

[52] Duncan, op. cit., 70–71.

Chapter 8
A Comic Plot with a Tragic Ending:
The Macdermots of Ballycloran

Trollope and Ireland

There is a certain continuity in the development of liberal British cultural nationalism observable by moving from Thackeray's *Barry Lyndon* to Anthony Trollope's novel *The Macdermots of Ballycloran* (1847). Trollope, who published a biography of Thackeray, admired and was influenced by him, claiming in his *Autobiography* that "I myself regard [*Henry*] *Esmond* as the greatest novel in the English language."[1] Like Thackeray, Trollope engaged romance in the depiction of Ireland for the purpose of highlighting historical developments and cultural assumptions. The two men were also friends, and both had connections with and a sympathy for Ireland and its people. However, this sympathy was not without limits. After the Famine, Trollope's increasingly pessimistic attitudes regarding the possibility of Irish assimilation into the British social body followed a trajectory of development similar to Thackeray's increasing negativity when the latter was confronted with what he saw as "intransigence" in Irish expressions of nationalism. It would be a mistake, however, to regard their distaste for Irish nationalism as necessarily, or excessively, hidebound or reactionary. If in the twenty-first century we regard the Irish republic as an inevitability, in the mid-nineteenth century it was anything but. In particular, in the years leading up to the Famine these writers imagined a Britain that included Ireland, and if in those visions is recorded an Irish difference which rendered assimilation problematic, difference is something which Irish nationalists insisted upon as well.

Although there are similarities in the two writers' early recognition of the impact of historical contingency on the difficulties of assimilating the Irish into the British body politic, there is a great deal of difference in the ways in which each writer records the deteriorating prospects of a fruitful and harmonious Union. *Barry Lyndon* offers an honest and straightforward statement of the causes and effects of the problem of assimilation, but does not imagine a remedy. By the end of the 1840s Thackeray imagines, in *Pendennis*, a Great Britain in which the ethnic Gaelic Irish are largely marginalized. More importantly, the narrative of Pen's renunciation of Emily encodes a justification for that exclusion – the Costigans "weren't made" to inhabit the same sphere as the Pendennises. Early in his career Trollope recorded the material causes of Irish social problems, and expressed

---

[1]   Trollope, Anthony. *An Autobiography* (1883). Oxford: Oxford University Press, 1980, 186.

the gradual diminishment of Irish difference (or, at least, the alienating effects of that difference) as something which could be accomplished by education and mutual efforts to ameliorate the causes of social displacement in *The Macdermots of Ballycloran*. Here Trollope echoes Lady Morgan in attributing a large part of Irish misery to colonial policy, with a suggested remedy of rapprochement through education that also is very different from Edgeworth's regime of domestic discipline.

Trollope's fiction offers interesting parallels with that of Thackeray, as well as connections with other British writers of "Irish" novels. Like Thackeray, he reworks in *The Macdermots of Ballycloran* the motifs and conventions of the national tale tradition in order to offer his own comment upon conditions in Ireland, where he began his long career as a Postal Surveyor in late 1841, not returning to reside permanently in England until December, 1859. His extended stay gave him deep insights into what in his fiction emerges as the most significant problem confronting a harmonious and productive Union between the two nations: the difficulty of assimilating into one body politic two peoples with very different histories and a long and troubled colonial relationship.

The Macdermots portrays the inability of the of Irish to assimilate as something which arises from each side's ignorance, or lack of education. A lack of political, economic, and social education prevents Irish entry into the British middle class. As in other representations of the Irish, the class conflict in *The Macdermots* is displaced in part onto a sexual conflict. While the heroine of this novel lacks a proper domestic education, Trollope also emphasizes the absence of a strong or responsible authority within the social structure he regards as necessary to rehabilitate her. And this absence, which is replicated in the social and economic realms as well – there is no responsible structure whatsoever, much less Burke's sacred polity – is central to the problem of assimilation in Trollope's vision. There exists in place of this authority a power structure whose representatives exploit, rather than regulate, the social order. This corrupt local authority is assisted by what might be termed a willful ignorance of the true nature of Irish political, economic and social conditions on the part of the "superior" partner in Union. In order to avoid addressing the true causes of economic and social disaffection, those in positions of power misrepresent or allow to be misrepresented the effects of those causes as strictly "political" discontent and violence, as the imperial government stands aloof and allows the adventuring to go on unchecked. With an unmistakable increase in severity over the course of his writing career, Trollope condemns the British for the continued failure to address this ignorance, and even more so for having entered into a Union "conceived" as unequal – in either the word's signification "begun, given life," or "imagined." His condemnation takes the form of a marriage plot rewritten as a seduction plot, featuring male heroes with explicitly dishonorable intentions, preying upon ignorant and vulnerable heroines.

The fictional project described here, as in the case of Thackeray, is augmented by some direct statements from the author in the public press (but to a lesser extent – Thackeray, unlike Trollope, made his living as a journalist as well as novelist). Trollope wrote a series of letters to the *Examiner* over the course of the year 1850 in which he sought to counteract what he saw as a distorted representation of Ireland in the British press. In these letters he decried the press's focus upon threats to landlords and merchants and accounts of mob violence, and its simultaneous exploitation of religious and class differences which resulted in understating the poor's distress. In one letter, dated June 15, 1850, Trollope denies an Irish predilection to political violence, while at the same time characterizing the "Irish temperament" as both susceptible to political agitators and pliable to a firm and responsible social regulation that the Empire should provide: "I do assert that the Irish are not a people naturally prone to political excitement. They are a passive, long-suffering people, personally indifferent to those principles to which the English attach so much importance; they are on that account the more inclined to follow implicitly the guidance of a master, and to submit in all things to command."[2] This characterization is of course a sweeping generalization, but not only is the temperament described here represented with a great deal of consistency in the characters of Thady and Feemy Macdermot (and in Kate O'Hara and her mother in *An Eye for an Eye*), but the "guidance of the master" is portrayed as wholly corrupt.

The Seduction Plot

As Thackeray had done in *Barry Lyndon*, Trollope engages Irish national tales in his first novel, *The Macdermots of Ballycloran*. The novel encapsulates Irish history in the story of a single family and recalls, but complicates, the comic ending of Lady Morgan's *Wild Irish Girl*. Trollope offers almost anthropological descriptions of people and customs in order to offset romantic representations of Ireland, following Edgeworth. He depicts a multi-layered society whose structure is responsible for the country's social and economic ills, echoing Lady Morgan's *Florence McCarthy*. Unlike any of his predecessors, however, Trollope eschews satire or a comic ending, and instead presents the events of the novel and their consequences in a tragic mode that anticipates the novels of Thomas Hardy. Trollope intertwines the themes of education, class, and domesticity in a way which at once recalls and departs from the national tales, in order to depict a society which is alienated from the rest of the British nation by identifiable and remediable circumstances.

The novel centers on the story of Thady Macdermot, who struggles against a rapacious landlord conniving to dispossess him and a Constabulary officer who is attempting to seduce his sister, all the while unable to collect the rents due him from tenants trying to eke out subsistence from plots on a "half-reclaimed bog." The "marriage" plot of Captain Ussher and Feemy Macdermot rewrites the comic resolution of the national tales as the seduction of an ignorant and defenseless girl, and ends in the death of both lovers, imagining a bitter possibility for Union.

---

[2]   Quoted in Dunleavy, Janet Egleson. "Trollope and Ireland," in *Trollope Centenary Essays*, ed. John Halperin. New York: St Martin's, 1982, 59.

The fate of Thady, who is hanged for Ussher's murder, figures the death of a middling class of Irish not violently disposed against the power structure, but driven by circumstances to strike out against it. These circumstances include the wretched conditions resulting from British colonial policy, as well as the harsh practices of unscrupulous land agents and a court system which represents the landed interests. The tragedy results from misunderstandings on both sides. Trollope's first novel might thus be regarded as a cautionary tale.

The Macdermots are a decayed family of Irish gentry who, at a point of former glory, built a house, which is now falling down around them. Trollope, in opening the novel with a description of their house, invokes a classic literary convention in which the country manor serves as a symbol of the larger society, in this case the Irish nation. In describing the house through the eyes of an English traveler who has taken a walk after dining at his hotel, Trollope directly evokes the opening of *The Wild Irish Girl* and its hero Horatio. Lady Morgan's novel itself was patterned in part on the Gothic romances of Radcliffe and others, in which ruin and decay allegorize a society whose forms and structures belong to an older culture and regime. The corrupt patriarchal authority and social institutions represented in these novels, usually depicted in the genre's depraved monks and aristocrats, are often located in Southern, Catholic Europe. The Gothic setting represents a cultural landscape that threatens to imprison and defile the heroine, but she is usually rescued by an emotionally sensitive male who represents the enlightened sensibilities and recuperated, benevolent paternal authority of modern metropolitan imperial culture. In *The Macdermots*, the living presence of Irish history encoded is as yet unchanged. Ireland's social structure – so corrupt it is characterized as criminal – is rotting, despite the relatively recent appearance of the British lion at the door, in Trollope's heavily symbolic description: "The entire roof was off; one could see the rotting joists and beams, some fallen, some falling, the rest about to fall, like the skeleton of a felon left to rot on an open gibbet ... The knocker was still on the door, – a modern lion-headed knocker."[3]

The romantic traveler's description intensifies the Gothic resonances of the scene, and at the same time directly ascribes the effects he views not to nature, but to historical circumstance: "I sat ... and meditated on this characteristic specimen of Irish life. The sun was setting beautifully behind the trees, and its imperfect light through the foliage gave the *unnatural ruin* a still stronger appearance of death and decay, and brought into my mind thoughts of the wrong, oppression, misery, and despair, to which someone had been subjected (italics added)."[4] The phrase "characteristic specimen of Irish life" clearly signals the metaphoric value of the house, and by extension the family which inhabits it, and the phraseology "unnatural ruin" emphasizes Trollope's point that the deterioration of this society is entirely a result of man-made causes. By these means Trollope makes evident that his novel

    [3]   *The Macdermots of Ballycloran* (1847). New York: Dover, 1988, 2. Hereafter referred to as *MOB*.

    [4]   *MOB*, 3.

encodes Irish colonial history, and it does so from the Elizabethan settlements through the 1830s, the time at which the main action of the novel is set.

Although Trollope opens his novel by utilizing Gothic motifs, he quickly shifts from the limited perspective of an unfamiliar wanderer to an omniscient narrator who explicitly attributes the characters' social and economic condition to the events of history.[5] Moreover, the events are depicted in historical time; however, the march of this history leads not to ever-uplifting progress, but directly to a disaster. The omniscient narration begins by allegorizing Irish history in a manner similar to that which will be used by Thackeray to record British public history in the private account of the Pendennis family. The narrator begins his tale by invoking Walter Scott's prototypical historical novel, *Waverley; or, 'Tis Sixty Years Since*:

> About sixty years ago, a something Macdermot, true Milesian, pious Catholic, and descendant of king somebody, died somewhere, having managed, through all the troubles of his poor country, to keep a comfortable portion of his ancestor's royalties ... He having two sons ... made over to them in some fictitious manner (for in those righteous days a Roman Catholic could make no legal will) to his eldest, the estate on which he lived, and to the youngest, that of Ballycloran – about six hundred as bad acres as a gentleman might wish to call his own.[6]

In this way Trollope records, as had Lady Morgan, the displacements onto unproductive lands and disabilities to which the Gaelic Irish were subjected (although he attempts to mitigate or perhaps create a sense of irony here by the assertion that "a comfortable portion" of the patrimony was retained, a claim the Gaelic Irish would dispute). He also makes direct reference to the continuing problems presented by the historical displacements of such landowners as "the fruitless endeavour to make his tenants pay thirty shillings an acre for half-reclaimed bog."[7] In describing the struggles of the hero's grandfather (also named Thady) and his father Larry, Trollope allegorically encodes British claims to any valuable Irish property: "Thady [the elder] got himself a wife with two thousand pounds fortune, for which he had to go to law with his brother-in-law. The lawsuit, the continual necessity for renewing the bills ... and a somewhat strongly developed aptitude for poteen, sent poor Thady to another world prematurely, and his son and heir, Lawrence, came to the throne at the tender age of twelve."[8] The "continual necessity for renewing the bills" may be a reference to the "tithe wars" of the 1830s, which gave rise to considerable Irish disaffection.[9] Larry, as representative

---

[5]   The shift in narrative voice is noted by F.W. Wittig in his essay "Trollope's Irish Fiction," *Eire-Ireland* 9:3, 101–2.

[6]   *MOB*, 4–5.

[7]   Ibid., 5.

[8]   Ibid.

[9]   "Tithe wars" was the name for the contention over mandatory Irish financial support of the Church of Ireland in the form of tithes, in effect a burdensome tax to support a church

of the family, also represents Ireland's middling classes, and his ascension to "the throne" at an immature age figures Ireland's entrance into a partnership between "two unequally advanced countries."

But Trollope is not uncritical of the Irish themselves, as Thady the elder's self-destructiveness, evidenced in his "somewhat strongly developed aptitude for poteen," gives proof. Larry is offered a lucrative alliance with the daughter of the builder of his house, but refuses it out of pride: "The builder from Carrick had made overtures about a daughter he had at home, and offered poor Larry his own house, as her fortune. But the blood of the Macdermots could not mix with the lime and water that flowed in the builder's veins; he therefore made an enemy where he most wanted a friend."[10] Larry's refusal to mix his blood with the lime and water in the builder's veins make clear reference to the failure to form a large and inclusive professional-gentry class similar to that in Britain which prefigured the emergence of the dominant middle class. In Ireland, the commercial middling class was comprised mostly of Anglo-Irish tradesmen, estate agents, and small landowners, with whom the Gaelic Irish had what can best be described as a troubled relationship – the Crawleys of *Florence McCarthy* are a memorable depiction of this class. So while Larry's refusal to join the middle class evinces a stiff-necked pride, Trollope suggests through the family's disputes with the builder that Irish pride was also in part a response to previous dealings in which the Gaelic Irish received less than fair treatment. The refusal to enter into what the novel represents as a familial relationship is predicated by a mutual distrust which under existing conditions cannot or will not be overcome:

> Mr Macdermot thus regarded his creditor as a vulgar, low-born blood-sucker, who, having by chicanery obtained an unwarrantable hold over him, was determined, if possible, to crush him. The builder, on the other hand, who had spent a long life of constant industry, but doubtful honesty, in scraping up a decent fortune, looked on his debtor as one who gave himself airs to which his poverty did not entitle him; and was determined to make him feel that though he could not be the father, he could be the master of a "rale gintleman."[11]

Larry's obstinacy is born of ignorance, and Trollope represents Irish resistance or failure to create a British-type middle class as the product of this ignorance, of not only how to secure their own best interests, but also what those interests are. While the Unionist Trollope is a critic of, rather than an apologist for Union,

---

to which only a small percentage of the mostly Roman Catholic population belonged. Tithes were collected every year until the passage of the Tithe Act in 1838, by which the onerous yearly tribute was commuted to a once-for-all rent charge and reduced by one quarter. See Foster (1988), pp. 309–10. Trollope's reluctance to represent the issue directly in 1847 may be explained by his view that the question was extraordinarily complex and difficult, as again evidenced by his brief allusion to the Tithe question in *Phineas Finn* (1869), published more than 20 years after *The Macdermots*. See Chapter 1.

    [10]   *MOB*, 5.
    [11]   Ibid., 9.

he nevertheless betrays an assumption of Irish inferiority in the depth with which he portrays Irish childlike ignorance in an otherwise sympathetic and insightful work. From an Irish nationalist point of view, this assumption is condescending in the extreme; Irish interests regarded in this light are clearly best served by the restoration of the rights, privileges and benefits which attend autonomy (to say nothing of the benefits restoration of confiscated lands would produce). Trollope's assumption of Irish inferiority (which is explicitly enunciated in his letter to the *Examiner* quoted above) is also present to a degree in Thady's inability to recognize his sister's danger until being informed of it by the priest. Recanting Gaelic Irish furthermore are represented as the as the chief villains of *The Macdermots* in the characters of Ussher, Hyacinth Keegan and his paid Catholic spies, and, to a lesser extent, Jonas Brown. This recalls Edgeworth's portrayal of Ulick O'Shane, another grasping convert whose policies represented a corrupt social order. While Catholics did enjoy increasing political and social power in the 1830s, this power was strictly circumscribed. Firstly, the Catholic Emancipation Act of 1829 actually disenfranchised many Catholics by raising the franchise from forty shillings to ten pounds. Catholics were moreover confronted with what R.F. Foster calls "the blatant continuation of many Protestant monopolies – in the civil service, the legal profession, and most of all local government ... the sense of an underlying alienation continued as a theme of rural life up to the 1830s."[12] While there were indeed cases of persons converting for the purpose of attaining professional or political advancement, these converts in no way dominated the professions, judicial system, or government. In fact, the phenomenon was relatively rare, owing to the social ostracism of recanters by Catholics and Protestants alike – a fact borne out by virtually all fictional representations of them from the period. Thus, Trollope's portrayal of oppression as a largely Gaelic-on-Gaelic phenomenon supported by the British power structure is somewhat misleading.

In fairness to Trollope, he forthrightly attributes the ignorance of his Irish characters to the deprivation, both material and cultural, that resulted from British colonial policies, policies which he just as straightforwardly represents. From his position as a loyal subject of the British Empire, his portrayal of the problems attending Irish assimilation, and even more his depiction of the causes of those problems, are both candid and realistic. His belief that Ireland benefited from its association with Britain was sincere, as was his evident hope that those benefits would continue to increase. He states in his *Autobiography*, written in 1883, that improvements in the standard of living since his arrival in 1841 are demonstrable: "I have sometimes wondered at the obduracy with which some people have spoken of the permanent ill condition of the country. Wages are now nearly double what they were then ... Banks have sprung up in almost every village. Rents are paid with more than English punctuality. And the religious enmity between the classes,

---

[12]   Foster. "Ascendancy and Union," in *The Oxford History of Ireland.* New York: Oxford University Press, 1989, op. cit., 156. Trollope himself came to Ireland to fill a job many Catholics presumably could have.

though it is not yet dead, is dying out."[13] Trollope believed that the suffering and privation of large numbers of people, though not eradicated, had been diminished, and his desire to share the benefits of the British citizenship which he felt himself fortunate to enjoy is a laudable sentiment; also laudable is his willingness both to admit that the nation of which he was so proud deprived the Irish of those benefits, and to seek to redress that injustice.[14] This was a willingness not shared by all of his fellow Britons. The Irish in *The Macdermots of Ballycloran*, like the real Irish people he met as a civil servant in the employ of the imperial government, are British subjects but, through dint of circumstances, do not enjoy full access to the British middle class. *The Macdermots*, considered as Trollope's exploration of a serious problem confronting his nation, seeks to be both pragmatic and humane.

Trollope portrays Irish ignorance as one of the chief obstacles to Irish assimilation throughout *The Macdermots*; he furthermore attributes this ignorance not to any inherent racial inferiority, but to a lack of adequate education afforded to the Irish under the colonial social dispensation. Thady's lack of education deprives him of the ability to attain a profession or properly manage his estates, and ultimately to protect Feemy from the advances of Ussher. Feemy's lack of education in domestic discipline makes her Ussher's easy prey. But Trollope addresses the British lack of education about Irish conditions as well. In *Florence McCarthy* Lady Morgan portrayed ruling and middling classes who misrepresented economic dissatisfaction as "rebellion" for the purpose of consolidating and furthering their own interests. Trollope engages in a similar project. In the denouement, Thady Macdermot is hanged for murdering Captain Ussher, head of the local constabulary and thus a member of government whom many of the Irish find particularly obnoxious for his zealous pursuit of illegal poteen distillers (he also hypocritically partakes of the illegal brew himself and allows his friends to drink it unmolested). However, Thady's act of violence was committed in the heat of passion in defense of his sister, who appeared to him as though she was being abducted by Ussher while she was unconscious. The chief witness against him, a spy in the pay of an unscrupulous land agent hoping to take over the Macdermot property, characterizes the deed as politically-motivated violence to the authorities, and Thady is convicted. To his judges, Ussher's murder represents an Irish rejection of the rule of law. Trollope's exposition of the true causes for Thady's act and its consequences constitute the didactic purpose of the novel. The novel attempts to educate the English reader

---

[13]   *Autobiography*, op. cit., 72.

[14]   Foster asserts that Trollope's belief that the Irish could indeed be fully assimilated into the British body politic is evidenced by his creation of the character Phineas Finn: "Trollope's Irish politics meant that he had to believe that Union worked – as it had triumphantly worked for him. Hence the choice of an Irish hero for his Parliamentary series of novels: the implicit message was that the Irish could be insiders too" (*Paddy and Mr Punch: Connections in Irish and English History*. London: Penguin, 1993, 145). However, if this message truly is implicit, it conflicts with other strong implications in the novel, as I discuss briefly in Chapter 1.

about the realities of Irish life, and to erase misconceptions about the real causes of Irish disaffection, in order that those causes might be eliminated.

Robert Tracy asserts that Larry Macdermot, the thoroughly broken-down patriarch of the clan, is a "revised version of Lady Morgan's proud and reclusive Prince in his ruined castle," and that the "learned and accomplished Glorvina ... is revised into the slatternly 'Princess' of Ballycloran, Feemy Macdermot."[15] While the comparison with the landlord who has been reduced to drunken inertia and madness leaves out a significant portion of the culture and history represented by the noble, learned and *distingué* Prince of Inismore, Trollope was indeed rewriting the marriage plot which figures Anglo-Irish Union, and invoking Lady Morgan's prototypical heroine. "Feemy" is a nickname for Euphemia, a name taken from the Greek *euphemos*, or "fair of speech." This is an oblique reference to Glorvina, whose name in Irish can be translated as "fair of voice." Trollope's description of Feemy makes the connection even more explicit: "Euphemia, or Feemy, was ... a tall, dark girl, with that bold, upright, well-poised figure that is so peculiarly Irish. She walked as if the blood of all the old Irish Princes was in her veins."[16]

However, Trollope immediately complicates the representation of nationhood in the female protagonist: "[S]he had a well-formed nose, as all coming of old families have; and a bright olive complexion, only the olive was a little too brown, the skin a little too coarse; and then, Feemy's mouth was, oh! Half an inch too long!"[17] There is more at work here than simple caricature. The narrator asserts that it is both poverty and lack of familiarity with imperial metropolitan culture which produce the characteristics in Feemy that Tracy describes as "slatternly": "In all, Feemy was a fine girl in eyes not too much accustomed to refinement ... though Feemy had as fine a leg as ever bore a pretty girl, she was never well shod, – her shoes were seldom clean, often slipshod, usually in holes ... But if the beautiful girls of this poor country knew but half the charms which neatness has, they would not so often appear as poor Feemy too usually appeared."[18] In describing the holes in Feemy's shoes and stockings Trollope calls attention to her poverty, which, however, he describes as no obstacle to her attractiveness: "No girls know better how to dress themselves than Irish girls, or can do it with less assistance or less expense."[19]

Her poverty does, however, relegate her to a life in which she has no access to or communication with the larger British society. Trollope makes clear that it is a lack of experience and education, of both Feemy and her family, which induce her to enter an unequal and personally disastrous alliance with Captain Ussher: "She would have been a fine creature had she been educated, but she

---

[15]   "'The 'Unnatural Ruin': Trollope and Nineteenth-Century Fiction," *Nineteenth-Century Fiction* 37:3 (December 1982), 366.

[16]   *MOB*, 6.

[17]   Ibid.

[18]   Ibid., 7.

[19]   Ibid., 61.

had not been educated…she did not know how to use what God had given her, and therefore, abused it."[20] Feemy's lack of education, particularly in that of domesticity, is perhaps the most significant factor contributing to the tragic ending of the marriage plot. Trollope attributes her downfall, as well as her brother's inability to save her from it, to this cause. What constitutes her education in this novel is the familiar motif of unregulated reading, recalling among others Barry Lyndon and the young Harry Ormond: "she was addicted to novels."[21] Captain Ussher, as the highest-ranking officer of the local Constabulary, represents the official Anglo-Irish power structure, and to Feemy "had all the chief ornaments of her novel heroes – he was handsome, he carried arms, was a man of danger, and talked of deeds of courage."[22] Trollope condemns the Ascendancy subtly and symbolically, but thoroughly in his description of the villain's background: Ussher is the "illegitimate son of a gentleman of large property ... and tolerably well-educated."[23] The sexual impropriety of their relationship is hinted immediately: "[P]eople had for some time been saying that he meant to marry Feemy. They now began to say that he ought to do so."[24] Ussher indeed promises to wed Feemy, but uses this promise to take advantage of her sexually: "Then he first told her she would be his wife ... and she had given all she had – her heart, her love, her obedience, her very soul – to him, without having any guarantee that she really had aught in return."[25] Although their sexual union is cloaked here in obscurantist language typical of Victorian novels, there is no mistaking its true nature when Feemy becomes pregnant. Despite his protestations to Feemy, however, Ussher has no real plans to marry her, as he reveals on numerous occasions: "[H]e could not decide what to do ... the only conclusion to which he could bring himself with certainty was this – that nothing should induce him to marry her."[26] Her naivety proves her undoing. In response to Thady's questions about whether she has ascertained Ussher's intentions in light of the seriousness of the relationship, which he can only guess at, she responds : "Oh heavens, Thady, sure we're to be married."[27] But in describing the enticements of a match with Ussher, the narrator makes clear that Feemy is incapable of negotiating an alliance in which her partner would be compelled to behave responsibly toward her: "He certainly did not intend to marry the poor girl; had she sufficient tact, she might, perhaps, have persuaded him to do so; but her fervent love and perfect confidence, though very gratifying to his vanity, did not inspire him with that feeling of respect with which any man would wish to have for the girl he was going to marry."[28]

---

20   Ibid., 37–8.
21   Ibid., 7.
22   Ibid., 17.
23   Ibid., 16.
24   Ibid., 14.
25   Ibid., 42–3.
26   Ibid., 164.
27   Ibid., 48.
28   Ibid., 141

Instead of marrying Feemy, Ussher persuades her to run off with him by means of threats and blandishments which allegorize the bribery and intimidation that paved the way for the 1801 passage of the Act of Union, against which Edgeworth had often complained. Feemy relents, despite her reservations: "At last he told her, somewhat roughly, that if she would not come with him in the manner he proposed, he would leave her forever ... [O]ld feelings, principles, religious scruples, the love of honour and fair fame, and the fear of the world's harsh word, were sorely fighting in her bosom ... Then he stooped to lift her up, and as he kissed the tears from her face, passion prevailed, and she whispered in his ear she would go."[29] Trollope here encodes what he describes in his *Autobiography* as "the treachery of the Union."[30] Ussher's mixture of coercion and cajolement recalls the notorious methods used by the Pitt government to induce the Irish Parliament to support the Act of Union. The Irish Parliament, under the leadership of Henry Grattan, had originally rejected the proposal by a narrow margin in January 1799. The Chief Secretary for Ireland, Lord Castlereagh, ordered those MPs with positions in government to support the Union or resign, while others were given jobs or aristocratic titles in exchange for support of the Act. Many seats changed hands as the government bought out opponents, and when the Parliament met in January of 1800 the measure passed, despite a moving appeal for its defeat by Grattan. The British Parliament passed the measure later that year, and the Act went into effect on January 1, 1801.[31] The two nations were thus joined in Union despite the opposition of Ireland's dominant political party (Grattan's Patriot Party) and the failure of the Act to address the most pressing issues facing the great majority of the populace, including tithe and education reform, relief for the poor, and removal of the Catholic (and to a lesser extent, Dissenter) disabilities. Many Patriot members of the Irish Parliament, including Maria Edgeworth's father, resigned in disgust. Thus Union was conceived in less than honorable conditions, and measures to ensure the responsible behavior of the stronger and protection of the weaker partners were avoided.[32]

Feemy is too ignorant and weak to protect herself from Ussher's dishonorable scheme, and likewise she has no one else to protect her. At the moment of her sexual surrender to Ussher, the narrator informs us that "there was no one to whisper caution to Feemy."[33] Her father has been reduced to a drunken, paranoid recluse (although his paranoia does not signify, as the saying goes, that no one is out to get him), and her nominal protector is her brother Thady. As a small landowner,

---

[29]   Ibid., 167.

[30]   *Autobiography*, op. cit., 73.

[31]   See Flanagan, Foster, et al.

[32]   As mentioned in a previous chapter, Pitt had promised the removal of some Catholic disabilities, including eligibility to hold administrative and legal positions, but when these proved impossible to effect (owing in large part to opposition from King George III, who believed among other things that approving these measures constituted an abdication of his responsibilities as Defender of the Faith) Pitt resigned as a point of honor.

[33]   *MOB*, 43.

he stands as an Irish counterpart to the British property owners and professionals who comprise the nation's dominant, or middle class. But unlike fictional British representatives of that class such as Arthur Pendennis, there is no structure in place to train him in the exercise of an idealized, responsible masculine authority. Thady, whose name recalls the narrator of Edgeworth's *Castle Rackrent*, has been ill prepared for effective participation in the rule of Ireland. His education and experience poorly equip him to confront the long-standing and complex problems he faces: "As had been the case with his father, he had been educated at a country school; he could read and write, but do little more: he was brought up to no profession or business; he acted as his father's agent over the property – by which I mean to signify that he occupied himself in harrowing the tenantry for money which they had no means of paying."[34] This unfitness to rule is further allegorized as an inability to exercise effective guidance over his family. When he becomes aware of Captain Ussher's advances towards Feemy, he is thoroughly unequipped to protect her: "[T]hough he would let no one injure Feemy if he could help it, he hardly knew how effectually to protect her."[35] His efforts to save Feemy from the dangers she faces, taken in any case too late to be of use (she is already pregnant), are awkward and unavailing, and the narrator emphasizes how ill-prepared he is to exert any authority:

> He certainly appeared but a sorry Mentor for a young lady in a love affair! ... He had come [to Feemy] with two high feelings, love for his sister ... and love and respect for his family name; he had wished to protect the former from insult and unhappiness; and to sustain the fallen respectability of the latter ... He was not aware how very uncouth his own manner had been ... At any rate, there he stood perfectly baffled.[36]

When Ussher and Feemy prepare to abscond, Feemy symbolically loses consciousness. Though she had agreed to accompany him as his mistress, Thady observes what at first appears to be a theft of property, and then the forceful abduction of his sister:

> It was Thady's idea that something had been stolen from the yard, which the thief was now removing, under cover of the darkness. By degrees, as he got nearer, he perceived it was a woman's form that the man was half dragging, half carrying, and then he heard Ussher's voice say loudly, and somewhat angrily, This is d – d nonsense, Feemy! You know you must come now." [37]

Thady's perception of theft or abduction accurately reflects the reaction of a significant portion of Ireland's population, from varying political backgrounds, to the "treachery" of Union. When Ussher hears Thady's footsteps behind him

---

[34]   Ibid., 6.
[35]   Ibid., 17–18.
[36]   Ibid., 49, 50.
[37]   Ibid., 216.

he drops the still insensible Feemy to the ground, but at the same instant is struck dead by Thady with a blow from his shillelagh. Feemy soon dies while Thady awaits trial in prison, and thus ends the marriage plot.

Striking at the Corrupt Power Structure, not Union

Although the Macdermots represent Ireland in microcosm, Trollope provides alternative models to the social structure that produced them. Like Edgeworth, he presents examples of good and bad landlords in Counsellor Webb and Jonas Brown. Webb is "kindhearted ... [and] ever anxious to ameliorate the condition of the poor,"[38] while, significantly, Brown's formula for maintaining his own power over the peasantry is to keep them in ignorance: "He ... was actuated by the most superlative contempt for the poor, from whom he drew his whole income. He was a clever, clear-headed, avaricious man; and he knew that the only means of keeping the peasantry in their present utterly helpless and dependent state, was to deny them education ... He dreaded any movement intended to teach them anything."[39] But in contrast to Edgeworthian characters such as Mrs Rafferty in *The Absentee*, Trollope offers a positive representation of a Gaelic, Catholic family from the commercial classes. At the heart of the novel is a chapter describing the McKeons, a middle-class Catholic family who represent the domestic ideal. Mrs. McKeon is enlisted by the parish priest to aid Feemy and protect her from Ussher (albeit, as in the case of Thady, too late; she is already pregnant, a fact which the other characters only ascertain at the end of the novel). Unfortunately, in the thirty-five years intervening between the representations of Mrs. Rafferty and Mrs. McKeon, prosperous Catholic families from the merchant classes remained rare enough in Ireland to perpetuate their relegation to the status of peripheral characters in novels depicting national life.

The character who embodies the Gaelic cultural ideal in *The Macdermots of Ballycloran* is instead the local parish priest, Father John McGrath. While he can hardly be said to represent a middle-class ideal in light of his priestly vow of poverty, he nevertheless personifies the virtues of wisdom, kindness, and sympathy to which the middle class characters Thady and Mrs. McKeon aspire. Although prone to good-natured teasing of his parishioners from time to time, he always offers them kind and wise advice, and discerns their problems with empathetic, nonjudgmental understanding. He has been educated in a manner unavailable to his flock absent a priestly vocation, however, and though Thady and Mrs. McKeon seek his direction when he points out to them Feemy's need of their aid, they had both been unequipped to recognize her danger or know what actions to take. Father John has been educated at the seminary at St Omer, in France, "and afterwards at Paris," and had "seen more of French manners and customs

---

[38]   Ibid., 264.
[39]   Ibid., 263.

than usually falls to the lot of Irish theological students."[40] Thus his education has availed him access to the unified metropolitan culture of Western Europe. It is this education and experience of metropolitan culture which set him apart from all the Irish characters of the middling classes in the novel. Trollope suggests that were a similar education afforded to ordinary Irish, the prospects for assimilation would be greatly improved. Although Father John has some character defects, such as his poor housekeeping skills and inability to properly manage his personal finances, these liabilities are dismissed by the narrator as insignificant, and moreover ascribed to that familiar marker of Irishness in British fiction, childish improvidence: "With all his acquirements, however, in many things Father John was little better than a child ... Though his zeal had enabled him to raise money for the church, he could never keep any of his own; he had always his little difficulties."[41] Father John's childishness accords with the stereotype Trollope enunciated in his letter to the *Examiner*, and if anything, would make him more likely to "submit in all things to command" to the senior partner in Trollope's imagined Union. Father John's attractiveness as a junior partner is impressed on the reader the more strongly through the contrast of him with Father Cullen, his curate.[42] Cullen has been educated at the Irish seminary at Maynooth, and is a thorough nationalist bigot – narrow-minded, provincial, prejudiced, and uncouth – in other words, the exact opposite of the fastidious, cultured, and empathetic Father John. *The Macdermots* thus offers a clear choice: properly educate the Irish to develop their qualities of sympathy, good humor, and personal neatness, and create a nation of conciliating Father McGraths, or provide them with a circumscribed education, limit their means and create a nation of rabble-rousing Father Cullens.

The narrative insists however that the rabble-rousing element is as yet a marginal presence in Irish society, despite sensationalist representations in the British press. Thady's act of violence is portrayed to the authorities, despite evidence to the contrary, as a political assassination perpetrated for the benefit of the local Ribbonmen, "Ribbonmen" was a term used indiscriminately to refer to the Catholic agrarian secret societies with vague aspirations to rid Ireland of the Protestant religion and British government. The movement was in fact mostly urban in origin, a small fringe of the small Irish working class, but as Trollope's use of the term in this novel suggests, it became a catch-all name for nationalist groups of the lower classes.[43] The few associated with the local group in *The Macdermots* exist lawlessly on the fringes of society, but enjoy some support

---

[40]   Ibid., 24.

[41]   Ibid., 24.

[42]   The name Cullen is perhaps a reference to the Rev. Paul Cullen, who later became Archbishop of Dublin and the first Irish Cardinal. Cullen, though opposed to Fenianism, nevertheless had strong associations with Catholic nationalism, and as rector of the Propaganda College at Rome sought to counteract British influence with the Vatican.

[43]   See M.R. Beames, "The Ribbon Societies: Lower-class Nationalism in Pre-famine Ireland," *Past and Present* 92 (1982), 157–71; also Foster (1988), 291–9, et al.

from their neighbors (much of it for their poteen production and opposition to the still-hunting revenue police); however, the majority of the characters in the novel have little to do with them. Trollope depicts a long-suffering middle-class Ireland which reluctantly entertains ideas of nationalism only because driven to extremity. Thady's murder of Ussher encodes a spontaneous strike against the corrupt power structure, not a repudiation of Union.

Trollope represents Ireland's continued misery, as had Lady Morgan, as largely a product of its legal and economic structures, which act in concert to the detriment of the great majority of the population and the benefit of a privileged few. He is careful to show that Thady's prosecution is conducted by the British government. This accurately reflects a British colonial presence which loomed large in 1830s Ireland. R.F. Foster describes the visible trappings of this power as including "the viceroy presiding over ... [the] court at Dublin Castle ... the appurtenances of a large army establishment, [a newly expanded, paramilitary] professional police force, and the dominating presence of solidly-built barracks in most provincial towns."[44] Moreover, the unjust verdict rendered to Thady is improperly influenced by the judge – at the trial the judge instructs the jury to disregard testimony which would exonerate Thady of capital murder. But Trollope records not only the utilization by corrupt officials of the power of the imperial government to maintain their position. He also attacks one of the chief distortions of which he complained in his letters to the *Examiner*, which he has contradicted throughout the narrative. Political violence in the narrative is confined to an extremist element within the lower classes, and not widespread, as its sensationalist coverage in the British press would suggest. This message is confirmed by the findings of modern historians.[45] The implication is clear enough – if the nation's real economic problems are not meaningfully addressed, disaffection is likely to increase, and formerly patient Irishmen like Thady may indeed resort to violence on a wide scale. Trollope represents a corrupt legal system which uses pre-emptive intimidation to prevent such developments. With the death of Thady, the younger generation of the Macdermot clan is wiped out. Thady's patience, combined with his untutored and thus ineffective industry, has availed him nothing, and Feemy's willingness to accommodate an irresponsible partner has destroyed herself and her unborn child. Trollope's allegory of the destruction of Union is portrayed mournfully, as an extinction, yet one that can still be avoided.

---

[44]   "Ascendancy and Union," in *The Oxford History of Ireland*, ed. R.F. Foster. New York: Oxford University Press, 1989, op. cit., 156.

[45]   Cf. Foster, an historian whose positions Perry Curtis has characterized as "revisionist or meliorist ... with regard to Anglo-Irish cultural discourses" (Curtis, *Apes and Angels*, op. cit., 116), who nevertheless asserts that "[i]n fact, levels of [political] violence [in the 1830s] were, by many criteria, quite low" (Foster 1989, 164).

Chapter 9
The Sacred, the Profane, and the Middle Class: Thackeray's Post-Famine Criticism and *Pendennis*

"Why Am I to Keep an Irishman?"

We have seen how in Thackeray's *Barry Lyndon* Irishness signifies alterity and is coded as premodern. At the time of its writing, Thackeray attributed the Irish inability to assimilate to historical contingency, and early in his career repudiated the use of romance as a means of representing Irish social aspirations. In a review which appeared in the London *Morning Chronicle* on 16 March, 1844 (which coincided with the serialization of *Barry Lyndon*), of the French author J. Venedey's novel *Irland*, Thackeray asserts, as he does elsewhere, that the discussion of Ireland's political, economic, and social problems is an improper subject for romance, and rather, demands "historical research": "[Venedey] makes too little allowance for the difficulties attending the linking of two such unequally advanced countries together; and instead of making it a matter of historical research, he treats it as a romance, personifying England as the villain of the tale, and Ireland as the heroine and victim."[1]

Alongside his frequent renunciations of romance, Thackeray's early reviews and essays evince a deep sympathy for Irish problems, including assimilation into the larger British body politic, as the above comment suggests. In the early part of the decade he could portray British public opposition to the visit of Czar Nicholas of Russia as "the work of low-minded, sordid knaves ... We are mighty angry with Nicholas about Poland; but until lately, has somebody else treated Ireland better?"[2] Thackeray often admitted that Britain had grossly mistreated Ireland in the past, but that current policy of the 1840s sought to redress old wrongs.

---

[1]   Quoted in *Thackeray's Contributions to the Morning Chronicle*, ed. Gordon Ray. Urbana: University of Illinois Press, 1966, 2.

[2]   *Punch*, Vol. VI, June 8, 1844, quoted in *Hitherto Unidentified Contributions to Punch*, ed. M.H. Spielmann. New York: Harper & Brothers, 1900, 78. Spielmann compiled numerous "hitherto unidentified" contributions of Thackeray to *Punch* from between the years of 1843 and 1848 utilizing an editorial day-book in which were entered authors' names and records of payment for individual contributions. I cite Spielmann's text since I rely on his research for the authenticity of these quotations (some of which, though appearing anonymously, still bear Thackeray's unmistakable style).

However, as Daniel O'Connell's Repeal of the Act of Anglo-Irish Union Movement began to share attention in the British press with more radical and violent Irish nationalist groups, Thackeray began to regard Irish political agitation as more obnoxious. In an "open letter" from "Mr. Punch" to Daniel O'Connell on the occasion of O'Connell's 1844 imprisonment on charges of sedition, Thackeray, while poking good-natured fun at Irish military chauvinism as was his wont, warns more seriously that violent threats from the nationalist movement are both imprudent and ill-founded, since the might of the British Empire assures that violent opposition will be crushed and that Ireland's wrongs will be ameliorated:

> The Irish are strong men, and won every battle that was fought ... I have no objection to think that Caesar's Tenth Legion came out of Tipperary; and that it was three hundred of the O'Gradys who kept the pass of Thermopylae. Nevertheless, have no more talk about bullying John Bull ... It's no use trying; we won't be beaten by the likes of you. But we have done you wrong, and we want to see you righted; and as sure as Justice lives, righted you shall be.[3]

Later that same year (1844), also in *Punch* in a blurb entitled "A Chance Lost," Thackeray regretted that Prince Albert and Queen Victoria had not extended their stay in Ireland long enough for the Queen to give birth to the Duke of Edinburgh, so that Her Majesty's newborn son "would have been born in Dublin on the birthday of Daniel O'Connell ... and the Queen might have numbered ONE LOYAL IRISH SUBJECT MORE."[4] While the suggestion is obviously made in a humorous, and probably ironic, vein, just as evident is its recognition of the desirability of strengthening ties between the two societies. At the same time, Thackeray was pursuing his own effort to delineate "the difficulties attending the linking of two such unequally advanced countries together" in his novel *Barry Lyndon*, which sought to satirize both the romance form and the allegorized "history" of the national tales of Lady Morgan and others, in what I have described as his project of anti-romance.

"Irish Beggary and Ruin Follows the March of Our History"

However, several developments of the mid-1840s, including increased political agitation by Irish nationalists and what Thackeray (and Trollope as well) regarded as Irish thanklessness towards British relief efforts for the Irish Famine, coupled with charges from some quarters that British misrule caused the famine,

---

[3]   *Punch*, VI, 1844, quoted in Spielmann Ibid., 80. It should be noted that O'Connell preached nonviolence. Threats of violence at this time arose mostly from the Young Ireland movement, a group of more radical nationalists comprised mostly of Protestants who eventually repudiated O'Connell, and other small, mostly disorganized groups who nevertheless attracted what Anthony Trollope characterized as an inordinate and misleading amount of press notice.

[4]   *Punch*, VI, August 17, 1844, ibid., 85.

induced Thackeray to seemingly abandon any hope or desire for Irish assimilation. By the time he published *Pendennis* in the late 1840s, Thackeray had become disgusted with continued Irish "ingratitude" towards what he regarded as the good-faith efforts to improve conditions in Ireland, and with increasing bitterness endorsed the Repeal Movement on several occasions in print.[5] In a letter headed "Young Ireland" and addressed from Mr. Punch to Mr. Davis, one of the movement's leaders, Thackeray "approves" with biting irony Davis's appeals for liberty: "Davis calls the QUEEN an alien; the army cowards; instigates 'triumph;' has no objection to blood; incites, infuriates, simple folk; and the British tyrant has not a word to fling at him. If his eloquence should bring about commotion, be the blood on the British tyrant's head, not on Davis's."[6] Thackeray effectively washed his hands of the Irish with a piece entitled "Mr. Punch for Repeal." In this piece Thackeray responds to a statement by John O'Connell, made after his father Daniel's funeral, scorning the "heartlessness of the statesmen, and legislators, and press-writers of wealthy England, who, after plundering us for centuries, refuse us the smallest assistance in the time of extremity which has been brought upon us by English misrule."[7] Incensed by the younger O'Connell's disregard of British relief efforts, Thackeray asks "What is the use of meddling? It is expensive and not useful."[8] Gone is the amusement with which he formerly regarded Irish military boasting, replaced by an undisguised asperity, when Thackeray goes on to compound the violent rhetoric of the Young Irelanders and others together with appeals for continued Irish aid in his attack on John O'Connell's ingratitude:

> We are – as you kindly and constantly show us – naturally cowardly and deceitful. You are open and courageous in Ireland. I admire the frankness of a man who holds out his hand and says, "For the love of Heaven, you infernal scoundrel, give me your money, and I should like to dash your brains out." I admire him; and that, I say, is why I am and declare myself a Repealer. I am for not being abused, for not having to pay money any more, and for not having my brains dashed out.[9]

Thackeray here has simplified the "Irish question" by amalgamating the positions of several Irish parties with differing agendas into a single (and somewhat self-contradictory) complaint. The infantilized and contradictory utterance he

---

[5]   Thackeray's increasing disenchantment with the Irish parallels that of *Punch* generally. See R.F. Foster's *Paddy and Mr. Punch*, Chapter 9, where he concludes: "'Grateful Paddy' apparently preferred to buy guns rather than bread, and therefore forfeited any sympathy that Mr. Punch might have left" (180).

[6]   *Punch*, 8, 205 (1845), quoted in Spielmann ibid., 147. Thomas Davis was a fiery leader of the Young Ireland movement and often preached in *The Nation*, Young Ireland's newspaper, that "Ireland can be a nation again."

[7]   Quoted in Spielmann Ibid., 219.

[8]   *Punch*, 14, 346 (February 26, 1848), quoted in Spielmann ibid., 81.

[9]   Ibid.

attributes to John O'Connell is moreover reminiscent of characters such as Corny O'Shane or his own Jack Costigan of *Pendennis*. Thackeray rightly points out that considerable relief efforts (to which he himself generously contributed) have already been made in England, but his paraphrase distorts O'Connell's remarks, creating a straw-man: "It is clear that the English press-writers and others have been plundering Mr. J. O'Connell and friends for centuries; that we have brought a potato-disease upon you and denied you the smallest relief; that four or five hundred thousand pounds paid over honestly, squeezed out of all sorts of pockets is not the smallest relief at all."[10] The distortion may be slight, but it is significant that in Thackeray's rephrasing O'Connell seems to place responsibility for the "plundering" of Ireland mainly on the press-writers. Clearly O'Connell was referring to "wealthy England" as the perpetrators of the plunder; the press-writers were heartless in O'Connell's estimation for reasons not noted by Thackeray. These reasons included the influential assertion by numerous commentators within the British press that any governmental assistance would foster dependence and sloth, and that assistance should be borne by private charities only.[11] Furthermore, Thackeray's ironic assertion that "we have brought a potato-disease upon you" seeks to dismiss by literalizing and thus reducing to absurdity the charge that Britain was indeed responsible for the famine. Most modern historians agree that a backward agrarian society, linked to a largely unindustrialized economy, was the product of a system in which most of the profitable land was devoted to cattle and sheep production supplying the British market, leaving a vast proportion of the rapidly expanding population dependent for subsistence on potatoes grown on tiny, subdivided holdings. Thus, while Thackeray is correct in suggesting through his irony that the fungus which caused the blight was not brought upon the Irish by the English, the misrule O'Connell refers to was indeed directly responsible for the disaster which ensued when it took hold of Ireland's dietary staple.

In more direct statements in the latter half of 1848, Thackeray seriously and persistently advances proposals to separate Ireland from the British Empire. In "A Letter to A Nobleman Visiting Ireland," he repeats his assertion of the futility of continued attempts at "righting old wrongs" while now denying kinship with the Irish: "I wish the Irishman every freedom and prosperity ... Last year I gave him money out of my own pocket, and was cursed for my pains. I will do so no more; never more. I prefer a quiet life, and have my own kindred to help out of my own superfluity .Why am I to keep an Irishman? He threatens me as he clutches my bread; he hates and insults me as I try to do him good."[12] In a bleak assessment

---

[10]   Ibid.

[11]   The reactions of government policy were inadequate by any modern standard, but Peel's government did alleviate the harshness of the suffering early on in the crisis. However, when Lord John Russell became Prime Minister in 1846 Peel's policies were replaced by more *laissez-faire* measures which sought to place the burden on Irish property rather than state handouts. The effects, which have been voluminously recorded, were disastrous.

[12]   *Punch*, 15, 373, quoted in Spielmann ibid., 257.

of any future prospects of harmony between the two peoples, Thackeray directly denies the possibility of assimilation as well. In citing differences between Saxon and Celt which recall Matthew Arnold's more thorough delineation of "racial" characteristics, Thackeray describes the Irish as remaining mired in cultural and economic stasis, viewing the march of the imperial metropolitan culture's progress in historical time from "outside" of history: "Fancy our persisting in governing Celts by Saxon laws, and that horrible figure of Irish beggary and ruin follows the march of our history into the future, hangs on in piteous chains and rags, preventing her progress – it is frightful to look at."[13]

In August of 1848 Thackeray announced in a letter to his mother that "I opened my fire yesterday with the first chapter of *Pendennis*."[14] In that first chapter he establishes not only Pen's infatuation for the Irish Emily Costigan, but also his uncle the Major's horror at this development and resolution to prevent it. The Major's reaction is based upon the certainty of the family's social ostracism should the affair result in marriage: "People will laugh at me so that I dare not show my head."[15] His characterization in *Punch* of an Ireland outside of history thus directly coincides with Thackeray's creation of the character Jack Costigan, a stage-Irish figure, and his daughter Emily. Emily, married in the novel to an effete and elderly aristocrat, represents an Irish nation which was united with Great Britain by the vote of a pre-Reform Parliament. Thackeray's imagined community of Britain from this point on is in large part defined, both as what it is and what it is not, by the unassimilability of the Irish. Although it is only strongly implied in *Pendennis*, Thackeray bluntly attributes responsibility for this alienation to the Irish in his journalism which was written simultaneously with the beginning of his novel and appeared in the same publication which serialized it.

Mythic Nation-building: *Pendennis*

In *The History of Pendennis*, Thackeray goes beyond merely providing a negative example of anti-domesticity and the inassimilable British subject to give full expression to an idealized national culture. In this novel, class conflict is displaced onto sexual conflict,[16] and national difference (including Irishness) is encoded as class difference. *Pendennis* depicts sexual alliances which are potentially disruptive of the social order and counterbalances them with a society which fully realizes Burke's sacred polity. Thackeray constructs an ideal in the hero's mother against which the model of Mrs. Barry may be measured, and in the marriage plot portrays "family affections [which] keep[] inseparable ... our state, our hearths,

---

[13]   Ibid.

[14]   Quoted in the Introduction to Scribner's 1917 edition of *Pendennis*, xvi.

[15]   Thackeray, William Makepeace. *The History of Pendennis: His Fortunes and Misfortunes, His Friends and His Greatest Enemy.* New York: Charles Scribner's Sons, 1947, 6. Hereafter *Pendennis*.

[16]   Cf. Armstrong, op. cit., esp. 178.

our sepulchres, and our altars."[17] However, in this novel Burke's patriarchal aristocratic ideal is replaced by a professionalized middle class, in which the hero Pen takes his place as a journalist and author of novels. And as in *Barry Lyndon*, Irishness plays a central role in Thackeray's imagined community.

Pendennis is a *bilduungsroman* that traces the social education of a boy who at a crucial period of his youth becomes fatherless. Like Edgeworth's Irish national tales, *Pendennis* is a comically structured work in which the hero establishes his legitimacy as a member of the ruling class; however, the ruling-class to which Pen belongs is Britain's newly dominant middle class. Recalling Edgeworth's *Ormond*, Thackeray endows his hero with a name encoding mythic overtones of nation-building. His first name, Arthur, associates him with the legendary king of the originary British national fable. His surname suggests *Pendragon*, a name familiar from the Arthurian romances, which is a term denoting the ancient British prince holding supreme power among the post-Roman Celts of England and Wales, and is etymologically derived from the Welsh *pen* or chief. His nickname is an obvious reference to the profession he assumes, but it might also be noted that history is proverbially written by the victors, and by mid-nineteenth-century Britain the social formation which had emerged victorious from the 1688 Revolution was the professionalized middle class.[18] Pen's private history therefore encodes that public victory.

Pen's father was an apothecary, and the recent emergence of the professions into legitimate membership within Britain's dominant caste is duly recorded in *Pendennis*. One might recall Croker's declassing of Lady Morgan by disparaging her language as "smelling vilely of the apothecary's shop" only one generation earlier, a period roughly contemporaneous with Pen's early life. In British history as allegorically rendered in *Pendennis*, Pen's father "had a Cornish pedigree which carried the Pendennises up to the time of the Druids – and who knows how much farther back! They had intermarried with the Normans ... and were related to all the great families of Wales and Brittany."[19] Pen's family history thus recapitulates in brief a long swath of English political history, encoding an idealized, ancient (and non-Irish) Celtic heritage. Thackeray then allegorizes more recent British social history by depicting Arthur's branch of the family as descended from a younger son excluded from the patrilineal succession by the laws of primogeniture. It is worth quoting the passage outlining this more recent Pendennis family history in its entirety, since a close reading of it reveals important details it records as it allegorically encapsulates British history from the time of the Revolution:

> There were those alive who remembered having seen [Pen's father's] name painted [below] a gilt mortar and pestle [over the door of] a very humble shop in the city of Bath. He had for a time struggled with poverty. but Lady Ribstone

---

[17] Burke, op. cit., 30.

[18] Cf. Benedict Anderson's description of the role the printed word plays in nation building in Chapter 2 of *Imagined Communities*, op. cit.

[19] *Pendennis*, 7.

happening to be passing to the Rooms with an intoxicated Irish chairman, who bumped her Ladyship up against Pen's very doorpost, and drove his chairpole through the handsomest pink-bottle in the surgeon's window, alighted screaming from her vehicle, and was accommodated with a chair in Mr. Pendennis's shop. Mr. Pendennis's manners were so uncommonly gentlemanlike and soothing, that her Ladyship ... appointed her Preserver, as she called him, apothecary to her person and family. In a word, he got the good graces of [her Ladyship's] family, and from that day began to prosper.[20]

Britain's "Glorious" Revolution pitted the Protestant William of Orange against the Catholic James II, and the interests of the Protestant aristocracy and middling classes coincided in the defeat of the Catholic Pretender. The crucial battles of this struggle took place in Ireland, where the overwhelmingly Catholic population supported James, and the Irish chairman's drunken agency in bringing together the Protestant aristocrat and "tradesman" encodes the violent circumstances attending the beginning of that alliance. The "soothing" manners of middle-class domesticity are aptly described as "gentlemanlike," because they are a cultural inheritance of the Burkean ideal. The professional classes (including "tradesmen") and the gentry (and small property owners) who now make up this middle class get "the good graces of the family," that is, conciliate the aristocracy and facilitate the development of a relationship founded upon mutual benefit. One result of this conciliation was the Reform Act of 1832, a large step in the political empowerment of the middle class.[21] The British aristocracy might well attribute its "preservation" to the middle classes; violent social upheaval of the type endured in Revolutionary France was avoided through the more gradual expansion of the ruling classes recorded here. Thackeray's characters have thus, in Ian Duncan's phrase, "transcended historical process in order to occupy a generic idyll of private life,"[22] since Thackeray has here encoded in Pen's private history the formation of the professional-gentry class.

But as in Edgeworth's Irish novels, Pen must merit inclusion in this class through the acquirement of an acceptable domestic discipline. Catherine Peters has aptly compared Pen to Edward Waverley in the acquisition of his social legitimacy: "A close[] literary relative is Waverley, who, like Pen, suffers from a desultory and inadequate education, and is a romantic who learns to abandon romanticism during the course of his adventures."[23] The most important aspect

---

[20]   Ibid., 6–8.

[21]   Middle-class political power emanating from this Act was of course limited. It expanded the franchise to include owners and tenants of property worth 10*l.* annually (and was only passed in the face of stiff opposition from aristocratic interests in Croker's Tory Party, headed by the Duke of Wellington). Subsequent Reform Acts of 1867 and 1884 extended the franchise further, but full enfranchisement of all British men and women only occurred in the twentieth century.

[22]   Duncan, op. cit., 55.

[23]   Peters, Catherine. *Thackeray's Universe: Shifting Worlds of Imagination and Reality.* New York: Oxford University Press, 1987, 174.

of this education is, as in *Ormond*, the hero's domestic education. Thus the novel begins with the introduction of Major Pendennis, Pen's uncle, receiving a letter from Pen's widowed mother announcing her alarm at Pen's infatuation with an Irish actress twelve years his senior, and pleading with the Major to come to Fairoaks (the home his father was enabled to purchase through his alliance with Lady Ribstone) to discipline the boy (Helen Pendennis's objections to Emily Costigan closely echo Croker's disapproval of Lady Morgan's marriage).

Although the class conflict is here partially obscured and displaced onto a sexual conflict, the implications of class difference are unmistakable. And like Lady Morgan's shortcomings in the criticism of Croker, the class difference of Pen's inassimilable object of infatuation is marked by her Irishness. Emily, or "La Fotheringay," is an actress with a reputation of numerous sexual intrigues. Her coarseness and greed (she is searching for an English husband from above her social class) are remarked repeatedly (straightforwardly by the narrator and other characters, but ingenuously by Pen, whose passion is depicted as blind). At the height of this infatuation the narrator compares her to a cheap, gaudy watch Pen had received from his father as a boy. As he had with the watch, he thinks of nothing but her by day, and dreams of her by night, and "at the very first moment of waking [each morning] hugged it and looked at it. – By the way, that first watch of Pen's was a showy, ill-manufactured piece: it never went well from the beginning, and was always getting out of order. And after putting it aside into a drawer and forgetting it for some time, he swopped it finally away for a more useful timekeeper."[24]

The rather heavy-handed metaphor of the gaudy watch is telling; it begins the narrative's thorough dehumanization of Emily. Pen goes night after night to see her perform, and considers her portrayals, in which Emily employs the same tones, inflections and gestures every time, evidence of great acting. In his youthful romanticism he considers this "artistry" proof of her elevated soul. But the narrator, as well as other characters who watch her closely, describe her as having a temperament characterized by "healthy dulness [sic] and cheerful insensibility."[25] or worse yet, a parrot or an automaton. She is unable to understand the lines she speaks or the poetry Pen writes to her, and her inane and self-absorbed prattle in response to Pen's high-minded proclamations of sentiment and passion, often cloaked in literary allusion, render her at best childlike in the manner of Edgeworth's Gaelic Irish characters. The smitten Bows, her music and dance teacher, who unlike Pen has some experience of the world and also unlike Pen remains devoted to her over the course of the novel, nevertheless affirms her lack of humanity:

> You are not the only one who has made a fool of himself about that woman. And I have less excuse than you, because I'm older and know her better. She has no more heart than the stone you are leaning on, and it or you might fall into the

---

[24]   *Pendennis*, 46–7.

[25]   Ibid., 164.

water, and never come up again, and she wouldn't care. She has no heart and no head, and no sense, and no feelings and no griefs or cares, whatever. I was going to say no pleasures – but the fact is, she does like her dinner, and she is pleased when people admire her.[26]

Even Emily's most ardent admirer admits she has no intellectual or emotional life, only appetites and vanity. Thackeray represents her as something less than human – a sexual threat who endangers Pen's domesticity. His interest in Emily is ultimately revealed to be only a romanticized lust, an unacceptable desire in a properly domesticated middle-class subject. This point is made clear by references linking her with pagan beauty; "the Louvre Venus – that delight of gods and men",[27] as well as the reaction to her of the all the novel's male characters, who remark repeatedly upon her beauty and physical desirability. Even an aged parson, an old friend of the Pendennis family, admires her in a way in which the sexual overtones are clear: "I must say, Major, she is endowed with very considerable personal attractions."[28] Although the novel adheres to Victorian convention and demurely retreats from any explicit description of Emily's sexuality, she is clearly a devouring female, a creature of appetite. She awakens in Pen unprincipled desires of his own (despite his romanticization of them) which require policing.

Irish anti-domesticity is further emphasized by the portrayal of Emily's father and their relationship. Captain Costigan might be regarded as a reimagination of Barry Lyndon, who this time escapes a similar fate in the Fleet because he has a daughter who can support him. Costigan is in many ways a stage Irishman, a stereotype of the nineteenth century with roots in English literature that stretch back beyond Shakespeare's Captain Macmorris. He is described in mock-heroic terms that recall Shakespeare's Bardolph, as a drunken adventurer "who manages to keep afloat ... [and] get his daily portion of whiskey and water" by whatever means he can, usually dishonest "wind-raising conspiracies in which he engages with heroes as unfortunate as himself ... through all the storms of life Jack had floated somehow, and the lamp of his nose had never gone out."[29]

Emily is his chief co-conspirator, and their sphere of operations is the marriage market to which Emily has gained entrée by means of her physical charms. Costigan contrives to play Pander, and urges Emily to encourage Pen for the purpose of entrapping him into marriage. Only when Major Pendennis informs Costigan that Pen has limited financial means does the father break off their relationship and accuse Pen of sexual impropriety: "He has been acting the part of viper to this fireside, and traitor to this familee ... He has deceived us in the most athrocious manner ... He has thrifled with your affections, and outraged my own fine feelings." In a state of infantile confusion (cf. Corny O'Shane),

---

26   Ibid., 149.
27   Ibid., 42.
28   Ibid., 106.
29   Ibid., 54.

Costigan insists that "an infernal swindle had been practiced upon him, and that he was resolved either on a marriage, or on the blood of both [Major Pendennis and Pen]." Emily, however, unemotionally points out to her father the impracticality of marrying Pen under such circumstances: "Sure, if he has no money, there's no use in marrying him, papa."[30]

That the relationship between Pen and Emily represents both socio-sexual impropriety and a transgression of class boundaries is evidenced by both parties' conclusions after the affair. Emily, who is also clear-sighted and worldly in sexual matters, points out to her father the consequences they both would face if Pen had made her pregnant: "[S]uppose there were a family? – why, papa, we shouldn't be as well off as we are now."[31] She offers a frank admission of her own and her father's class ambitions, while at the same time giving as explicit an indication as was possible in a Victorian novel that those hopes were based on her sexual relationship with Pen: "And there's an end to all the fine talk about Mrs. Arthur Pendennis of Fairoaks Park – the Member of Parliament's Lady ... Pretty carriages and horses we should have to ride! ... But it's always the same. If a man looked at me, you fancied he was going to marry me."[32]

On the other side, the Pendennis camp offers forthright admissions of Irish exclusion from the middle class. The Major affirms Pen's class superiority when Pen's friend Foker assesses his position: "Connection not eligible. Too much beer drunk on the premises. No Irish need apply. That I take to be your meaning' The Major said it was, exactly."[33] Later the Major fumes to himself "The impudent bog-trotting scamp ... Dare to talk of permitting the Costigans to marry with the Pendennises!"[34] Pen does not dare reveal to his mother Costigan's relationship to Emily, identifying him merely as "a Peninsular officer ... Pen did not say more. And how was Mrs Pendennis to know that Mr. Costigan was the father of Miss Fotheringay?"[35] The Major explicitly warns Pen that an alliance with Emily will exclude him from the ruling class: "[The diplomatic service] at once is closed to you. The public service is closed to you. Society is closed to you[36]" Pen is willing, for a time, to throw away his opportunities in the public sphere, but his uncle's argument about the domestic ramifications of this marriage has greater effect on him: "[You will be] the young husband of an old woman, who, if she doesn't quarrel with your mother, will at least cost that lady her position in society, and drag her down into that dubious caste into which you must inevitably fall."[37] Pen comes to his senses when the Major again reminds him of Helen's reduction

---

30   Ibid., 127–8.
31   Ibid., 129.
32   Ibid.
33   Ibid., 109.
34   Ibid., 132.
35   Ibid., 69.
36   Ibid., 95.
37   Ibid.

in status. He asks and receives his mother's forgiveness for exposing her to the threat: "'Be a man, and remember that your mother is a lady. She was never made to associate with that tipsy old swindler or his daughter' [said the Major]. 'Be a man and comfort your mother, my Arthur,' Helen said ... Seeing that the pair were greatly moved, the Major went out of the room ... He had won a complete victory."[38]

The Major seems to invoke Burke's naturalization of the social order in stating "your mother was never made to associate with" the Costigans, but in so doing also calls to light the complicated nature of Thackeray's class attitudes. In both *Barry Lyndon* and *The Irish Sketch Book*, as well as in his journalism, Thackeray attributed Irish difference to historical contingency, and he repeats his conviction again in *Pendennis* through the narrator's descriptions of Jack Costigan: "I take it no foreigner understands the life of an Irish gentleman without money ... all these are mysteries to us inconceivable."[39] Thackeray refers to the Irishman's lack of resources, which he attributed often in his fiction and elsewhere to British colonial policy. He also faithfully records the Major's naturalization of this difference, which was perhaps a prevalent attitude in his society. That the Major's class attitudes are wrong-headed in Thackeray's social vision is perhaps demonstrated at the novel's denouement when he is "punished" by his own valet. Morgan (the valet) proves to have amassed a fortune and has secretly established himself as the Major's landlord, and in one of the novel's final scenes turns him out of his Mayfair lodgings.

However, it is important to note the ambivalence that even the Morgan sequence betrays in Thackeray's class attitudes. Morgan's triumph over the Major seems appropriate retribution for the Major's petty tyrannies over him despite Morgan's instrumentality in maintaining "old Wigsby's" prominent position in society, as well as for the Major's attempts to undermine the marriage plot with Laura (whom Pen finally marries) over objections to what he regards as her inappropriate origins. What the Major regards as inappropriate is directly connected to wealth; his disapproval of Laura is counterbalanced by his regard for Pen's friend Foker, son of a wealthy brewer, and he plots to ally Pen with the rich Blanche Amory, of whose low birth he is aware. The Major appears to endorse a social mobility limited to "natural-born" English, perhaps reflecting his own status as descendant of a younger son. His downfall momentarily seems to overturn for good the classism in *Pendennis*. Yet in the next scene Thackeray reverses this reversal, and after Morgan attempts to blackmail the Major, the elder Pendennis easily cows him and once more demonstrates his superiority. Similarly, although the narrator attempts to sympathize with Costigan by hinting, however slightly, that his primitiveness is conditioned by material circumstances in Ireland, the narrative nevertheless endorses the Major's opinion that people such as Emily "aren't made" to inhabit the same sphere as Helen Pendennis.

---

[38] Ibid., 141.

[39] Ibid., 54.

Pendennis's preoccupation with class is evidenced in other sexual conflicts as well: in the desire of Pen's tutor, the hapless Smirke, for Pen's widowed mother, and in those of Blanche Amory, the object of another love intrigue of Pen's. In the Smirke episode the class conflict is explicitly enunciated. When in a drunken conversation with his tutor, whom he regards as a servant, Pen learns that the object of Smirke's desire is Helen Pendennis, again an older woman of a higher social class, he is dismayed: "'My mother!' cried out Arthur, jumping up and sober in a minute. 'Pooh! damn it, Smirke, you must be mad – she's seven or eight years older than you are ... My tutor, I say *my tutor*, has no right to ask a lady of my mother's rank of life to marry him (italics in original)."[40] But while in the Smirke sequence class values are straightforwardly voiced, the class ideals evinced through Blanche are both more subtle and more complicated. Blanche is the low-born daughter of the novel's villain[41] and a mother who, after Blanche's birth, marries a corrupt aristocrat. While her stepfather's title gives her entrée into Pen's social world, Blanche (whose real name, Betsy, the narrator notes as a marker of her lower class origins) nevertheless frequently exhibits her inability to assimilate. Her anti-domestic cruelty to her parents and half-brother, her prodigious reading of romantic novels and poetry, and her coquetry among several of the novel's male characters, often encouraging more than one of them at the same dinner party, all code her as an unacceptable object of desire for Pen.

Pendennis's class scheme is complicated and hierarchical. Blanche's role in delineating this scheme is most revealing in the plot sequences involving her father's chef, Miroblant. Introduced as a ridiculous rival whom Pen at one point almost assaults for his class presumption, Miroblant is portrayed as a stage-Frenchman, another long-standing comic stereotype. In speaking to a townswoman, he imagines that all the women, including Blanche and her mother, are in love with him:

> To inspire hopeless passion is my destiny ... Is it my fault that that young woman [Blanche] deperishes and languishes ... consumed by a flame which I can not return? The governess of the young Milor has encountered me in my walks, and looked at me in a way which can bear but one interpretation. And Milady herself, who is of mature age, has once or twice addressed compliments to the lonely [culinary] artist which can admit of no mistake.[42]

Both Miroblant and his desire for Blanche are rendered ridiculous by the narrative. Since Miroblant is a foreigner and a servant, even the *parvenue* Blanche is out of his social reach, in spite of her dubious inclusion within Pen's world (a dubiety Pen only recognizes belatedly, and the Major denies owing to her family's wealth). Corrupt aristocrats are also marginalized from the dominant caste and punished in Thackeray's imagined community. Blanche's step-father, a baronet and wastrel,

---

[40]   *Pendennis*, 174–5.
[41]   However, this detail is not revealed until the denouement.
[42]   *Pendennis*, 264.

is a pariah, plagued by prodigious gambling debts and only kept from total ruin by a faithful retainer, the army veteran Chevalier Strong. Emily finally marries an elderly and effete aristocrat, and, significantly, they remain childless, a comment on their social legacy. They throw decadent *soirées* at which all the other *louche* members of high society Pen has met over the course of the novel congregate to ridicule them. As Emily's fate makes clear, members of the aristocracy who are corrupt and idle do not occupy the highest rank in Thackeray's idealized national culture; rather, like foreigners and servants, they are marginalized.

These examples of sexual and social impropriety and class difference serve as counterpoints to the sanctified domesticity elaborated in the marriage plot. The domestic ideal is enshrined in the self-sacrificing angel of the house, and Pen's domestication is partly the project of an idealized female. In *Pendennis* ideal femininity is first embodied by the hero's mother, who then transmits her power (and, seemingly, her *identity*) to Laura Bell, his cousin whom his mother has adopted. The reason for the transmutation is that the self-sacrifice and devotion Helen exhibits are not enough to inculcate in Pen proper domesticity. They must be accompanied by a regimen of discipline through which the woman can transmit her moral power to the man. Laura for a time repudiates Pen for improprieties which his mother is ready to overlook. Helen's failure in this regard is rehabilitated in the novel by Laura's assumption of Helen's authority. In this way Laura becomes a de-sexualized embodiment of a female kinship – at once mother, sister, cousin and wife. But unlike in Armstrong's formulation where "middle-class authority rest[s] in large part upon the authority that novels attribute[] to women,"[43] properly domestic females in *Pendennis* empower the men and in turn submit to their paternal authority. Thackeray makes clear from the opening passages, when Helen Pendennis appeals to the Major for help in the Fotheringay affair, that a responsible masculine authority is necessary to regulate the social order. However, neither is the Major himself a properly domesticated male. Rather, he is a worldling, a Regency buck adept at maintaining a place for himself at the dinner tables of the rich and powerful but not fit for ruling over a family, and his social legitimacy is limited in this novel because of that unfitness. The Major is a childless bachelor, and despite the assumptions of other characters such as Foker that Pen will inherit from him, he significantly and symbolically has no patrimony to leave. While his worldly advice is sometimes useful in the public and social spheres, Pen must draw on the moral power of the feminine ideal in order to obtain the legitimacy required to exercise his paternal authority.

At the outset of the novel, Pen's father dies suddenly, leaving him master of Fairoaks. Pen's domestic education has been neglected thus far, and his reading unregulated: "He never read to improve himself out of school-hours, but, on the contrary, devoured all the novels, plays, and poetry on which he could lay his hands."[44] When at sixteen years old his father dies, Pen must discontinue his schooling as well.

---

[43] Armstrong, op. cit., 4.
[44] *Pendennis*, 17.

Pen, who hates school, feels "a sort of secret triumph and exultation. He was the chief now and lord."[45] He enjoys his status as lord of the manor and indulges himself in expensive hobbies, one of which is attending the theater every night, where he encounters Emily. This continues until his uncle intervenes, at which time Pen resolves to learn a profession. He goes to "Oxbridge," but his desultory efforts at university get him "plucked," and he must return home in disgrace, after having seriously depleted his mother's financial resources by throwing extravagant parties for the "men" of the college and indulging in frequent gambling.

Pen's desire must be disciplined, and feminine moral authority provides him with the strength to regulate it. This moral authority is derived from feminine purity. Helen is described as a paragon, regarded by other characters as the equal of any of the nobility Pen encounters (in part owing to her lineage – like Pen's father she has noble antecedents). Despite his disdain for her provinciality, the Major "pronounced [her], and with perfect truth, to be as fine a lady as any in England. Indeed, Mrs. Pendennis's tranquil beauty, her natural sweetness and kindness, and that simplicity and dignity which a perfect purity and innocence are sure to bestow on a handsome woman, rendered her quite worthy of her brother's praises."[46] Thackeray invests this naturalized and pure domesticity with a sanctity recalling Burke. Upon the death of Pen's father, the narrator describes motherhood in terms that also compound "our hearths, our sepulchers, and our altars" into a domestic ideal: "The maternal passion is a sacred mystery to me. What one sees symbolized in the Roman churches in the image of the Virgin Mother with a bosom bleeding with love, I think one may witness (and admire the Almighty bounty for) every day."[47] It is interesting to note that Thackeray continues this idealization, begun with a reference to Catholic veneration of Mary, with an image of another Jewish mother, thus representing a sanctified domesticity among two groups socially excluded from the British polity. The implication is that sacred domesticity is a cultural legacy, like Anglo-Irish legitimacy in Edgeworth's Ireland, transmitted by more primitive peoples to the modern British nation-state:

> I saw a Jewish lady, only yesterday, with a child at her knee, and from whose face towards the child there shone a sweetness so angelical, that it seemed to form a sort of glory round both. I protest I could have knelt before her too, and adored in her the Divine beneficence in endowing us with the maternal *sorge*, which began with our race and sanctifies the history of mankind.[48]

Despite Thackeray's mystification of the feminine ideal, he also suggests that it requires disciplining in order to (re)produce the properly domesticated subject. Helen's devotion to Pen causes her to neglect his domestic discipline, and there are early signals in the narrative of the dangers even of feminine purity if left unregulated:

---

[45]   Ibid., 23.

[46]   Ibid., 15.

[47]   Ibid., 23.

[48]   Ibid., 23.

> There was a very blank anchorite repast when Pen dined from home: and he
> himself headed the remonstrance from the kitchen regarding the deteriorated
> quality of the Fairoaks beer. [Helen] was becoming miserly for Pen. Indeed, who
> ever accused woman of being just? They are always sacrificing themselves *or
> somebody* for somebody else's sake (italics added).[49]

Pen's complaint about the beer is an example of Thackeray's subtly compressing
rich significance into compact prose, for it economically signals the types of excess
to which Pen's unregulated desires lead him. Helen is scrimping to accommodate
him, but the term "miserly" codes Helen's sacrifices as unhealthy as well. The
assertion that women are "always sacrificing themselves or somebody" signifies
that in addition to herself, she in fact is sacrificing Pen. The corrosiveness of
Helen's devotion is fully revealed in what the narrator frankly describes as her
sexual jealousy of Blanche, which not accidentally coincides with the beginning
of Helen's fatal illness: "[Helen] watch[ed] over the pair with that anxiety with
which brooding women watch over their sons' affections – and in acknowledging
which, I have no doubt there is a sexual jealousy on the mother's part, and a secret
pang – when Helen saw that the intimacy appeared to make progress ... the poor
widow's heart began to fail her – her darling project (of marrying Pen to Laura)
seemed to vanish before her."[50] Helen becomes even more jealous later in the
novel when she witnesses Pen's emotional attachment to another Irish girl, Fanny,
a servant in Pen's London lodging house. Pen's interest in the beautiful Fanny is
this time innocent. He becomes ill and she nurses him back to health. However, on
a visit to his sickbed Helen observes their emotional intimacy, leaps to the wrong
conclusion, becomes consumed with jealousy and dies.

The Helen character, and with her a normative domesticity, is rehabilitated
through the figure of Laura. Laura is the daughter of Helen's cousin, with whom
Helen had her own romantic attachment before she met Pen's father. Mr. Bell
was, however, engaged to an older woman who forced him to honor a loveless
commitment out of spite. After Laura's parents die, Helen adopts her as the
daughter she never had. Laura, a blood cousin, has thus been raised as a sister to
Pen. This relationship is emphasized throughout the novel, but the narrator reveals
the sexual attraction between them by describing their efforts to suppress it: "For
some time past, an agreeable practice, known since times ever so ancient, by
which brothers and sisters are wont to exhibit their affection towards one another,
and in which Pen and his little sister Laura had been accustomed to indulge pretty
frequently in their childish days, had been given up by mutual consent of those
two parties."[51] Despite her attraction, however, Laura is ready to renounce Pen
for his unprincipled conduct. While Helen makes excuses for Pen, claiming that
his academic exertions are responsible for his failure to return home and visit his
mother over the holidays, Laura sees through him: "'It is better that he should lose

---

[49]   Ibid., 32–3.
[50]   Ibid., 269.
[51]   Ibid., 225.

a[n academic] prize than forget his mother: and indeed, mamma, I don't see that he gets many prizes. Why doesn't he come home and stay with you instead of passing his vacations at his great friends' fine houses?' ... Laura declared stoutly that she did not love Pen a bit when he did not do his duty to his mother."[52] Helen is aware that Pen is making excuses for his unregulated conduct, but "she tried to believe that she believed them, and comforted herself with the maternal infatuation." [53] Laura, by contrast, refuses to validate Pen's actions, and the narrator makes clear that it is Pen's undisciplined domesticity of which Laura disapproves:

> Arthur's later talk and ways ... shocked and displeased Laura ... he spoke lightly and laxly of women in general; was less courteous in his actions than in his words ... It offended Miss Laura that he should smoke his horrid pipes in the house; that he should refuse to go to church with his mother, or on walks or visits with her, and be found yawning over his novel in his dressing gown, when the widow returned from those duties.[54]

Laura also disapproves of Pen's sexual intrigue with Emily, but it is Pen's undutifulness to his mother, specifically Pen's willingness to abase Helen, for which she would repudiate him for good: "The Fotheringay affair ... vastly shocked and outraged Laura. A Pendennis fling himself away on such a woman as that! ... to fall on his knees to an actress, and drink with her horrid father! A good son to bring such a man and such a woman as that into his house, and set them over his mother! 'I would have run away, mamma, I would, if I had had to walk barefoot over the snow!'"[55] Because Laura is devoted to Helen, she retains a sisterly interest in Pen too, but when Pen nonchalantly courts Blanche, in whom Laura has observed non-domestic conduct, she regards him as an unsuitable match for herself:

> After the affair with Blanche, a difference ever so slight, a tone of melancholy, perhaps a little bitter, might be perceived in Laura's converse with her cousin. She seemed to weigh him, and find him wanting, too; the widow saw the girl's clear and honest eyes watching the young man at times, and a look of almost scorn pass over her face.[56]

Laura's disapprobation weighs heavily on Pen, and he himself begins to recognize that it is Laura's moral strength from which he gains the power to regulate his desires and take his place in society. This is figured symbolically in her paying off his debts and paying for his schooling when he returns to Oxbridge; and the sense of obligation Pen feels and heeds when he learns of her responsibility (he scrupulously repays her as soon as he is able) mark a new stage in his moral development:

---

[52]   *Pendennis*, 227.

[53]   Ibid.

[54]   Ibid.

[55]   Ibid., 228.

[56]   Ibid., 285.

One day [Helen] told him of these projects [to establish Pen in a profession], and who it was that had formed them; how it was Laura who insisted on his going to London and studying; how it was Laura who would not hear of the – the money arrangements when he came back from Oxbridge – being settled just then [and thus allowing Pen to finish his education].[57]

Thackeray explicitly announces that it is Laura's agency which allows Pen to finally both rehabilitate himself and find the gumption to enter a profession and "shoulder his way in the world," in short, to become a full-fledged member of the ruling class:

On hearing that news [of Laura paying his debts and sending him back to Oxbridge] Pen blazed up with pleasure ... "O mother, I've been wearying myself away for months here, longing to work, and not knowing how. I've been fretting over the thoughts of my shame, and my debts, and my past cursed extravagance and follies ... If I can get a chance to redeem the past, and to do my duty to the best mother in the world, indeed, indeed, I will. Heaven bless you! God bless Laura!"[58]

The bulk of the novel from this point forward details Pen's entrance into the professional world, aided by Laura's moral strength. It is not until he finds success, however, that he is ready to marry her, at which time she willingly gives up her power to him. She has assumed the same sanctified purity which characterized Helen, tempered with a discipline marked by renunciation. Despite her love she would have repudiated Pen were he unsuitable, but since he has proven himself worthy she is prepared to completely sacrifice herself to him either as wife or sister. She proves this when, under the mistaken impression that Pen really does love Blanche, only now with a pure love not based upon greed as before, she blesses his supposed passion: "You take Blanche without money, without a bribe. Yes, thanks be to Heaven, dear brother. You could not have sold yourself away."[59]

Thackeray is at great pains to establish that Pen's love for Laura is not based upon sexual desire, but rather an idealized domestic affection that recalls the terms with which he mystified the love of the Jewish mother and child: "The fulness of innocent love beamed from [Laura] ... A smile heavenly pure, a glance of unutterable tenderness, sympathy, pity, shone in her face – all which indications of love and purity Arthur beheld and worshiped in her, as you would watch them in a child, as one fancies one might regard them in an angel."[60] Having thoroughly policed Pen's unprincipled male sexuality, Laura is now ready to submit to him and render to him a devotion identical to Helen's, now acceptable because Pen has proven himself worthy: "And to think that he is to be mine, mine! and that I

---

57 Ibid., 287.

58 Ibid.

59 Ibid., 832.

60 Ibid.

am to marry him, and not to be his servant as I expected to be only this morning; for I would have gone down on my knees to Blanche to beg her to let me live with him."[61] Laura also assumes more than just Helen's devotion. The narrative goes on to suggest that she is accompanied by Helen's spirit, or has somehow mystically incorporated her identity: "'Oh mother! mother, that you were here!' Indeed, she felt that Helen were there – by her, actually, though invisibly. A halo of happiness beamed from her. She moved with a different step, and bloomed with a new beauty."[62]

In empowering Pen, Laura transcends the roles of female relationship to men, and becomes at once Pen's wife, sister, mother, and even daughter, which is signaled by the way in which he infantilizes Laura in the final few pages: "[H]e marked the solemn little tragedy airs and looks, the little ways, the little trepidations, vanities of the little bride."[63] Thackeray thus enshrines the marital bond which cements the social order in a way which elides sexuality. In Thackeray's imagined Britain exclusion is obscured as well in the portrayal of members of other groups to whom this normative domesticity is "foreign," who represent Burke's "alien cyons." The final line of the novel paraphrases the slogan of the British abolitionist movement in order to sum up Pen's history, and ironically refers to the desexualized familial relations glorified in the domestic ideal: "[L]et us give a hand of charity to Arthur Pendennis, with all his faults and shortcomings, who does not claim to be a hero, but only a man and a brother."[64] Despite the obvious generosity of these sentiments, the limits of this brotherhood seem only to extend as far as a carefully defined national identity.

---

[61] *Pendennis*, 859.

[62] Ibid.

[63] Ibid., 861.

[64] Ibid., 890.

Chapter 10
Allegory for the End of Union:
Trollope's *An Eye for an Eye*

Seduction Plot: Suite

Thackeray's response to increased violence and political agitation in part is expressed, in *Pendennis*, through an imagined Great Britain in which the ethnic Gaelic Irish largely define otherness. More importantly, the narrative of Pen's renunciation of Emily encodes a justification for Irish exclusion – the Costigans "weren't made" to inhabit the same sphere as the Pendennises. Anthony Trollope experienced a similar disillusionment in regard to the creation of a cohesive social body out of Union, but in his last completed Irish novel, any bitterness expressed is largely reserved for Britain's role in the fiasco.[1] In *An Eye for an Eye*, Trollope allegorizes the colonial relationship between the two nations, which was not substantially altered with the 1801 Union, as an alliance in which Britain never countenanced a full partnership with Ireland, and therefore bore large responsibility for the increasingly radicalized and violent Irish nationalist movement. As in Lady Morgan's *Wild Irish Girl*, the partnership in *An Eye for an Eye* is figured as a marriage plot, but as in *The Macdermots*, the ending is tragic, not comic. The ambivalent hero makes an insincere marriage offer, which is condemned in the narration as a betrayal of the bride's good faith as well as of his own better principles, and union never takes place. Robert Tracy quotes the "hero" of *An Eye for an Eye* asking a priest "to do for him something romantic, something marvelous, perhaps something almost lawless" to assert that these are "three terms that accurately describe the Ireland of Trollope's fiction."[2] However, Fred Neville (an English hero who in part recalls Morgan's Horatio) finds that the priest will do no such thing to assist him in escaping responsibility for his reckless adventuring. Far from being a romantic setting, Ireland becomes for Neville and, by extension, for England, a site which he wished to romanticize, but where realities too long ignored, or worse, purposely distorted, must be faced.

An Eye for an Eye, like *The Macdermots*, is an allegorical account of the seduction of an Irish girl through promises of marriage which are neither kept, nor even seriously entertained by the hero. When adopted by his noble uncle, Fred Neville is raised from the status of commoner to titled legatee of a vast patrimony,

---

[1]   *The Land Leaguers* (an uncompleted novel was published posthumously in 1884), although unfinished, also exhibits much pessimism and bitterness, and does focus on a perceived deterioration in Irish attitudes (and condemns Irish-American influences on Irish agitation).

[2]   Robert Tracy. "'The Unnatural Ruin': Trollope and Nineteenth-Century Fiction," *Nineteenth-Century Fiction* 37:3 (December 1982), 360–61.

but he insists upon being allowed to spend a year in Ireland with his army regiment before assuming his responsibilities over his uncle's demesne. Trollope here allegorizes the ascension of the middle class to a share in political power, much as Thackeray had done in *Pendennis*. At the same time he also encodes the Irish colonial experience. Fred justifies his conquest of the "wild Irish girl" as something undertaken in a "spirit of adventure," but his adventuring is further metaphorized in his pointless and destructive habit of shooting seagulls. Trollope's narrative excoriates an enterprise which should be engaged responsibly towards the colonized, much as he had in *The Macdermots*, but goes even further here. Ireland is again personified as a woman victimized by a suitor who makes false promises in the marriage plot, but this time she is the mother of the girl ruined as a result of her conquest. *An Eye for an Eye* thus reverses the transformation of Kathleen Ni Houlihan. The beautiful young woman representing Irish nationhood is replaced by a crone – a madwoman isolated from the British nation in an asylum (in "the West of England") and consumed by a thirst for revenge. There is no longer any apparent hope for assimilation. However, *An Eye for an Eye* makes no attempt to depict actual Irish political or economic grievances or British colonial policy; it merely allegorizes the relationship between Britain and Ireland, with unmistakable references to the national tales. The central theme in this work is what Trollope regards as the tragedy of that relationship, and the most damning consequence of the allegorized critique of Irish colonialism is the end of Union. What differentiates Trollope's treatment of this theme here from in *The Macdermots* most significantly is the fact that in *An Eye for an Eye* the chance to unite two peoples under terms of mutual responsibility and good will has been completely obliterated. Since the increased intransigence of Irish nationalists contributed greatly to Trollope's pessimism, it will be helpful to recall some of the more important developments in the nationalist movement, which the novel engages through Mrs. O'Hara.

Perhaps most significantly, radical nationalist rhetoric had become much more violent since the publication of *The Macdermots*, and one of the chief contributing factors was the decline of Daniel O'Connell's influence. O'Connell, whose own positions had become more inflammatory by the close of the 1830s despite his continued adherence to a policy of nonviolence, founded the National Repeal Association in April 1840. He no longer merely advocated social justice for Catholics within the Empire. By Repeal he meant a recognition of the illegitimacy of Union and the inauguration of an alternative mechanism of government, but not necessarily an immediate and total severance of ties: "A parliament inferior to the British parliament I would accept as an installment ... I will never ask for or work for any other, save an independent legislative, but if others offer me a subordinate parliament, I will ... accept that offer."[3] Some historians suggest he indicated a type of devolution, with one King and two legislatures, but many members of the British public perceived his plan as the beginning of the dismemberment of the Empire. However, in 1843, O'Connell's ability to influence events in Ireland

---

[3]   Speech to Dublin Corporation, 1843, quoted in Oliver MacDonagh's *States of Mind: A Study of Anglo-Irish Conflict 1780–1980*. London: Allen and Unwin, 1983, 58.

rapidly waned. When the government banned a mass or "monster" meeting called for the purpose of summoning an alternative parliament, threatening to use force if necessary, O'Connell, who believed in constitutional measures and shunned violence, backed down and cancelled the meeting. His retreat was perceived as weak by many of his own constituents, upon whom the notion of Repeal had a strong emotional pull. Upon his defeat, the Young Ireland movement, whose leadership was comprised mostly of Protestants (as were the United Irishmen of the 1790s, whom they admired), splintered away from the Repeal movement. Though still venerated as "the Liberator" of the Catholics, O'Connell never regained his pre-eminence in Irish politics.

The Young Irelanders, in contrast to O'Connell, embraced violent means to achieve their goals, and now eclipsed his influence – R.F. Foster estimates the readership of their newspaper, *The Nation*, to be possibly as high as 250,000 by 1843.[4] Dismissing O'Connell's plea for Young Ireland's repudiation of physical violence, T.F. Meagher's call for British blood typifies the inflated rhetoric of the movement (and like the speech of Mrs. O'Hara, echoes the language of the Old Testament):

> Be it for the defence, or be it for the assertion of a nation's liberty, I look upon the sword as a sacred weapon. And if ... it has sometimes reddened the shroud of the oppressor like the anointed rod of the high priest, it has at other times blossomed into flowers to deck the freeman's brow ... Abhor the sword and stigmatize the sword? No, no.[5]

Violence like that espoused by Young Ireland was also embraced by the smaller, secret agrarian societies and other groups. Then came the Famine, which was characterized as genocide by some Irish, and which further polarized British and Irish factions. On the British side, we have seen the reaction of Thackeray, a hitherto sympathetic observer of Irish affairs, to Irish political agitation in the Famine's wake.[6]

By the time Trollope wrote *An Eye for an Eye*, Young Ireland had given way to new organizations (in the aftermath of a failed rising in 1848), but the pattern they established of a romantic nationalism, characterized by the ideology of a spiritual rebirth through nationhood, which was to be achieved by a racial community throwing off the domination of a demonized oppressor by whatever means necessary, was firmly entrenched. One of Young Ireland's more extreme but influential off-shoots was the Irish Confederation, which espoused militarism, separation, 1798 revivalism, and along with all this, Francophilia. In *An Eye for an Eye* this traditional nationalist resort to France for aid and succor as a kindred revolutionary, Anglophobic, Celtic nation – cf. *Barry Lyndon* – is noted in one of

---

[4] Foster, 1988, op. cit., 311.

[5] Debating O'Connell's motion, July 27, 1846. Quoted in Foster 1988, op. cit., 312.

[6] A comprehensive account of the political and social developments throughout this period is K.T. Hoppen's *Elections, Politics and Society in Ireland 1832–85*. Oxford: Oxford University Press, 1984.

the final sequences, when Kate O'Hara, the girl seduced by Fred Neville, flees to France to live with her reprobate father after Fred's child, whom she has been carrying, is stillborn, a symbolic touch that comments starkly on the author's view of the prospects for Union. Trollope embodies the increasingly intransigent nationalism which came to be known as Fenianism,[7] wholly committed to the use of force, in Kate's mother. Fenianism embraced the ethos of the Ribbon societies, Young Ireland, and other groups, as well as an hysterical Anglophobic ideology that viewed Britain as a satanic power on earth. Mrs. O'Hara's constant recitation of the Old Testament dictum "an eye for an eye" economically conveys the inexorability and self-righteousness of this ideology and at the same time records the moribund prospects for a successful Union.[8]

Against this political backdrop, Trollope unfolds the troubled relationship of a revised wild Irish girl and her English suitor. The allegorical resonances of *An Eye for an Eye* are obvious from the beginning. The novel opens with an Introduction which figures Ireland as a place of profound alienation, and rejects any prospect of assimilation: "At a private asylum in the West of England there lives ... an unfortunate lady, as to whom there has long since ceased to be any hope that she should live elsewhere."[9] Trollope allegorizes the more radical manifestations of Irish nationalism, including the rising influence of Fenianism, as the woman's obsessive quest for vengeance: "She has present to her, apparently in every waking moment of her existence, an object of intense interest ... She is ever justifying some past action of her life. 'An eye for an eye,' she says, 'and a tooth for a tooth.' And those words she will repeat daily, almost from morn till night."[10] The narrator further records the loss of good will on the part of former British sympathizers such as Thackeray: "Friends who would be anxious for her recovery, who would care to see her even in her wretched condition, she has none."[11] He implies that the imperial government expends great amounts of money on the maintenance of Ireland, and that much of this aid is spent on the paramilitary police and other governmental services: "But though she has no friends – none who love her – she has all the material comfort which friendship or even love could supply. All that

---

[7]   The Gaelicist label Fenian (a name derived from the Fianna army in the medieval saga of Fionn Mac Cumhail, or the anglicized "Finn McCool") was often used as an umbrella term, first applied to the Irish Republican Brotherhood in 1858, although this group initially avoided naming itself altogether. Like "Ribbonmen," it was a loose term applied to varying types of organizations, but it connoted an increasingly radical and violent opposition to membership in the Union. The IRB was founded by two Young Irelanders, James Stevens and John O'Mahoney, who fled to France after the failure of 1848.

[8]   Three valuable studies of the political movements summarized here and British reactions to them are Charles Townsend's *Political Violence in Ireland: Government and Resistance Since 1848.* Oxford: Oxford University Press, 1984; Patrick O'Farrell's *England and Ireland Since 1800.* Oxford: Oxford University Press, 1975; and Foster, 1988, op. cit.

[9]   Trollope, Anthony. *An Eye for an Eye* (1879). London: Penguin, 1993, 1. Hereafter *An Eye for an Eye.*

[10]   *An Eye for an Eye*, 1–2.

[11]   Ibid., 2.

money can do to lessen her misery, is done ... This lady has her own woman to attend her; and the woman, though stout and masterful, is gentle in language and kind in treatment."[12] Trollope, the former Irish civil servant, here seems to be suggesting that the services rendered in Ireland by the British government are administered in a "kindly" manner. One does not doubt the sincerity of his belief; however, the implication is at odds with many historical accounts as well as contemporary nineteenth-century Irish perceptions, a fact also attested to by the increase in nationalist radicalism.

However, *An Eye for an Eye* is not an attack upon Irish nationalism, nor does it, like *The Macdermots*, explore the causes which produce it; rather, it concentrates all of its rhetorical energy on the condemnation of a corrupt British colonial enterprise. This is made clear at the opening of the novel proper through allegorical references in the description of Fred's patrimony: "The Earl of Scroope lived at Scroope Manor ... an Elizabethan structure of some pretensions, but no fame."[13] Scroope Manor serves, as had the Macdermot house, as a metonymy, but in this case, of British colonialism in Ireland. Its characterization by Trollope as "an Elizabethan structure of some pretensions, but no fame," refers to a period which is significant for the consolidation of British power in Ireland. The 1580s and 90s witnessed the first massive confiscations and resettlements of Irish estates. This transfer of Irish property to English ownership consolidated Protestant power in Ireland, and brought much of colonial Ireland, hitherto rather weakly and ineffectively ruled, under firm British control.[14] The confiscations, together with the numerous other abrogations of Irish rights and privileges which characterized this long domination, informed the current political radicalism, rankling the Irish like a long-festering wound.

At the same time, Trollope, a "constant reader of Shakespeare,"[15] like Morgan and Edgeworth references the *Henriad* through the use of the name Scroope, which recalls two significant but not particularly prominent figures in a group of works including Prince Hal, Falstaff, Hotspur, King Richard II, and other more memorable characters. In *Richard II*, Sir Stephen Scroop brings news to the king that disaffection with his rule extends throughout society:

> White beards have armed their thin and hairless scalps
> against thy majesty; boys with women's voices
> ... clap their female joints
> in stiff unwieldy arms against thy crown
> ... distaff women manage rusty bills
> Against thy seat: both old and young rebel.[16]

---

[12] Ibid., 2–3.

[13] Ibid., 5.

[14] See Canny, *Kingdom and Colony: Ireland in the Atlantic World 1560–1800*. Baltimore: Johns Hopkins University Press 1988, et al.

[15] Richard Mullen with James Munson, *The Penguin Companion to Trollope*, 164.

[16] Shakespeare, William. *Richard II*, 3.2.112–15, 118–19.

The widespread nature of Irish discontent in 1870 makes this reference seem apposite enough, but several speeches of Richard Scroop, Archbishop of York in *Henry IV Part 2*, directly invoke rebellion against an irresponsible government. Scroop's description of his party's rebellion against Henry IV echoes Trollope's condemnation of the British colonial regime in both *The Macdermots* and *An Eye for an Eye*:

> I sent your Grace
> The parcels and particulars of our grief,
> The which hath been with scorn shoved from the court,
> Whereon this Hydra son of war is born.[17]

The invocation of the *Henriad* here is telling. Scott canonically invoked the Henry IV plays as a model for historical fiction, perhaps borrowing the idea from Lady Morgan (see Chapter 2 above), citing *Henry IV Part 2* on the title page of *Waverley*, and taking from Shakespeare civil war as the event through which history and the nation become visible. The nation which becomes visible in Trollope's novel is, however, a Great Britain which cannot include Ireland. As in Shakespeare's second history tetralogy, two of the main concerns of *An Eye for an Eye* are rebellion and the legitimacy of rulers. Trollope suggests through the marriage plot that Britain's rule in Ireland is illegitimate, insofar as its policies constitute a corrupt exercise of power by a ruling authority out of touch with its society's ideals. It is the irresponsibility of the superior partner of the Union towards the Irish, and the resulting intransigent disaffection of the weaker, that comprises the "argument" of *An Eye for an Eye*.[18]

The allegorical references to the British colonial project are continued in descriptions of Scroope Manor's library and grounds. The proximity of a small percentage of dwellings to the Manor and to the church, while the great majority are prevented from making "such encroachments," records the political and economic favoritism accorded the Anglo-Irish: "Close to the Manor and again near to the Church, some favoured few had been allowed to build houses ... but these tenements must have been built at a time in which landowners were very much more jealous than they are now of such encroachments from their humbler neighbours."[19] The disconnection of the Protestant ruling classes from the Catholic

---

[17]   Shakespeare, William. *Henry IV Part 2*, 4.2.35–8. See the description of the events surrounding passage of Union in Chapter 8 above.

[18]   Cf. Foster's description of the presence of the imperial government in Ireland in the 1830s (cited above in the discussion of *The Macdermotts*), a situation which had not appreciably changed by the 1870s. Added to this were new grievances, among them significantly the *laissez-faire* policies of the Russell government in response to the famine, thought by many in Ireland to have consigned millions to death or emigration. The large-scale evictions by many landowners in the wake of the Famine increased the traditional hostility between landlords and tenants, and the bitterness of the nationalists was expressed more implacably and violently.

[19]   *An Eye for an Eye*, 6.

religion and culture is suggested by the Manor library's disused books: "There was a vast library filled with old books which no one ever touched, – huge volumes of antiquated and now all but useless theology, and folio editions of the least known classics."[20] To the ruling classes Catholicism may well have seemed antiquated, and in terms of career advancement it was certainly useless as well, albeit no longer an explicit disadvantage since Catholic Emancipation.[21] In describing the Manor's servants, Trollope also alludes to the size and prosperity of the civil servant class, while characterizing such jobs as sinecures: "The household [staff] was very large ... All these [servants] lived well under the old Earl. There was much to get and almost nothing to do. A servant might live forever at Scroope Manor, – if only sufficiently submissive to Mrs. Bunce, the housekeeper. There was certainly no parsimony at the Manor, but the luxurious living of the household was confined to the servants' department."[22] Trollope makes the connection between Scroope Manor and Britain's longstanding colonial regime unmistakable by noting the prohibitions against Catholic participation in public life: "None were taken into service but they who were or called themselves members of the Church Establishment."[23]

Like Captain Ussher, Fred uses insincere promises of marriage to obtain sexual favors. That he represents the British colonial project is evidenced by Trollope's direct invocation of Lady Morgan's hero Horatio. Fred similarly happens upon a beautiful Irish girl in a Connaught remarkable for its "wildness and strangeness."[24] But Fred's spirit of adventure, for which he often congratulates himself, is rapacious, and the narrator frequently compares him to a wolf, whose attraction for a naïve girl is enhanced by the smooth manners which reflect his metropolitan background: "Men so often are as ravenous as wolves, merciless, rapacious, without hearts, full of greed, full of lust, looking on female beauty as prey ... It might be that [Fred] was a wolf, but his manners were not wolfish."[25] After his conquest of the girl, Fred concocts a confused and impracticable scheme to offer her not a marriage but an arrangement that would make her his concubine: "Then he gave the reins to some confused notion of an Irish bride, a wife who should be half a wife and half not, – whom he would love and cherish tenderly but of whose existence no English friend should be aware. How could he more charmingly indulge his

---

[20] Ibid., 7–8.

[21] The numbers among the Catholic middling classes had increased in the aftermath of Emancipation, but by how much is a matter of some contention among historians. Thomas Drummond, Under-Secretary for Ireland 1835–1840, opened positions on the bench and in the Solicitor and Attorneys General's offices and instituted other reforms. But his premature death dampened the new spirit of co-operation and reform. Moreover, Catholics were still virtually excluded from the imperial government in the predominantly Catholic country.

[22] Ibid., 9–10.

[23] Ibid., 13. Those who "called themselves members" is probably a sly reference to recanters such as Ulick O'Shane.

[24] *An Eye for an Eye*, 105.

[25] Ibid., 95, 97.

spirit of adventure than by some such arrangement as this?"[26] To emphasize to the reader that the narrator's irony reflects more than a mildly indulgent mid-Victorian disdain for Regency-type immorality (of the kind attached negatively to Thackeray's Major Pendennis), Trollope codes Fred's adventuring as predation, by placing the conquest and Fred's projected means of conducting the affair in immediate juxtaposition with his other customary indulgence of his spirit of adventure – the shooting of seagulls, whose wanton destruction is analogous to that of Kate and her mother: "Then he got into his canoe, and, having succeeded in killing two gulls on the Drumdeirg rocks, thought that for that day he had carried out his purpose as a man of adventure very well."[27] This is high Victorian dudgeon, expressed in biting sarcasm.

The inescapable conclusion here is that the cultural nationalism being constructed in this novel is exclusionary, but in a way very unlike that of *Pendennis*. Irishness is written out of Britishness, but in this novel, it is done regretfully. What is portrayed as most un-British in *An Eye for an Eye* is the Irish colonial project itself. Fred's enterprise is represented as divorced from the social and political ideals of the larger British society through various narrative threads, but perhaps most tellingly in the subplot involving Fred's brother Jack. The narrator comments upon the name as a marker of commonness: "For an old family coachman it beats all names."[28] But it is clear that as an ordinary middle-class Briton, Jack also embodies values very different from those of the rapacious Fred. Upon his uncle's death, Fred turns to his brother ostensibly for advice on how to begin his life as the new Earl of Scroope, but in reality seeking approval for his bid to extract himself from his promise to marry Kate. Jack informs Fred that honour should be every man's highest ideal: "How can I advise you? ... As a rule a man should keep his word ... A man should keep his word certainly. And I know no promise so solemn as that made to a woman when followed by conduct such as yours has been."[29] Fred refuses to heed his brother's advice, and instead returns to Ireland to inform Kate and Mrs O'Hara that he will not make Kate Countess of Scroope. In his interview with Kate's mother on cliffs overlooking the ocean, she becomes infuriated, and demands that Fred act honorably: "Tell me, man, that she shall be your lawful wife." Fred replies "It cannot be so," and Mrs O'Hara pushes him off of the cliff.[30] Upon Fred's death, Jack becomes Earl of Scroope.

By restoring to the ruling class the ideals Jack embodies, Trollope is elaborating a national identity that privileges fair play and honor, encoded in a well-regulated male sexuality not unlike that championed by Edgeworth and Burke. But the unequal partnership Edgeworth envisioned at the beginning of the century has resulted in a disaster that Trollope forthrightly documents. Though Jack, who

---

26   Ibid., 133.
27   Ibid., 134.
28   Ibid., 56.
29   Ibid., 319.
30   Ibid., 410–11.

represents a renewed commitment to traditional "British" values, wishes to treat Mrs O'Hara fairly, no more can be done for her than the provision of her physical comfort: "When it was at last decided that the law should not interfere at all as to the personal custody of the poor maniac who had sacrificed everything to avenge her daughter, the Earl of Scroope selected for her comfort the asylum in which she still continues to justify from morning to night, and, alas, often all the night long, the terrible deed of which she is ever thinking … 'An eye for an eye, and a tooth for a tooth!'"[31] In this way Trollope characterizes the relationship of the two societies, which, it is now clear, are and will remain two distinct societies: one consumed by a thirst for revenge beyond all reason, the other disposed, in Thackeray's phrase, to "right old wrongs" but prevented by the circumstances of the other's hatred from doing more than providing the means for material support.

Mrs. O'Hara embodies an Irish nationalism vastly more radical and implacable than that espoused by the social outcasts who fleetingly entice a desperate Thady to consider hearing them out in *The Macdermots*. That he has portrayed the madwoman's vengeance as understandable, if not justifiable, renders Trollope's vision in some ways far more sympathetic than many of his contemporary countrymen's. However, the impossibility of Union is insisted upon. Fred's frequently stated but ill-formed plans to keep Kate without allowing her to become Countess of Scroope allegorize England's entrance into a Union in which Ireland was never offered full partnership. *An Eye for an Eye*, in the classic romantic national tale tradition, figures this irresponsible political conduct as rogue male sexuality. It also makes clear that this irresponsibility in large part precipitates Mrs. O'Hara's act. Her murder of Fred is unpremeditated; when the fullness of his insincerity is revealed she becomes "maddened" with a rage with which Trollope's middle-class readership could readily sympathize, if not excuse, and she uses the proximity of the steep cliff to exact her revenge: "The peril of his position on the top of the cliff had not occurred to him … Nor had that peril … ever occurred to her. She had not brought him there that she might threaten him with that danger, or that she might avenge herself by the power which it gave her. But now the idea flashed across her maddened mind."[32]

Unimagined Community

In *The Macdermots of Ballycloran*, the climax of the plot also hinged on an unpremeditated murder. But in that earlier novel, the "victims" of the murder and its fallout – Ussher, Feemy, and Thady – were all representative of "local" elements of Irish society. In *An Eye for an Eye*, Fred's death represents the end of the corrupt colonial enterprise, as Jack's assumption of the Earldom represents for Trollope the commencement of the good-faith policies of the British government

---

[31]   Ibid., 425–6.

[32]   Ibid., 411.

towards Ireland,[33] and the material support represented by Mrs. O'Hara's upkeep. But the necessity of her confinement from the general population itself represents the insuperable alienation of a preponderant segment of the Irish population, a circumstance Trollope denied in *The Macdermots*. The marriage plot structure utilized by the liberal Unionist Lady Morgan to express great hope for a future in which Britain and Ireland are united thus provides the liberal Unionist[34] Trollope a regrettably fitting means by which to record the death of those hopes: "Indeed, there is no one left ... by whom such a hope could be cherished."[35]

Despite Trollope's palpable sympathy for the "poor maniac" and regret for the estrangement of the two societies, however, the fact that Mrs. O'Hara has murdered the representative of British colonial power places final responsibility for the schism squarely on the Irish. Though clearly driven to it, she still is mad, and a murderess. This characterization seems monstrous in comparison with that of the young but careless and heedless "victim," and despite Trollope's forthright portrayal of the evident British reluctance to embrace the Irish as equals that characterized the "conversation" from the beginning, this lack of a fair British perspective, as I argued in the first chapter, was integral to the failure of the enterprise. While many of the Irish people never embraced Union, perhaps had they been offered "true" Union, they might have – we can never know. By the waning years of the nineteenth century, what was becoming evident was that the Union was doomed from the beginning. Trollope's portrayal of Britain's colonial enterprise as thoroughly corrupt was prescient insofar as it paralleled the belief common among the Irish revolutionary generation, which was just then being born, which identified all English cultural norms with corruption.[36] As far as the Union of Great Britain and Ireland was concerned, if communities are imagined, there was a failure of imagination on all sides. Lady Morgan was more prophetic than perhaps she realized when she decided *not* to depict Gorvina walking down that aisle.

---

[33]   For Trollope these probably began with the Catholic Emancipation Act of 1828, and included parliamentary reform, the repeal of the Tithe Act, Famine relief, some legal and judicial reforms, the second Parliamentary Reform Act of 1867, the disestablishment of the Irish Church in 1869, and Gladstone's attempt to introduce some principles of tenant protection in the Land Act of 1870.

[34]   Ironically, by the late 1880s the term "liberal Unionist" came to mean a staunch opponent of Home Rule and follower of Joseph Chamberlain; here, however, I'm using it more loosely to characterize the views of both Morgan and Trollope (who died in 1882 a staunch opponent of Home Rule) with wider connotations of both the terms "liberal" and "Unionist."

[35]   *An Eye for an Eye*, 1.

[36]   Foster, 1993, op. cit., 299.

Bibliography

Works Cited: Primary Sources

Colquhoun, Patrick. *A Treatise on the Police of the Metropolis*. London: H. Fry, 1797.

Croker, John Wilson. "Review of *Woman: Or Ida of Athens*," *The Quarterly Review* 1 (1809), 49–63.

———. "Review of France," *Quarterly Review* 32 (April 1817), 260–86.

Edgeworth, Maria. *The Absentee* (1812). Edited with an Introduction by McCormack, W.J., and Kim Walker. Oxford: Oxford University Press, 1988.

———. *Castle Rackrent* (1800). London: Penguin, 1992.

———. *Belinda* (1801). London: Baldwin and Cradock, 1832.

———. *Ormond: A Tale* (1817). London: Macmillan, 1895.

———. *Practical Education*. London: Joseph Johnson, 1801.

Fielding, Henry. *An Enquiry Into the Causes of the Late Increase of Robbers, &c.* (1751). Middletown, CT: Wesleyan University Press, 1988.

Kay, James. *The Moral and Physical Condition of the Working Classes Engaged in the Cotton Manufacture in Manchester (1832)*. Shannon: Irish University Press, 1971.

Owenson, Sydney (Lady Morgan). *Florence McCarthy* (1818). New York: D. & J. Sadlier (n.d.).

———. *France* (1817).

———. *The O'Briens and the O'Flahertys* (1828).

———. *O'Donnel, A National Tale* (1814).

———. *Patriotic Sketches of Ireland* (1807).

———. *The Wild Irish Girl* (1807). London: Oxford University Press, 1999.

Report of the Select Committee on the Police of the Metropolis (1816), 510, vol. V.

Report of the Select Committee on Mendacity in the Metropolis (1816), vol. V.

Report of the Select Committee on the Police of the Metropolis (1817), 231, vol. XVII.

Report of the Select Committee on the Police of the Metropolis (1828), vol. VI.

Report of the Select Committee on Drunkenness (1834), vol. VIII.

Report of the Select Committee on the State of the Irish Poor in Great Britain (1836), vol. XXXIV.

Report of the Royal Commission to Inquire into the Best Means for Establishing an Efficient Constabulary Force in the Counties of England and Wales (1839), 169, vol. XIX.

Thackeray, William Makepeace. *The Memoirs of Barry Lyndon, Written by Himself* (1844). Lincoln: University of Nebraska Press, 1962.

————. "A Box of Novels," *Fraser's* 29:2 (February 1844), 153–69.

————. *The History of Pendennis: His Fortunes and Misfortunes, His Friends and His Greatest Enemy*. New York: Charles Scribner's Sons, 1947.

————. *Hitherto Unidentified Contributions to Punch*, ed. M.H. Spielmann. New York: Harper & Brothers, 1900.

————. *Thackeray's Contributions to the <u>Morning Chronicle</u>*, ed. Gordon Ray. Urbana: University of Illinois Press, 1966.

————. *The Irish Sketch Book* (1843). New York: T.Y. Crowell, (n.d.).

Trollope, Anthony. *An Eye for an Eye* (1879). London: Penguin, 1993.

————. *An Autobiography* (1883). Oxford: Oxford University Press, 1980.

————. *The Macdermots of Ballycloran* (1847). New York: Dover, 1988.

————. *Phineas Finn, the Irish Member* (1869). Oxford: Oxford University Press, 1992.

Works Cited: Secondary Sources

Anderson, Benedict. *Imagined Communities: Reflections on the Origins and Spread of Nationalism*. London: Verso, 1991.

Armstrong, Nancy. *Desire and Domestic Fiction: A Political History of the Novel*. New York: Oxford University Press, 1987.

Ayers, P.K. "Fellows of Infinite Tongue: *Henry V* and the King's English," *Studies in English Literature* 34:2 (Spring 1994), 253–77.

Bellamy, Liz. "Regionalism and Nationalism: Maria Edgeworth, Walter Scott, and the Definition of Britishness," in *The Regional Novel in Britain and Ireland, 1800–1990*, ed. K.D.M. Snell. Cambridge: Cambridge University Press, 1998, 54–77.

Bradshaw Brendan, Andrew Hadfield, and Willy Maley, eds, *Representing Ireland: Literature and the Origins of Conflict*. London, 1975.

Braudy, Leo. *The World in a Frame*. New York: Doubleday/Anchor, 1977.

Brennan, Timothy, "The National Longing for Form," in *Nation and Narration*, ed. Homi Bhabha. New York: Routledge and Keegan Paul, 1990, 44–70

Brewer, Kenneth L. Jr. "Colonial Discourse in William Makepeace Thackeray's *Irish Sketch Book*," *Papers on Language and Literature* 29:3 (Summer 1993), 259–83.

Brown, Terence. "Saxon and Celt: The Stereotypes," in *Literary Interrelations: Ireland, England and the World (Vol. 3, National Images and Stereotypes)*, eds Wolfgang Zach and Henry Kosok. Tubingen: Gunter Narr Verlag, 1987, 1–9.

Burke, Edmund. *Reflections on the Revolution in France* (1790), ed. Conor Cruise O'Brien. London: Penguin, 1986.

Butler, Marilyn. *Maria Edgeworth: A Literary Biography*. Oxford: Oxford University Press, 1972.

Campbell, Mary. *Lady Morgan: The Life and Times of Sydney Owenson*. London: Pandora, 1988.

Carlyle, Thomas. *Chartism* (1839). New York: James B. Millar, 1885.

Colby, Robert A. "*Barry Lyndon* and the Irish Hero," *Nineteenth-Century Fiction* 21 (1966), 109–30.

Colgan, Maurice. "After *Rackrent*: Ascendancy Nationalism in Maria Edgeworth's Later Irish Novels," in *Studies in Anglo-Irish Literature*, ed. Heinz Kozok. Bonn: Bouvier Verlag Herbert Grundmann, 1982, 37–42.

Conley, Carol. *The Unwritten Law: Criminal Justice in Victorian Kent*. Oxford: Oxford UP, 1991.

Corbett, Mary Jean. "Public Affections and Familial Politics: Burke, Edgeworth, and the 'Common Naturalization' of Great Britain," *English Literary History* 61 (1994), 877–97.

Curtis, L. Perry. *Apes and Angels*. Washington, D.C.: The Smithsonian Institution, 1997.

Davidoff, Lenore and Catherine Hall. *Family Fortunes: Men and Women of the English Middle Class*, 1780–1850. Chicago, 1987.

Davis, Graham. "Little Irelands," in *The Irish in Britain 1815–1939*, eds Roger Swift and Sheridan Gilley. London: Pinter, 1989.

Disraeli, Benjamin. *Sybil, or The Two Nations* (1845). Ware (Hertfordshire): Wordsworth Classics, 1995.

Duncan, Ian. *Modern Romance and Transformations of the Novel: The Gothic, Scott, Dickens*. Cambridge: Cambridge University Press, 1992.

Dunleavy, Janet Egleson. "Trollope and Ireland," in *Trollope Centenary Essays*, ed. John Halperin. New York: St Martin's, 1982.

Dunne, Tom. "Fiction as 'The Best History of Nations': Lady Morgan's Irish Novels," in *The Writer as Witness: Literature as Historical Evidence*, ed. Tom Dunne. Cork: Cork University Press, 1987, 133–57.

Eagleton, Terry. "Form and Ideology in the Anglo-Irish Novel," in *Literary Interrelations: Ireland, Egypt and the Far East*, eds. Wolfgang Zack and Henry Kosok. Tubingen: Gunter Narr Verlag, 1987, 135–46.

Edwards, Owen Dudley. "Anthony Trollope, the Irish Writer," *Nineteenth-Century Fiction* 38:1 (June 1983), 1–42.

Ferris, Ina. *The Achievement of Literary Authority*. Ithaca: Cornell University Press, 1991.

———. "Narrating Cultural Encounter: Lady Morgan and the Irish National Tale," *Nineteenth-Century Literature* 51:3 (December 1996), 287–303.

———. "Writing on the Border: The National Tale, Female Writing, and the Public Sphere," in *Romanticism, History, and the Possibilities of Genre*, eds Tilottama Rajan and Julia M. Wright. Cambridge: Cambridge University Press, 1998.

Finnegan, Frances. *Poverty and Prejudice: A Study of Irish Immigrants in York 1840–75*. Cork: Cork University Press, 1982.

Flanagan, Thomas. *The Irish Novelists 1800–1850*. New York: Columbia University Press, 1959.

Foster, R.F. "Ascendancy and Union," in *The Oxford History of Ireland*. New York: Oxford University Press, 1989.

————. *Modern Ireland 1600–1972*. London: Penguin, 1988.

————. *Paddy and Mr. Punch*. London: Penguin, 1993.

Foucault, Michel. *Discipline and Punish*, trans. Alan Sheridan. New York: Vintage, 1995.

Gamer, Michael. *Romanticism and the Gothic: Genre, Reception, and Canon Formation*. Cambridge: Cambridge University Press, 2000.

Gilley, Sheridan. "English Attitudes to the Irish in England 1789–1900," in *Immigrants and Minorities in British Society*, ed. Colin Holmes. London, 1978.

Greenblatt, Stephen. *Renaissance Self-Fashioning*. Chicago: University of Chicago Press, 1982.

Hack, Daniel. "Inter-Nationalism: *Castle Rackrent* and Anglo-Irish Union," *Novel: a Forum on Fiction* 29:2 (1996), 145–64.

Highley, Christopher, "Wales, Ireland, and *Henry IV*," *Renaissance Drama* 21 (1990), 91–114.

Hollingworth, Brian. *Maria Edgeworth's Irish Writing: Language, History, Politics*. New York: St Martin's, 1997.

Innes, C.L. *Woman and Nation in Irish Literature and Society, 1880–1930*. Athens: University of Georgia Press, 1993.

Jennings, Louis J. *The Croker Papers*. New York: Scribner's, 1884.

Kelly, Gary. "Jane Austen and the English Novelists of the 1790s," in *Fetter'd or Free? British Women Novelists, 1670–1815*. Athens: Ohio University Press, 1986, 285–306.

————. *Women, Writing and Revolution 1790–1827*. Oxford: Clarendon Press, 1993.

Klancher, Jon. *The Making of the English Reading Audiences, 1790–1832*. Madison: University of Wisconsin Press, 1987.

Klotz, Gunther. "Thackeray's Ireland: Image and Attitude in The Irish Sketch Book and Barry Lyndon," in *Literary Interrelations: Ireland, England and the World (Vol. 3, National Images and Stereotypes)*, eds Wolfgang Zach and Henry Kosok. Tubingen: Gunter Narr Verlag, 1987, 95–102.

Leerssen, Joseph. *Remembrance and Imagination: Patterns in the Historical and Literary Representation of Ireland in the Nineteenth Century*. Notre Dame, IN: University of Notre Dame Press, 1997.

Lees, Lynn. *Exiles of Erin: Irish Migrants in Victorian London*. Ithaca: Cornell University Press, 1979.

Lew, Joseph W. "Sydney Owenson and the Fate of Empire," *Keats-Shelley Journal* 39 (1990), 39–65.

Lukacs, Georg. *The Historical Novel* (1937), trans. Hannah and Stanley Mitchell. Lincoln: University of Nebraska Press, 1983.

Lynch, Deidre. "Nationalizing Women and Domesticating Fiction: Edmund Burke and the Genres of Englishness," *Wordsworth Circle* 25 (Winter 1994), 45–9.

MacDonagh, Oliver. *States of Mind: A Study of Anglo-Irish Conflict 1780–1980*. London: Allen and Unwin, 1983.

Mellor, Anne K. *Romanticism and Gender*. New York: Routledge, 1993.

Miller, Julie Anne. "Acts of Union: Family Violence and National Courtship in Maria Edegworth's *The Absentee* and Sydney Owenson's *The Wild Irish Girl*," in *Border Crossings: Irish Women Writers and National Identities*, ed. Kathryn Kirkpatrick. Tuscaloosa: University of Alabama Press, 2000.

Mullen, Richard and James Munson, eds. *The Penguin Companion to Trollope*. New York: Penguin, 1996.

Murphy, Andrew. "Shakespeare's Irish History," *Literature and History* (3rd series) 5:1 (Spring 1996).

Neill, Michael. "Broken English and Broken Irish: Nation, Language, and the Optic Power in Shakespeare's Histories," *Shakespeare Quarterly* 45:1 (Spring 1994), 20–49.

Newcomer, James. *Lady Morgan the Novelist*. London: Associated University Presses, 1990.

O'Tuathaigh, M.A.G. "The Irish in Nineteenth-Century Britain: Problems of Integration," in *The Irish in the Victorian City*, eds R. Swift and S Gilley. London: Pinter, 1985.

Parker, Patricia. *Literary Fat Ladies: Rhetoric, Gender, Property*. London: Methuen, 1987.

Paulson, Ronald. *Representations of Revolution, 1789–1820*. New Haven: Yale University Press, 1983.

Peters, Catherine. *Thackeray's Universe: Shifting Worlds of Imagination and Reality*. New York: Oxford University Press, 1987.

Poovey, Mary. *Making a Social Body*. Chicago: University of Chicago Press, 1996.

Richardson, Clem. "The Irish in Victorian Bradford," *The Bradford Antiquary*, ix, 294–316.

Said, Edward. *Culture and Imperialism*. New York: Vintage, 1994.

———. *Orientalism*. New York: Vintage, 1979.

Shakespeare, William. *Henry IV Part 1*. New York: Signet, 1986.

———. *Henry IV Part 2*. New York: Signet, 1988.

———. *Henry V*. New York: Signet, 1988.

———. *Richard II*. New York: Dorset, 1988.

Stallybrass, Peter and Allon White. *The Politics and Poetics of Transgression*. Ithaca: Cornell University Press, 1986.

Stevenson, Lionel. *The Showman of Vanity Fair*. New York: Scribners, 1947.

———. *The Wild Irish Girl: The Life of Lady Morgan*. New York: Scribners, 1950.

Stocking, George. *Victorian Anthropology*. New York: Free Press, 1987.

Swift, Roger. "Another Stafford Street Row: Law, Order, and the Irish in Mid-Victorian Wolverhampton," *Immigrants and Minorities*, 3:1 (March 1984), 5–29.

———. "Crime and the Irish in Nineteenth-Century Britain," in *The Irish in Britain 1815–1939*, eds Swift, Roger and Sheridan Gilley. London: Pinter, 1989, 163–82.

Tracy, Robert. "Maria Edgeworth and Lady Morgan: Legality versus Legitimacy," *Nineteenth-Century Fiction* 40:1 (June 1985), 1–22.

———. "'The Unnatural Ruin': Trollope and Nineteenth-Century Fiction," *Nineteenth-Century Fiction* 37:3 (December 1982), 358–82.

Trumpener, Katie. *Bardic Nationalism: The Romantic Novel and the British Empire*. Princeton: Princeton University Press, 1997.

———. "National Character, Nationalist Plots: National Tale and Historical Novel in the Age of *Waverley*, 1806–1830," *English Literary History* 60 (1993), 685–731.

Wallace, Martin. *A Short History of Ireland*. New York: Barnes and Noble, 1986.

Wiener, Martin. *Reconstructing the Criminal: Culture, Law, and Policy in England 1830–1914*. Cambridge: Cambridge University Press, 1990.

Wittig, F.W. "Trollope's Irish Fiction," *Éire-Ireland* 9:3, 97–118.

Wollstonecraft, Mary. *A Vindication of the Rights of Woman* (1792). London: Penguin, 1992.

Further Reading

Allen, Michael and Angela Wilcox, eds. *Critical Approaches to Anglo-Irish Literature*. Gerrards Cross: Colin Smythe, 1988.

Altick, Richard D. *The English Common Reader: A Social History of the Mass-Reading Public*. Chicago: Chicago University Press, 1957.

Andrewes, Elmer. "Aesthetics, Politics, and Identity: Lady Morgan's *The Wild Irish Girl*," *Canadian Journal of Irish Studies* 12:2 (December 1987), 7–19.

Arac, Jonathan, and Harriet Ritvo, eds. *Macropolitics of Nineteenth-Century Literature: Nationalism, Exoticism, Imperialism*. Philadelphia: University of Pennsylvania Press, 1991.

Armstrong, Nancy, and Leonard Tennenhouse. "A Novel Nation, or How to Rethink England as an Emergent Culture," in *Modern Language Quarterly* 54:3 (September 1993), 327–44.

Ashcroft, Bill, Gareth Griffiths, and Helen Tiffin. *The Empire Writes Back: Theory and Practice in post-Colonial Literature*. London: Routledge, 1989.

Asmundson, Doris R. "Trollope's First Novel: A Re-Examination," *Éire-Ireland* 6 (Autumn 1971), 83–91.

Atkinson, Colin B. and Jo Atkinson. "Sydney Owenson, Lady Morgan: Irish Patriot and First Professional Woman Writer," *Éire-Ireland* 15 (1980), 60–90.

Azim, Firdouz. *The Colonial Rise of the Novel*. New York: Routledge, 1993.

Bakhtin, Mikhail. *The Dialogic Imagination: Four Essays by MM Bahktin*, ed. Michael Holquist. Austin: University of Texas Press, 1981.

Barfoot, C.C. ed., *Literature of Politics, the Politics of Literature: Ritual Remembering – History, Myth and Politics in Anglo-Irish Drama*. Amsterdam: Rodopi, 1995.

Beames, M.R. "The Ribbon Societies: Lower-class Nationalism in Pre-famine Ireland," *Past and Present* 92 (1982), 157–71.

Beckett, J.C., *The Anglo-Irish Tradition*. London: Faber and Faber, 1976.

———. *The Making of Modern Ireland 1603–1923*. London: Faber and Faber 1966.

Berlatsky, Joel. "Roots of Conflict in Ireland: Colonial Attitudes in the Age of the Penal Laws," *Éire-Ireland* 18 (1983), 40–56.

Bhaba, Homi. *The Location of Culture*. New York: Routledge, 1994.

———. "The Other Question: Difference, Discrimination, and the Discourse of Colonialism," in *Literature, Politics, and Theory: Papers from the Essex Conference, 1976–84*. New York: Methuen, 1986.

Binchy, Maeve. "Introduction," in *An Eye for An Eye*. London: Trollope Society Edition, 1993.

Boerner, Peter. *Concepts of National Identity: An Interdisciplinary Dialogue*. Baden-Baden: Nomos Verlagsgesellschaft, 1986.

Boulton, James T. *The Language of Politics in the Age of Wilkes and Burke*. London: Routledge and Kegan Paul, 1963.

Bourdieu, Pierre. *The Field of Cultural Production*. New York: Columbia University Press, 1993.

Bowen, Kurt. *Protestants in a Catholic State: Ireland's Privileged Minority*. Dublin: Gill & Macmillan 1983.

Brantlinger, Patrick. *Rule of Darkness: British Literature and Imperialism, 1830–1914*. Ithaca: Cornell University Press, 1988.

Braudy, Leo. *The World in a Frame*. New York: Doubleday/Anchor, 1977.

Buckland. Patrick. *The Anglo-Irish and the New Ireland, 1885–1922*. Dublin: Gill and Macmillan, 1972.

Butler, Marilyn. Introduction to *Castle Rackrent* and *Ennui*. Harmondsworth: Penguin, 1992.

———. *Romantics, Rebels and Reactionaries: English Literature and Its Background, 1760–1830*. Oxford: Oxford University Press, 1981.

Canny, Nicholas P. *The Elizabethan Conquest of Ireland: a Pattern Established 1565–76*. Sussex: Harvester Press 1976.

———. *From Reformation to Restoration: Ireland 1534–1660*. Dublin: Criterion/ Helicon 1987.

———. *Kingdom and Colony: Ireland in the Atlantic World 1560–1800*. Baltimore: Johns Hopkins University Press 1988.

———. "Identity Formation in Ireland: The Emergence of the Anglo-Irish," in *Colonial Identity in the Atlantic World, 1500–1800*, eds Canny and A. Pagden. Princeton University Press 1987.

Carey, John. *Thackeray: Prodigal Genius*. London: Faber and Faber, 1977.

Carroll, David. "Narrative, Heterogeneity, and the Question of the Political: Bakhtin and Lyotard," in *The Aims of Representation: Subject/ Text/ History*, ed. Murray Krieger. New York: Columbia University Press, 1987.

Chatterjee, Partha. *The Nation and Its Fragments: Colonial and Postcolonial Histories*. Princeton: Princeton University Press, 1993.

Cockshut, A.O.J. "An Eye for An Eye," in *Anthony Trollope: A Critical Study*. London: Collins, 1955.

Colby, Robert. *Thackeray's Canvass of Humanity: An Author and His Public.* Columbus: Ohio State University Press, 1979.

Colley, Linda. *Britons: Forging the Nation 1707–1837.* New Haven: Yale University Press, 1992.

Collins, Kevin. *The Cultural Conquest of Ireland.* Cork: Mercier Press, 1991.

Comerford, R.V. *The Fenians in Context: Irish Politics and Society 1848–82.* Dublin: Wolfhound Press, 1998.

Conley, Carolyn A., "Wars Among Savages: Homicide and Ethnicity in the Victorian United Kingdom," *Journal of British Studies* 44:4 (2005), 775–95.

Connelly, Joseph F. "Transparent Poses: Castle Rackrent and The Memoirs of Barry Lyndon," *Éire-Ireland: A Journal of Irish Studies* 14:2 (1979), 37–43.

Connolly, Claire. "'I Accuse Miss Owenson': The Wild Irish Girl as Media Event," *Colby Library Quarterly* 36 (2000), 98–115.

———. "Introduction," in *The Wild Irish Girl: A National Tale*, ed. Sydney Owenson. London: Pickering and Chatto, 2000.

———, ed. *Theorizing Ireland.* London: Palgrave Macmillan, 2003.

Corbett, Mary Jean. *Allegories of Union in Irish and English Writing 1790–1870: Politics, History, and the Family from Edgeworth to Arnold.* Cambridge: Cambridge University Press, 2000.

Crawford, Jon G. *Anglicising the Government of Ireland: The Privy Council and the Expansion of Tudor Rule 1556–1578.* Irish Academic/Irish Legal Hist. Soc., 1993.

Crawford, Robert. *Devolving English Literature.* New York: Oxford University Press, 1992.

Cronin, John. *The Anglo-Irish Novel, Vol. 1: The Nineteenth Century.* Belfast: Appletree, 1980.

———. "Trollope and the Matter of Ireland," in *Anthony Trollope*, ed. Tony Bareham. New York: Barnes and Noble, 1980.

Crotty, Raymond. *Ireland in Crisis: A Study of Capitalist colonial Underdevelopment.* Dingle: Brandon, 1968.

Curtis, L. Perry (Lewis Perry). *Apes and Angels: The Irishman in Victorian Caricature.* Washington, D.C.: Smithsonian Institution Press, 1996.

———. *Anglo-Saxons And Celts; A Study Of Anti-Irish Prejudice In Victorian England.* New York: New York University Press, 1968.

Curtis, Liz. *Nothing But the Same Old Story: The Roots of Anti-Irish Racism.* London: Turnaround Distribution, 1985.

David, Deidre. *Rule Britannia: Women, Empire, and Victorian Writing.* Ithaca: Cornell University Press, 1995.

Deane, Seamus. "Civilians and Barbarians," in *Ireland's Field Day.* Field Day Theatre Company. Notre Dame: University of Notre Dame Press, 1986, 33–42.

———. "Fiction and Politics: Irish Nineteenth-Century National Character 1790–1900," in *The Writer as Witness: Literature as Historical Evidence*, ed. Tom Dunne. Cork: Cork University Press, 1987, 90–113.

————. "Maria Edgeworth, Romanticism and Utilitarianism," *Gaeliana* 8 (1986), 9–15.

————. "National Character and National Audience: Race, Crowds and Readers," in *Critical Approaches to Anglo-Irish Literature*, eds Michael Allen and Angela Wilcox. Gerrards Cross: Colin Smythe, 1989, 40–52.

Decap, Roger. "*Barry Lyndon*: Thackeray et 'l'ailleurs,'" in *Caliban, Vol. 28*. Toulouse, France, 1991, 37–48.

De Nie, Michael. *The Eternal Paddy: Irish Identity and the British Press, 1798–1882*. Madison: University of Wisconsin Press, 2004.

Dennis, Ian. *Nationalism and Desire in Early Historical Fiction*. London: Macmillan, 1997.

Duggan, G.C. *The Stage Irishman: A History of the Irish Play and Stage Characters from the Earliest Times*. Dublin: Talbot Press, 1937.

Dunne, Tom. "Haunted by History: Irish Romantic Writing 1800–50," in *Romanticism in National Context*, eds Roy Porter and Mikuláš Teich. New York: Cambridge University Press, 1988.

————. *Maria Edgeworth and the Colonial Mind*. Cork: University College Cork, 1984.

Duytschaever, Joris and Geert Lernout, eds. *History and Violence in Anglo-Irish Literature*. Amsterdam: Rodopi, 1988.

Dyer, Gary. *British Satire and the Politics of Style, 1789–1832*. Cambridge: Cambridge University Press, 1997.

Eagleton, Terry. *Heathcliff and the Great Hunger*. New York: Verso, 1995.

————. Fredric Jameson, and Edward Said. *Nationalism, Colonialism and Literature*. Minneapolis: University of Minnesota Press, 1990.

Edgeworth, Maria. *Letters from England 1813–1844*, ed. Christina Colvin. Oxford: Clarendon Press, 1971.

Edgeworth, Richard, and Maria Edgeworth. "Essay on Irish Bulls," in *Tales and Novels, Vol. 4*, ed. Maria Edgeworth.

Edwards, Owen Dudley. "Anthony Trollope, the Irish Writer," *Nineteenth-Century Fiction* 38:1 (1983–84), 1–42.

Edwards, Philip. *Threshold of a Nation: A Study in English and Irish Drama*. Cambridge: Cambridge University Press, 1979.

Elliott, Marianne. *Partners in Revolution: The United Irishmen and France*. New Haven: Yale University Press, 1982.

Ellis, S.G., *Tudor Ireland: Crown, Community and the Conflict of Cultures*. London: Longman, 1985.

Elsaesser, Thomas. "Tales of Sound and Fury: Observations on the Family Melodrama," in *Monogram*, No. 4. London: British Film Institute, 1972, reprinted in *Film Theory and Criticism,* eds Gerald Mast et al. New York: Oxford University Press, 1992.

Emsley, Clive. *Crime and Society in England 1750–1900*. London: Longman, 1987.

Ferguson, Moira. *Colonialism and Gender Relations from Mary Wollstonecraft to Jamaica Kincaid*. Columbia University Press, 1993.

Ferris, Ina. *The Romantic National Tale and the Question of Ireland.* Cambridge: Cambridge University Press, 2002.

———. *William Makepeace Thackeray.* Boston: Twayne, 1983.

Fitzpatrick, David. "Ireland and the Empire," in *The Oxford History of the British Empire, vol. 3: The Nineteenth Century*, ed. Andrew N. Porter. Oxford: Oxford University Press, 1999, 495–521.

Fitzpatrick, W.J. *Lady Morgan: Her Career, Literary and Personal* London: C.J. Skeet, 1860.

Foster, R.F. "Stopping the Hunt: Trollope and the Memory of Ireland," in *The Irish Story: Telling Tales and Making It Up in Ireland.* London: Penguin, 2001.

Foucault, Michel. *The History of Sexuality, vol. 1*, trans. Robert Hurley. New York: Pantheon Books, 1978.

Friedman, Geraldine. "Rereading 1798: Melancholy and Desire in the Construction of Edgeworth's Anglo-Irish Union," *European Romantic Review* 10 (1999), 175–92.

Froude, J.A. *The English in Ireland in the 18th Century.* 1878.

Gallagher, Catherine. *The Industrial Reformation of English Fiction: Social Discourse and Narrative Form, 1832–1867.* Chicago: University of Chicago Press, 1985.

———. *Nobody's Story: The Vanishing Acts of Women Writers in the Marketplace, 1670–1820.* Berkeley: University of California Press, 1994.

Gates, Henry Louis, Jr. *"Race," Writing, and Difference.* Chicago: University of Chicago Press, 1986.

Gellner, Ernest. *Nations and Nationalism.* Ithaca: Cornell University Press, 1983.

Gibbons, Luke. "Between Captain Rock and a Hard Place: Art and Agrarian Insurgency," in *Ideology and Ireland in the Nineteenth Century*, eds Tadhg Foley and Seán Ryder. Dublin: Four Courts Press, 1998, 23–44.

———. *Edmund Burke and Ireland: Aesthetics, Politics, and the Colonial Sublime.* Cambridge: Cambridge University Press, 2003.

Gledhill, Christine. "The Melodramatic Field: An Investigation," in *Home is Where the Heart Is*, ed. Christine Gledhill. London: British Film Institute, 1987, 255–67.

Glendenning, Victoria. *Anthony Trollope.* New York: Knopf, 1993.

Goldsmith, Oliver. "The History of Carolan, the Last Irish Bard" in *Collected Works, 5 vols.* Oxford: Clarendon Press, 1966.

Gossman, Lionel. *Between History and Literature.* Cambridge: Harvard University Press, 1990.

Green, Martin Burgess. *Dreams of Adventure, Deeds of Empire.* New York: Basic Books, 1979.

Grubgeld Elizabeth. "Class, Gender, and the Forms of Narrative: The Autobiographies of Anglo-Irish Women," in *Representing Ireland: Gender, Class, Nationality*, ed. Susan Shaw Sailer. Gainesville: University Press of Florida, 1997.

Hall, N. John. *Anthony Trollope: A Biography.* New York: Oxford University Press, 1993.

Halpern, John. *Trollope and Politics: A Study of the Pallisers and Others*. London: Macmillan 1977.

Hamer, Mary. "Putting Ireland on the Map," *Textual Practice* 3:1 (1989), 184–201.

Harvie, Christopher. *The Centre of Things: Political Fiction in Britain from Disraeli to the Present*. London: Routledge, 1991.

Hatfield, Andrew, and John McVeagh, eds. *Strangers to That Land: British Perceptions of Ireland from the Reformation to the Famine*. Gerrards Cross: Colin Smythe, 1994.

Hayley, Barbara. "'The Eerishers are marchin' in leeterature': British Critical Reception of 19th-Century Anglo-Irish Fiction," in *Literary Interrelations: Ireland, England, and the World Reception and Translation*. Tubingen: Gunter Narr Verlag 1987.

Hechter, Michael. *Internal Colonialism: The Celtic Fringe in British National Development 1536–1966*. Berkeley: University of California Press, 1975.

Herbert, Christopher. *Culture and Anomie*. Chicago: University of Chicago Press, 1991.

Hickman, Mary J. "Incorporating and Denationalizing the Irish in England: the Role of the Catholic Church," in *The Irish World Wide. Vol. 5: Religion and Identity*, ed. Patrick O'Sullivan. London: Leicester University Press, 1996.

Hobsbawm, Eric. *Nations and Nationalism Since 1780: Programme, Myth, Reality*. Cambridge: Cambridge University Press, 1990.

Hoppen, K.T. *Elections, Politics and Society in Ireland 1832–85*. Oxford: Oxford University Press, 1984.

Hurst, Michael. *Maria Edgeworth and the Public Scene: Intellect, Fine-Feeling, and Landlordism in the Age of Reform*. London: Macmillan, 1969.

Hutchinson, John. *The Dynamics of Cultural Nationalism: The Gaelic Revival and the Creation of the Irish Nation State*. London: Allen and Unwin, 1987.

Hynes, John. "*An Eye for An Eye*: Anthony Trollope's Irish Masterpiece," *Journal of Irish Literature* 16 (1987), 54–8.

Ignatiev, Noel. *How the Irish Became White*. New York: Routledge, 1995.

Jeffares, A. Norman. *Anglo-Irish Literature*. New York: Schocken Books, 1982.

Jeffery, Keith, ed. *An Irish Empire?: Aspects of Ireland and the British Empire*. Manchester UK: Manchester University Press, 1996.

Jones, Ann H. *Ideas and Innovations: Best Sellers of Jane Austen's Age*. New York: AMS Press, 1986.

Kearney, Hugh. *The British Isles: A History of Four Nations*. New York: Cambridge University Press, 1989.

Kee, Robert. *The Green Flag*, 3 vols. Harmondsworth: Penguin Books, 1989.

Kelly, Gary. "Class, Gender, Nation, and Empire: Money and Merit in the Writing of the Edgeworths," *Wordsworth Circle* 25:2 (Spring 1994), 89–93.

————. *English Fiction in the Romantic Period, 1789–1830*. London: Longman, 1989.

————. *The English Jacobin Novel, 1780–1805*. Oxford: Clarendon Press, 1976.

————. "Revolutionary and Romantic Feminism: Women, Writing, and Cultural Revolution," in *Revolution and English Romanticism: Politics and Rhetoric*, eds Keith Hanley and Raman Selden. London: Hemel Hempstead, 1990, 107–30.

Kelly, James. *Prelude to Union: Anglo-Irish Politics in the 1780s*. Cork: Cork University Press, 1989.

Kelly, R.J. "Anthony Trollope and Ireland," *The Irish Book Lover*, 18:2 (March and April 1930), 46 ff.

Kenneally, Michael. *Irish Literature and Culture*. Savage, MD: Barnes and Noble, 1992.

Kenny, Colum. "The Exclusion of Catholics from the Legal Profession in Ireland," *Irish Historical Studies*, 25 (November 1987), 337–57.

Kiberd, Declan. *Inventing Ireland: The Literature of the Modern Nation*. Cambridge: Harvard University Press, 1996.

Kincaid, James. "Introduction," in *An Eye for An Eye*. New York: Arno Press, 1981.

Kirkpatrick, Kathryn J. *Border Crossings: Irish Women Writers and National Identities*. Tuscaloosa, AL: University of Alabama Press, 2000.

Kittler, Friedrich. *Discourse Networks 1800–1900*, trans. Michael Meteer and Chris Cullens. Stanford: Stanford University Press, 1990.

Kowaleski-Wallace, Elizabeth. *Their Fathers' Daughters: Hannah More, Maria Edgeworth, and Patriarchal Complicity*. New York: Oxford University Press, 1991.

Lacaita, Francesca. "The Journey of the Encounter: The Politics of the National Tale in Sydney Owenson's *The Wild Irish Girl* and Maria Edgeworth's *Ennui*," in *Critical Ireland: New Essays in Literature and Culture*, eds Alan A. Gillis and Aaron Kelly. Dublin: Four Courts Press, 2001, 148–54.

Lamb, Lady Caroline. *Glenarvon* (1816). London: Everyman, 1995.

Lebow, R.N., *White Britain and Black Ireland: The Influence of Stereotypes on Colonial Policy*. Philadelphia: Institute for the Study of Human Issues, 1976.

Lecky, W.E.H. *A History of Ireland in the Eighteenth Century. New ed. Vol. V.* London, 1892. New York: AMS, 1969.

Leersen, Joep et al., *Forging in the Smithy: National Identity and Representation in Anglo-Irish Literary History*. The Literature of Politics, the Politics of Literature: Proceedings of the Leiden IASAIL Conference, vol.1. Amsterdam and Atlanta: Editions Rodolpi B.V., 1995.

————. *Mere Irish & Fíor-ghael: Studies in the Idea of Irish Nationality*. Amsterdam: John Benjamins, 1986.

————. "On the Treatment of Irishness in Romantic Anglo-Irish Fiction," *Irish University Review* 20 (1990), 251–63.

Levine, Philippa. *Feminist Lives in Victorian England*. London: Basil Blackwell, 1990.

Levy, Anita. *Reproductive Urges: Popular Novel-Reading, Sexuality, and the English Nation*. Philadelphia: University of Pennsylvania Press, 1999.

Lloyd, David. *Anomalous States: Irish Writing And The Post-Colonial Moment*. Durham: Duke University Press, 1993.

———. *Nationalism and Minor Literature: James Clarence Mangan and the Emergence of Irish Cultural Nationalism*. Berkeley: University of California Press, 1987.

MacConville, Michael. *Ascendancy to Oblivion: The Story of the Anglo-Irish*. London: Quartet, 1986.

MacDonagh, Oliver. *The Nineteenth-Century Novel and Irish Social History: Some Aspects*. Dublin: National Library of Ireland, 1970.

———. *States of Mind: A Study of Anglo-Irish conflict 1780–1980*. George Allen and Unwin, 1983.

———. *Irish Culture and Nationalism 1750–1950*, eds W.E. Mandle, Pauric Travers. London: Macmillan, 1983.

MacGrath, Kevin. "Writers in *The Nation* 1842–5," *Irish Historical Studies* 6 (1948), 189–223.

Malcolmson, A.P.W. *John Foster, The Politics of the Anglo-Irish Ascendancy*. London: Oxford University Press, 1978.

Marcus, Steven. *Engels, Manchester and the Working Class*. New York: Random House, 1974.

Marx, Karl and Frederick Engels. *Ireland and the Irish Question. Selected Letters and Papers*, trans. S. Ryazanskaya et al. Moscow: Progress Publishers, 1971.

Mayhew, Henry. *London Labour and the London Poor (4 vols, 1861–2)*. New York: Dover, 1968.

McCarthy, Conor. "Edward Said and Irish Criticism," *Éire-Ireland* 42:1–2 (Spring/Summer 2007), 311–35.

McCaw, Neil. "Some Mid-Victorian Irishness(es): Trollope, Thackeray, Eliot" in *Writing Irishness in Nineteenth-Century British Culture* ed. Neil McCaw; Aldershot (UK): Ashgate, 2004, 129–57.

McCormack, W.J. *Ascendancy and Tradition in Anglo-Irish Literary History From 1789 To 1939*. New York: Oxford University Press, 1985.

———. *Dissolute Characters: Irish Literary History Through Balzac, Sheridan Le Fanu, Yeats, And Bowen*. Manchester: Manchester University Press 1993.

———. *From Burke to Beckett. Ascendancy Tradition and Betrayal in Literary History*. Cork: Cork University Press, 1994.

———. "The Genesis of Protestant Ascendancy," in *1789: Reading Writing Revolution*, eds Francis Barker et al. Colchester: University of Essex, 1982, 303–23.

McHugh, Roger and Maurice Harmon. *A Short History of Anglo-Irish Literature*. New York: Barnes & Noble, 1982.

Mellor, Anne. *Romanticism and Gender*. New York: Routledge, 1993.

Meyers, Susan. *Imperialism at Home: Race and Victorian Women's Fiction*. Ithaca: Cornell University Press, 1996.

Michie, Elsie. "The Yahoo, Not the Demon: Heathcliff, Rochester, and the Simianization of the Irish," in *Outside the Pale. Cultural Exclusion, Gender Difference, and the Victorian Woman Writer*. Ithaca: Cornell University Press, 1993.

Millat, Gilbert ed., *Angleterre ou Albion, Entre Fascination et Répulsion: de l'Exposition Universelle au Dôme du Millénaire: 1851–2000* (Travaux & recherches) (Villeneuve-d'Ascq: Éditions du Conseil Scientifique de l'Université Charles de Gaulle-Lille III, 2006.

Monsarrat, Ann. *An Uneasy Victorian: Thackeray the Man. 1811–63*. London: Cassell, 1980.

Moody, T.W. and F.X. Martin, eds. *The Course of Irish History*. Cork: Mercier Press, 1967.

Morgan, Peter F. *Literary Critics and Reviewers in Early 19ᵗʰ-Century Britain*. London: Croom Helm, 1983.

Moskal, Jeanne. "Gender, Nationality, and Textual Authority in Lady Morgan's Travel Books." *Romantic Women Writers: Voices and Countervoices*, eds Paula Feldman and Theresa Kelley. Hanover: University Press of New England, 1995.

Moynahan, Julian. *Anglo-Irish: The Literary Imagination in A Hyphenated Culture*. Princeton, NJ: Princeton University Press, 1995.

Munich, Adrienne Auslander. *Andromeda's Chains. Gender and Interpretation in Victorian Literature and Art*. New York: Columbia University Press, 1989.

Myers, Mitzi. "Canonical 'Orphans' and Critical *Ennui*: Rereading Edgeworth's Cross-Writing," *Children's Literature* 25 (1997), 116–36.

———. "Goring John Bull: Maria Edgeworth's Hibernian High Jinks versus the Imperialist Imaginary," in *Cutting Edges: Postmodern Critical Essays on Eighteenth-Century Satire*, ed. James E. Gill. Knoxville: University of Tennessee Press, 1995.

Nairn, Tom. *The Break-up of Britain: Crisis and Neo-Nationalism*. London: Verso, 1981.

Nandy, Ashis. *The Intimate Enemy: Loss and Recovery of Self Under Colonialism*. Oxford: Oxford University Press, 1983.

O'Brien, Conor Cruise, ed. *The Shaping of Modern Ireland*. London: Routledge & Kegan Paul, 1960.

O'Brien, Gerard. *Anglo-Irish Politics in the Age of Grattan and Pitt*. IAP, 1987.

O'Farrell, Patrick. *England and Ireland Since 1800*. Oxford: Oxford University Press, 1975.

———. *England's Irish Question: Anglo-Irish Relations 1534–1970*. London: Batsford, 1971.

Ó Gallchoir, Clíona. "Maria Edgeworth's Revolutionary Morality and the Limits of Realism," *Colby Library Quarterly* 36 (2000), 87–97.

———. "Gender, Nation and Revolution: Maria Edgeworth and Stephanie-Felicite de Genlis," in *Women, Writing, and the Public Sphere, 1700–1830*, eds Elizabeth Eger, Charlotte Grant, Clíona Ó Gallchoir, and Penny Warburton. Cambridge: Cambridge University Press, 2001.

Panayi, Panikos. *Immigration, Ethnicity and Racism in Britain 1815–1945*. New York: St. Martin's Press, 1994

Partridge, A.C. *Language and Society in Anglo-Irish Literature*. Dublin: Gill and Macmillan, 1984.

Paulin, Tom. "English Political Writers on Ireland: Robert Southey to Douglas Hurd," in *Critical Approaches to Anglo-Irish Literature*, eds Michael Allen and Angela Wilcox. Gerrards Cross: Colin Smythe, 1989, 132–45.

Perera, Suvendrini. *Reaches of Empire: The English Novel from Edgeworth to Dickens*. New York: Columbia University Press, 1991.

Poovey, Mary. *Uneven Developments: The Ideological Work of Gender in Mid-Victorian England*. Chicago: University of Chicago Press, 1988.

Price, R.G.G. *A History of Punch*. London: William Collins Ltd, 1957.

Rauchbauer, Otto ed. *Ancestral Voices: The Big House in Anglo-Irish Literature*. Dublin: Lilliput, 1992.

Ray, Gordon. *The Age of Wisdom 1847–1863*. New York: McGraw-Hill, 1972.

———, ed. *The Letters and Private Papers of William Makepeace Thackeray, Vols 1–2*. Cambridge: Cambridge University Press, 1945–46.

———. *Thackeray: The Uses of Adversity 1811–1846*. New York: McGraw-Hill, 1955.

Rich, Paul B. "Social Darwinism, Anthropology and English Perspectives of the Irish, 1867–1900," *History of European Ideas* 19:4–6 (1994), 777–85.

Richards, Shaun, and David Cairns. *Writing Ireland: Colonialism, Nationalism, and Culture*. Manchester: Manchester University Press, 1988.

Richards, Thomas. *The Imperial Archive: Knowledge and the Fantasy of Empire*. London: Verso, 1993.

Robbins, Ruth, Julian and Wolfreys, eds. *Victorian Identities: Social and Cultural Formations in Nineteenth-Century Literature*. New York: Macmillan, 1996.

Said, Edward W., ed. *Literature and Society*. Baltimore: Johns Hopkins University Press, 1980.

———. *The World, the Text, and the Critic*. Cambridge: Harvard University Press, 1983.

Samuel, Raphael, ed. *Patriotism: The Making and Unmaking of British National Identity, 3 vols*. London: Routledge, 1993.

Sharpe, Jenny. *Allegories of Empire: The Figure of Woman in the Colonial Text*. Minneapolis: University of Minnesota Press, 1993.

Shattock, Joanne. *Politics and Reviewers: The Edinburgh and the Quarterly*. London: Leicester University Press, 1989.

Shillingsburg, Peter. *William Makepeace Thackeray: A Literary Life*. Basingstoke: Palgrave, 2001.

Simmons, Clare A. *Reversing the Conquest: History and Myth in Nineteenth-Century British Literature*. New Brunswick: Rutgers University Press, 1990.

Sloan, Barry. *The Pioneers of Anglo-Irish Fiction, 1800–1850*. Gerrards Cross: Colin Smythe, 1986.

Speare, Morris E. *The Political Novel: Its Development in England and America*. New York: Oxford University Press, 1924

Stepan, Nancy. *The Idea of Race in Science: Great Britain, 1800–1960*. Hamden, CT: Archon Books, 1982.

Stevenson, Lionel. *Dr Quicksilver: The Life of Charles Lever*. New York: Charles Scribners and Sons, 1939.

Sutherland, John. "Introduction," in *An Eye for An Eye*, ed. John Sutherland New York: Oxford University Press, 1992.

Swift, Roger. "Behaving Badly? Irish Migrants and 'Crime,'" in *Criminal Conversations: Victorian Crimes, Social Panic, and Moral Outrage*, eds Rowbotham, Judith and Kim Stevenson. Columbus: Ohio State University Press, 2005.

Swift, R. and S. Gilley, eds. *The Irish in the Victorian City.* London: Croom Helm, 1985.

———. *The Irish in Britain 1815–1939*. London: Pinter, 1989.

Taylor, John Tinnon. *Early Opposition to the English Novel: Popular Reaction from 1760 to 1830*. New York: King's Crown Press, 1943.

Tessone, Natasha. "Displaying Ireland: Sydney Owenson and the Politics of Spectacular Antiquarianism," *Éire-Ireland* 37 (2002), 169–86.

Thrall, Miriam. *Rebellious Fraser's: Nol Yorke's Magazine in the Days of Maginn, Thackeray, and Carlyle*. New York: Columbia University Press, 1934.

Tingay, Lance O. "The Reception of Trollope's First Novel," *Nineteenth-Century Fiction* 6:3 (December 1957), 195–200.

Tompkins, J.M.S. *The Popular Novel in England 1770–1800*. London: Methuen, 1932.

Townsend, Charles. *Political Violence in Ireland: Government and Resistance Since 1848*. Oxford: Oxford University Press, 1984.

Townsend, Molly. *Not by Bullets and Bayonets: Cobbett's Writings on the Irish Question: 1795–1835*. London: Sheed and Ward, 1983.

Tracy, Robert. *Trollope's Later Novels*. Berkeley: California University Press, 1978.

———. *The Unappeasable Host: Studies in Irish Identities*. Dublin: University College Dublin Press, 1998.

Tracy, Thomas. "The Mild Irish Girl: Domesticating the National Tale," *Éire-Ireland* 39:1–2 (Spring and Summer 2004), 81–109.

Trollope, Anthony. *Castle Richmond* (1860).

———. *The Kellys and the O'Kellys; or Landlords and Tenants* (1848).

———. *The Land Leaguers* (1884).

Vance, Norman. "Celts, Carthaginians, and Constitutions: Anglo-Irish Literary Relations 1780–1820," *Irish Historical Studies* 22:87 (March 1981), 216–38.

———. *Irish Literature: A Social History, Tradition, Identity, and Difference*. Oxford: Basil Blackwell, 1990.

Wallace. *A Short History of Ireland.* New York: Barnes and Noble, 1996.

Warner, Alan. *A Guide to Anglo-Irish Literature*. Dublin: Palgrave Macmillan, 1982.

Watt, Ian. *The Rise of the Novel*. Berkeley: University of California Press, 1957.

Whelan, Kevin. *The Tree of Liberty: Radicalism, Catholicism and the Construction of Irish Identity, 1760–1830*. Notre Dame: Notre Dame University Press, 1996.

White, Terence De Vere. *The Anglo-Irish.* London: Gollancz, 1972.

Williams, Leslie. "Irish Identity and the *Illustrated London News*, 1846–1851: Famine to Depopulation," in *Representing Ireland: Gender, Class, Nationality*, ed. Susan Shaw Sailer. Gainesville: University Press of Florida, 1997.

Williams, Patrick, and Laura Chrisman, eds. *Colonial Discourse and Postcolonial Theory: A Reader.* New York: Columbia University Press, 1994.

Wright, Julia M. "'The Nation Begins to Form': Competing Nationalisms in Morgan's *The O'Briens and the O'Flahertys*," *ELH* 66 (1999), 939–63.

———. "National Erotics and Political Theory in Morgan's *The O'Briens and the O'Flahertys*," *European Romantic Review* 15 (2004), 229–41.

Index